LANDING ON MY FEET

LANDING ON MY FEET

—— My Story ——

Mike Catt

HODDER &
STOUGHTON

First published in Great Britain in 2007 by Hodder & Stoughton
An Hachette Livre UK company

1

Copyright © Mike Catt 2007

A CIP catalogue record for this title is available from the British Library

ISBN 978 0 340 93660 3

Typeset in Sabon by Hewer Text UK Ltd, Edinburgh
Printed and bound by Clays Ltd, St Ives plc

Hodder & Stoughton policy is to use papers that are natural, renewable
and recyclable products and made from wood grown in sustainable
forests. The logging and manufacturing processes are expected to
conform to the environmental regulations of the country of origin.

Hodder & Stoughton Ltd
A division of Hodder Headline
338 Euston Road
London NW1 3BH

www.hodder.co.uk

Contents

Acknowledgements

My life has been a team game on the field and no different off it. For their love and support in bad times as well as good, I will always be indebted to Dad, Mum and my brothers Doug, Pete and Rich. To Jill, my uncle Doug, Kathleen, Fiona and Jayne – thank you. To Chris, Jan and Duncan, for looking after Evie and Ali when I have not been there, I am forever grateful. Likewise to Abdullah and the doctors at the Princess Diana Hospital in Birmingham, for giving our daughter the care she needed. And to Martin, Karen, Maddie, Phil, Yolanda and boys – thanks to you for teaching me about life outside rugby.

My career has been an incredible adventure, one I would have been unable to make without all the coaches, from school through to international level, from whom I learned so much. Thanks to Grey High School for all the foundations they put in place to enable me to succeed; to JAB, Ian and Carey for their support; and to Bath, London Irish and England, for making my dreams come true. It has been a fantastic journey. I have seen places and lived experiences that so few are privy to.

The good times far outweigh the bad, but none would have been possible without the support and talent of my team-mates at club level, and with England and the British and Irish Lions. I feel honoured and incredibly fortunate to share such memories with so many good people.

For the opportunity to chronicle my life in this book my thanks go to Roddy Bloomfield and Hannah Knowles at Hodder & Stoughton, to Mike Martin at Paragon Sports Management and to Alex Spink, rugby correspondent of the *Daily Mirror*, for helping me tell my story and making it both easy and enjoyable to express my feelings.

Above all I would like to acknowledge the love and support of my strong, lively, beautiful wife Alison. You have been my cornerstone for so long. You have put your heart and soul into Evie. You have given me the opportunity to succeed in what I do.

I dedicate this book to you, Ali, and to our precious Evie.

Photographic Acknowledgements

The author and publisher would like to thank the following for permission to reproduce photographs:

Action Images, Vincent Almavy/Getty Images, Steve Bardens/Rex Features, Shaun Botterill/Getty Images, Gabriel Bouys/Getty Images, Action Images/Jason O'Brien, Reuters/Howard Burditt/Action Images, David Cannon/ Getty Images, Russell Cheyne/Allsport, Chris Cole/Getty Images, David Davies/PA Wire/PA Photos, Reuters/Kieran Doherty KD/CP Reuters/Action Images, Matt Dunham/ AP/PA Photos, Mike Egerton/Empics Sport/PA Photos, Colorsport/Colin Elsey, Christophe Ena/AP/PA Photos, Franck Faugere/Flash Press/Action Images, Stu Forster/Getty Images, Action Images/Stuart Franklin, Getty Images, John Gichigi/ Getty Images, Tim Graham/Getty Images, Stuart Hannagan/Getty Images, Action Images/Paul Harding, Action Images/Richard Heathcote, Tony Henshaw/Action Images, Colorsport/Matthew Impey, Reuters/Eddie Keogh/Action Images, Ross Kinnaird/Empics Sport/PA Photos, Warren Little/Getty Images, Jamie McDonald/ Getty Images, Colorsport/Stuart Macfarlane, John Marsh/Empics Sport/PA Photos, Clive Mason/Getty Images, Taamallah Mehdi/ABACA/PA Photos, Reuters/Action Images, Craig Prentis/Action Images, Andrew Redington/Getty Images, David Rogers/Getty Images, Ross Setford/AP/PA Photos.

All other photographs are from private collections.

Introduction
Acceptance at Last

Stade de France, Paris, 20 October 2007

I did not pinch myself, just in case. Here I was, a month past my thirty-sixth birthday, lining up to play in the final of the Rugby World Cup. Four years earlier it had been extraordinary enough. Only selected to the England squad the weekend before it left for Australia, I came home with a World Cup winners', medal.

Could this really be happening to me and could the opposition really be South Africa, my country of birth, the nation I had grown up dreaming of playing for? Could England, a team given no chance by anybody outside our squad, really have made it through to the final?

Not for the first time, I had landed on my feet. This would be my final game in an England jersey and this time it would be my choice. I had decided I would go out on my own terms. What a way to go. Almost 16 million watching at home, my wife Ali and daughter Evie in the stands, so too my dad and three brothers.

It had been a rollercoaster ride to acceptance, both my own career and England's World Cup campaign. The team had managed it in five weeks, from losing 36–0 to South Africa in the pool stages to reaching the final with fantastic wins over Australia and hosts France in the knock-out stages. It had taken me rather longer.

For thirteen years I had been dropped and recalled by England more times than I could remember. I had won everything in the game, yet came into my final year feeling there was still something missing. And then, it happened.

'Catty, got a minute?'

I turned around to see Brian Ashton, England's head coach, striding towards me. It was March 2007 and we were in Bath, the city where my English rugby adventure had begun, and where I spent the happiest years of my career before the club was bought by multi-millionaire Andrew Brownsword and I was ditched to save a few quid.

Since my previous Six Nations outing for England in 2001 I had become a husband, a father and a World Cup winner. I had also, in the minds of an awful lot of people, become a former international.

Was that what Brian wanted to tell me as he cut across the corner of England's training pitch at the university and caught up with me? That my time had gone. After sixty-eight caps dating back to 1994, was this it?

At least Brian would tell me straight, I knew that. In all the years I had known him, he had never gone in for bullshit. Never talked round a subject, never used two words when one was enough. The guy gets straight to the point. I always admired him for that.

'There's something I want to tell you,' he said, his expression giving nothing away. 'You're playing against France on Saturday. One other thing. I'm thinking of making you captain.'

There are those who feel passionate about playing for their country and others who are just passionate about the sport. I fit the second category. I am obsessive about rugby and always have been. For years politics and what jersey I wore didn't really matter to me. At least that is what I told myself.

Born into a world of apartheid, I spent too many years feeling discriminated against. Not in terms of my human and civil rights, but my rugby. In South Africa, where I lived until I was twenty-one, my progress was restricted because I was 'English' rather than Afrikaner. Then when I moved to England it seemed I was suddenly not English enough.

So I put up a barrier. I said to myself, I'm not doing it for you lot, I'm doing it because I love rugby. That enabled me to roll with the punches and keep coming back for more when I was dropped by England, booed by the Twickenham crowd and written off in the press.

It was a natural defence mechanism in response to not feeling fully integrated, loved, appreciated – call it what you want. Only at Bath did I feel I belonged. And even there it turned sour when the money men took over and the family silver – Bath people who had made the club great – was sold off.

For years rugby was my be-all and end-all, my reason for being, and I was, perhaps, overly sensitive to criticism. That changed in the spring of 2002 when my life was turned upside down by a deep personal trauma that came perilously close to taking the lives of my wife and new-born child.

I saw Ali fit violently and heard doctors voice fears of brain damage. I saw Evie wired up in an incubator with her chest open after undergoing heart surgery. And all of a sudden I saw rugby for what it is. A game. Confronted by matters of life and death, rather than such relative trivialities as selection, I found a new perspective in my life.

Armed with that, I forced my way back into the England reckoning and convinced Clive Woodward that he should take me to the World Cup the following year. I kept battling, helped England through a sticky patch against Wales in the quarter-finals, won a starting place in the semis against France and applied the finishing touch in the final against Australia, kicking the ball into touch to end the game and spark the mother of all parties.

Almost overnight the boo boys became back-slappers. People went from wanting me dropped to wanting my autograph. I smiled and duly obliged, acknowledging that sport is a fickle business. I also took it on the chin, albeit with extreme reluctance and complete disgust, when Bath showed me the door only months later.

I am not one to kick up a fuss or to lash out. That has never been my style. I bottle up my frustration with the intention of using it to my advantage further down the line. That made me bitter at times but it also took me to the side of a training pitch in Bath staring wide-eyed at Brian Ashton as he asked me what I thought about captaining England.

'What do I think?' I said. 'I think damn right, I'd love to.'

Brian offered his hand and I shook it warmly. I felt pride, an almost child-like excitement but also anxiety. I wondered how the rest of the squad would react to my sudden elevation. A stranger to the squad all season, only four starts since the World Cup, and now, out of the blue, captain. I began to feel almost embarrassed. Brian could have picked Martin Corry or Jason Robinson, and he chose me. What would they think?

I wondered how my appointment would play in South Africa. Then I was struck by the irony of being handed this supreme honour in the city that I'd been effectively forced out of when Bath decided I was only worth a £20,000 contract three years earlier.

For a few minutes, as I strolled down to the River Avon and past my beloved former club, I cursed the management that I blame for ruining it. As the emotion welled up in me I turned my contempt towards those who had given me such a hard time over the years, those whose definition of me was always framed by negativity. Can't kick goals, can't tackle Jonah Lomu, what can he do?

Then a strange thing happened. I stopped and listened to myself. And something inside of me yelled, 'enough'.

You're happy and settled at London Irish. Your family are healthy, you're back in the England team and you've just been made captain of your country. Whether you keep it for one game or more, it's in the record books. They can't take it away from you. You have exceeded your wildest dreams. Life doesn't get better than this.

I still had the match against France to play and a fairytale victory to celebrate, then there would be a fourth World Cup and that amazing journey through to the final which would stop the nation in its tracks. After that, a move into a new player-coaching role with London Irish. But at that moment I was struck by a realisation. The acceptance I had spent my whole life craving had arrived.

1
LIVING WITH PREJUDICE

Port Elizabeth, 3 April 1984

Six o'clock in the morning and I had one thing on my mind. I wanted to be a Springbok. I wanted to follow in the footsteps of Danie Gerber and Naas Botha and the du Plessis brothers. I wanted to pull on the green and gold jersey of South Africa.

The day before had been the same, the day before that too. Up at first light, always with the same thought in my head. I was a sports freak. Nothing else in life mattered to me. School was what I did when I wasn't playing sport, woodwork being my best subject. Home was where I ate and slept and had my kit washed.

Dad's knock on the bedroom door woke us, just as it did every morning at the same time. I am one of four brothers and three of us shared a room together. Pete had the single bed, Richard and I had the bunks. Doug, being the oldest by three years, had his own room.

The first race of the day was on, for first use of the bathroom. From there the competition moved outside. Our parents never forced sport on us, they didn't need to. When you are four brothers everything is a contest, and the Eastern Cape, with its year-round sunshine and average temperature which ranged between 20° and 25° Celsius, was the perfect setting.

I lived in a world of apartheid, a legal system which classified people into four racial groups: white, black, Indian and Coloured. I didn't see it at the time. What mattered to me was that I was Under-13 Sportsman of the Year at Grey Junior School.

Life was brilliant for us. Superb weather, wonderful opportunities, not a care in the world. We were outdoors all of the time, the beach was five minutes away and we had a great school. All our mates lived within five or ten minutes of each other and we ran or cycled everywhere. We did life-saving and athletics and on a Saturday I would play rugby in the morning and football in the afternoon.

Home was a three-bedroom bungalow with a really big garden, in which were parked two-seater fibreglass hovercrafts that my dad, Jimmy, made. Dad manufactured electrical components for a living, having started up by making fluorescent lights in the garage. But in his spare time he made hovercrafts and rockets. I'm not quite sure why. He also dug us a pool in the front garden.

Pete, Rich and I shared that room until I was eight, when we moved to another bungalow, which dad converted into two floors, closer to school. It was there that we became really serious about our sport. All four of us boys were natural athletes and were pretty successful in the sports we played. Pete, being two years older than me, was the one most on my radar. More so than Doug, who has five years on me, and Rich, who is two years younger. Pete represented Eastern Province in triathlon, athletics, diving and soccer at Under-16 level. He used to hate it when I beat him, which only made me more determined.

I followed him into all those sports and all those teams, with the exception of the South African triathlon team for which he competed in Canada at the 1992 World Championships and finished thirteenth in his age group. I specialised in middle distance running: 800 metres, 3,000 metres flat and steeplechase and cross-country. I won all my cross-country races, running barefoot, and still remember the day Pete and I completed a family double around a local golf course; me winning the Under-9s race and him the Under-13s.

At Grey it was compulsory to do two winter sports and two summer sports. We had two and a half hours of sport each day, but for me that was still not enough. Which is why we were up at six every morning for an hour's speed work or skills training on the cinder athletics track, followed by a swim, before school. And why on this morning, like so many before, I was standing at one end of the beach which fringed Algoa Bay about to start running hard towards my target, placed on the sand five kilometres away. It was actually a tyre, but in my mind's eye it was my Springbok jersey.

All white South African boys are brought up to believe that representing the Springboks is the ultimate achievement and I was no different. It was the mid-1980s and the nation, never mind the sport, had a long way to go before it even started to become racially inclusive. Black Africans played football, whites played rugby. The racial demarcation did not end there. It extended to geographical areas. This was apartheid, which in Afrikaans means 'separateness', and the government was very clever at implementing it. They must have been, because it never once occurred to me to question why a black person had no rights, why he could not drink from a certain water fountain, use the same restroom as a white person or even live in a particular area.

We were taught about the Boer War and the Zulus, how the colonies started, and the murder of white Prime Minister Hendrik Verwoerd in parliament in 1966. But nothing that led us to call into question apartheid. Government censorship ruled. You never read anything in the newspapers, or saw or heard anything on the television and radio, which led you to query the status quo. And you didn't step outside the white areas and into the townships, so you had no idea what was going on. Only when I came over to the UK would I discover the truth. Only then would I be shocked by the images of violence on my television screen.

These in no way tallied with my experience of the country and my happy, sheltered life in Port Elizabeth. There was no crime, let alone the riots that were shown on television in the outside world. The only time our home was broken into was when some guy, high from sniffing glue, tried to get through a downstairs window one night. He was halfway through it when our English bull terrier, Dodger, sorted him out.

During the day we would leave the doors open, that was how secure we felt. Some of my friends, mostly from farming families, did carry hand guns but I was completely opposed to firearms and said so. There was absolutely no need for them and I always felt that if you had a gun and there was a situation when you pulled it, you would have to use it. The consequences of that would be too awful.

I saw no reason to be worried about anything and I didn't look for any. Mum says she now finds it extraordinary that she accepted that a black man couldn't go on to a beach that was labelled 'white only'. She is English, from near Biggin Hill in Kent, and says she can't believe we lived like that, but we did. She admits she was not a political animal, it was not her country, and so she was living in a fool's paradise. But for her, and us, it did seem like paradise.

Only later would she begin to realise that it actually wasn't, when the activists – freedom fighters or terrorists, depending on your viewpoint – managed to get film out of the country and the whole truth became known to the world. But when mum first arrived, having met and married dad in England where my two older brothers were born, it was a new country and she felt she needed to get on with it, so she did what she had to do to bring up her children to the best of her ability.

In that she received a significant amount of help from our nanny, Constance, whom we regarded as a second mother. Mum gave her a wooden spoon with which she was told she could wallop our backsides if we were bad, providing she could catch us. No chance. Constance lived with us through the week in a room out at the back of the house and brought us up brilliantly and pretty much on her own whilst dad was working twenty hours a day building his business and mum, a music teacher who played flute, piccolo and piano, was requalifying at the university to enable her to teach in South Africa.

When I was tiny Constance would carry me around on her back while she cleaned the house. When I suffered badly with colic, and used to cry a lot in the evenings, Constance would look after me. She did everything for us boys, despite having children of her own. They would often come to the house and we would play with them. But

They couldn't stay with her, because Constance was black. She would pack a bag at the weekend and take a bus out of town to be with them.

I began playing rugby at school when I was six and played barefoot all the way through to the Under-13s, when I moved from Grey Junior to Grey High. Most of the boys did that, very few left after junior school. Rugby was the number one sport and we had half a dozen teams in the Under-10s and played pretty competitive matches. We played barefoot not just from a safety point of view but because some of the schools we came up against couldn't afford boots. Many a time I remember running around barefoot at half past eight in the morning with frost on the ground. It was all a far cry from today where boots, gum shields and head gear are mandatory. Nowadays, there is no tackling for the first few years. We were doing it from the age of six.

We also had the competitive edge instilled in us from an early age. You had to be in the 'A' team, you had to win. It was not about the taking part. If you were dropped from a rugby team, you were distraught. It was just not the done thing. At the same time we also learned the meaning of discipline. The cane was regularly dished out to boys from the age of six upwards. I managed to avoid that but I did once come home with my mouth sellotaped shut.

I was never particularly academic but I excelled when it came to talking. I never stopped. And one day I was sent home early by my teacher. Mum was in her music studio and she noticed I had a black line around my mouth. 'What's been going on, Michael?' she asked. 'Sellotape,' I said. 'I was talking too much.'

As I grew older I got a bit more feisty. Once I suffered a bang to the head playing rugby. The coaches weren't sure whether it was concussion – which it was – and I insisted it was nothing of the sort and they should get me straight back on. So they did and I promptly ran with the ball in the wrong direction. That was bad enough but when the parents sitting in the stand started yelling at me, I turned round and very loudly told them to fuck off.

Grey was an all-white school and it was considered very English in a province where there was a big rivalry between the English and the Afrikaners, Port Elizabeth having been founded as a town in 1820 to house British settlers. I consider Afrikaners to be generally arrogant, aggressive, narrow-minded and hard because that was the way I found them. Pretty much every time you played rugby against them you got intimidated or beaten up. Most of those I came up against were from farming stock and were extremely strong.

The only time I really put myself in an Afrikaner environment was on a rugby pitch. At school everyone was English. We didn't really associate with Afrikaners at all. But being English and wanting to progress in South African rugby was to become a major problem for me.

I learned Afrikaans at school but because I was never in surroundings where I could use it I was not motivated by the subject and felt it was a waste of time. All my mates spoke English and while a lot of them grew up on farms and could speak the language we never socialised with Afrikaners. To be honest we were pretty much scared of them because they were big hard buggers. In my own school environment I was exceptionally confident, yet in the company of Afrikaners I didn't have the self belief to talk in their lingo. I understood it all but being able to speak it was a completely different matter. I would rather keep quiet than embarrass myself by trying to say something.

If I thought matters would improve as I grew older I was mistaken. Our school team was very successful, roaming unbeaten through Under-14 and Under-15 level and losing only twice at Under-16s, but when the provincial trials came along, however good you were, if you were English you would not get picked. It was like, 'Sorry, pal, wrong school.' Unless they were short of Afrikaner players you would, at best, be left on the bench. Very few English guys ever broke through at an early age.

We might have been kept apart from black Africa but there was no escaping this white on white prejudice in rugby circles. The Afrikaners were very dismissive of the English, not least because more often than not the English were a lot smaller as they didn't come from a background of physical labour. When we were away at rugby camps we learned to keep our mouths shut and just get on with it. It was a lesson which, generally speaking, has served me well down the years. Let your rugby do your talking. If you perform well enough then they have to pick you.

Not in Eastern Province they didn't. My silence was their cue to take the mickey out of me. At school I was nicknamed 'Costus' by my pals, as in 'you've cost us the game'. It was said with good humour. There was none that I could see in the names the Afrikaners called me. *Soutpil* was one, *rooinek* another. *Soutpil* literally means 'salty dick', as in you have one foot in South Africa and one foot in the UK, with your dick hanging in the sea. *Rooi* means red and *rooinek* is a nickname given to all Englishmen who visit South

Africa. The theory being that they arrive, unaccustomed to the heat of the African sun, and burn their necks.

This sort of teasing was all new to me and with the difficulty I had communicating with the rest of the side I found it a tough environment to be in. Take the Eastern Province initiation ceremony as an illustration of what I faced. You would have to tell a three-second joke in Afrikaans standing on a chair. If you failed to do so, or simply couldn't manage it, you had to bend over a table while other players took turns whacking your backside. If that wasn't enough you would then be made to sing the National Anthem in Afrikaans. Get it wrong and your rear got another beating.

My first club league game was at the age of eighteen for Crusaders Technikon against Despatch, for whom the legendary Danie Gerber was playing. He remains one of South Africa's greatest ever centres and it took me no time at all to learn that the hard way. I was playing at full-back and the first time I got the ball he was onto me in a flash and crushed me into the turf. They stuck up an up-and-under, I caught it and Gerber absolutely munched me. I weighed eighty-four kilos, he must have been a hundred. As he got up he sneered at me in Afrikaans, 'Welcome to the real world. Welcome to the big league.' I felt massively intimidated.

Intimidation is commonplace in South African rugby, especially at club level where teams look to target someone on the opposition side that they can beat up and mouth off to. And yet the only time I ever felt scared was not on the rugby field at all, but out in the bush in the middle of nowhere on a school camp during my final year in 1989.

The camp was called Sonop, which means 'sun up' in Afrikaans, and the idea was that boys, aged thirteen and fourteen, who were new to Grey spent weekends at Sonop where they were given a form of initiation into the school. A dozen or so of the top year were appointed as counsellors to look after these young kids and organise activities for them.

This particular weekend, however, was specifically for us counsellors to go and devise the programme of events we would lay on. We were half an hour out of town in a big hut which had no electricity, just candles inside and a camp fire out in the clearing. It was early evening and we were sitting around the fire when out of the bush walked two guys, one of whom I recognised as a school-leaver from the year before.

His name was Joe, all of us knew him pretty well and we beckoned him over to join us. His friend had brought him out to see our religious guidance teacher, Mr Grobelaar, as his father had recently died and he was struggling badly to cope without him. Mr Grobelaar greeted Joe and took him off for a chat in private. It must have been two hours later that they returned and what followed still, to this day, gives me goosebumps.

Mr Grobelaar announced that he needed to talk to three or four of us. Half a dozen counsellors, including me, stayed seated with Joe while the others got up and followed him towards the combi minibus parked at the far side of the clearing.

'How you doing, Joe?' I said.

'Who's Joe?' he replied looking straight ahead at the flames. Strange, I thought, but at that moment our teacher called us over so I let it go.

'Look guys,' Mr Grobelaar said to us. 'I'm in a bit of a dilemma here. I think this guy is possessed and I'd like us to try something if none of you object.'

'You're having a laugh, sir,' I said.

Mr Grobelaar continued. He explained that when he and Joe had gone away for their initial chat he had tried to calm him with hypnotism, a discipline he was qualified to practise. And that when he had him under his spell he had asked: 'Can you hear the train whistle in the distance?' Joe answered: 'No, I can only hear the screaming in the chambers.'

I tried and failed to suppress a smirk.

Again the teacher ignored me. He said that he wanted us to lie Joe down on his back on the ground and for everybody to touch him with a finger whilst saying together, 'In the name of Jesus Christ we demand that you leave his body.'

I looked him straight in the eye. 'You can't be serious.'

But he was. The colour in his face, or rather lack of it, told us that. He was as white as a sheet, completely drained from having spent two hours in the bush trying to calm this guy. Minutes later, miles from anywhere, Joe lay flat on his back beside the fire while we prodded him and said what we had been asked to say.

As we did it he curled up into a ball and let out this primal scream, that's the only way I can describe it. All of a sudden I had run out of smart-arse quips. We repeated the mantra again and again for what must have been ten minutes but the guy remained curled up in the foetal position, sobbing his eyes out. I was now pretty spooked. Our teacher called a halt to proceedings and got up, saying he was going to the hut to phone a priest he knew back in town.

He returned minutes later saying that we should get Joe into the combi posthaste because the priest wanted to see him immediately. Six boys were sequestered to accompany Joe and the teacher back into town. I was to stay behind but I helped them get him into the minibus. It was then Joe laughed, but not as you and I would. I can only describe it as how I imagine the Devil might.

Now I know what you are thinking. But I hadn't been drinking, nor had I been on the weed. I had not even been eating too much cheese before bedtime. I heard what I heard and others who were there will back me up on this. I was genuinely petrified.

Off they went and, believe me, I was not sorry to see the back of them. The rest of us headed for our sleeping bags and made sure the door of the hut was locked. I didn't sleep a wink and I was still awake, staring up at the ceiling, when headlights through the grilled window signalled their return. I heard a key turn in the lock, then Mr Grobelaar walked in, followed by the guys. And Joe.

The hut had a flat roof where we would go and sunbathe when we had a bit of down time and Mr Grobelaar gestured to me to follow him up there, where he explained that the priest had tried to exorcise whatever spirit had hold of Joe and had ended up passing out himself. I can't find the words to articulate exactly how far beyond making a joke of this I was by this stage.

Fair play to the teacher, who was by no means a big man, while the rest of us decamped up on to the roof in a hurry, he remained with Joe in the locked hut. Thankfully there was no further incident and when the sun rose we packed up and headed off home. We were asked not to tell anyone at school about what had happened. As it was towards the end of our final term and we had study leave prior to exams that was easier to do than it would otherwise have been.

To be quite honest I didn't want to talk about it with anyone. I wanted to shut the memory away in a box and bury it in the back of my mind. I heard nothing more about Joe for three months when word reached us that he was okay. The rage, or whatever it was inside him, had subsided. The trauma brought on by his dad's death had passed. But the memory has stayed with me.

Before then I had never believed in the Devil. I thought it was a lot of nonsense. A bit like ghosts. Unless you are given a solid reason to believe, you tend to dismiss it as the conversation of the crazed; the sort of stuff you see in horror movies like *The Exorcist* and *The Omen*. I have never watched either. Nor will I be starting any time soon.

I don't need to because I saw this with my own two eyes and it taught me a lesson. It taught me not to dismiss things which might seem out of the ordinary. I had not experienced anything even remotely similar before and there has been nothing since. But I am spooked by what I witnessed to this day. I am not religious in any way, despite having gone to Sunday School as a very young kid. But do I believe there is a dark side? Yes, I do.

By this time there had been a major upheaval at home. When I was thirteen, mum and dad announced they were getting divorced. It really hit me hard. I remember sitting in the lounge with Rich and both of us bursting into tears. We could not believe what was going on. Pete just sat there and said, 'I told you so, I knew it was going to happen.'

There had never been much emotion expressed amongst our family before then. Mum's mum had been as hard as nails, had apparently not really wanted kids and had sent mum to boarding school at the age of six. So she grew up very independent and very much a tough nut in her own right. She very rarely gave any love or hugs or anything during our upbringing. She was the one who disciplined us and she was pretty strict. I guess she needed to be with four boys. She was very successful in her own right as well, as a music teacher and a flautist in the orchestra. She would take us down to athletics meetings and she'd be the mother screaming from the crowd, urging us to run faster. But the emotion stayed on the touchlines. We knew mum and dad cared but it was never shown. I don't think either ever told us that they loved us.

Mum spent a lot of time in her music studio out in the back garden, where Doug went to play bassoon, Peter and Richard the clarinet, and I took them cold drinks. School once gave me an E-flat horn, a sort of baby euphonium, but after making a noise which sounded like a sick cow I gave music up as a bad job. Mum and dad used to fight a lot. They say they don't remember that but we do. It had a huge effect on us. We blamed ourselves but I think it was just one of those things. At first they stayed in separate rooms in the house, which we couldn't really understand. Then mum moved three kilometres up the road to a two-bedroom house, which had a little extension out the back where Rich and I lived. Pete moved into the main house with mum, Doug stayed with dad as he was just finishing school.

I had not seen it coming, then again I had not been looking out for it. My mind was always on sporting fields. It was not until I was eighteen or nineteen that I sat mum down and asked her questions about what actually happened. I wanted to finally figure out what had gone wrong. Then I went to have a beer with dad and asked him the same. Dad found himself a girlfriend pretty soon after leaving home, to whom he is now married. As a teenager you always blame that person, saying she broke up everything. But mum and dad insisted that was not the case and I realised it was for the best that they split up.

Mum remembers it this way. 'The boys have always been very close and supported each other hugely but they all suffered during that time, they all retreated into their shells I think. But when you're in the middle of a divorce it takes you about two years to get yourself right, let alone have the mind, time and insight to be able to analyse four little boys and see where they're at. I didn't love them any less, you must understand, but it was a difficult time.

'I didn't realise at the time that you have to keep telling them that it's not their fault that you're getting divorced. It has nothing to do with them. And that was exactly the case. They are all an absolute godsend and without them I wouldn't have got through it half as well as I did.'

After dad moved out we didn't really see him, other than at sporting events. Compare that with the way things had been, with dad waking us up and taking us for a run almost every morning. He worked so hard that the only time we would see him was when we were very successful at sport. But we were caught up in what we were doing – sport had taken over our lives – and because we were successful we didn't feel we really needed a father figure in our lives. We had ourselves and we had mum and we had a fantastic school.

*

Rugby was my life by the time I left Grey High School in 1989 at the age of eighteen. It saved me from National Service, which at the time was compulsory for South African men between the ages of 18 and 19, and it earned me a sports bursary to Technikon, the equivalent of an English technical college, worth about £300 at the time. I played rugby for them and also for the Crusaders club in Port Elizabeth.

National Service was no holiday and I can remember vividly the day Doug went into the army, standing in tears with mum and Rich as he and all the other new recruits lined up in their brown uniforms. He was nineteen and he was bound for the Angolan border. Whereas Pete went up to the border two years later and spent six months sunbathing and shooting at wild animals, Doug was in the townships when the army got drafted in to quell the riots. I've heard from others that it was a really bad scene up there. Doug never went into details when he came home, other than to say it was tough.

I wanted to get National Service out of the way as soon as I left school, but two weeks before I was due to go into the forces I broke my arm playing rugby and they would not take me. I never did make it, as National Service later became voluntary. Instead I went to Technikon where I lasted all of four months studying mechanical engineering, before baling out to concentrate on rugby. I had just broken into the Eastern Province senior side and wanted to devote my full attention to training for rugby as well as triathlon.

In order to make ends meet I worked in a sports shop for six months on the main road in Port Elizabeth before going to work for a while for my dad's electrical company, manufacturing home alarms. A family friend, Peter Sharman, used to buy alarms from dad and install them locally where he lived in Jeffrey's Bay, a holiday resort forty-five minutes from Port Elizabeth. I began helping him with installations and after a while he offered me £120 a month to go and work for his company, Coastal Security, and also agreed to let me live with him.

It was while I was working for Peter that I made my first big breakthrough in rugby, coming on as a replacement for the Eastern Province senior side in a Currie Cup match against Western Transvaal. The match was played at Olen Park, deep in the corn veldt. Not for nothing is it known as the Graveyard, with its bone-hard pitch surrounded by old wooden stands packed full of maize farmers. I was just eighteen and, if that wasn't exciting enough, I replaced Springbok centre Michael du Plessis for the last five minutes. I touched the ball twice and we won convincingly.

I thought it was just the start, but over the next two years I played only five games for Eastern Province before getting dropped, for the first time since I was nine, shortly before my twenty-first birthday. The reason, I was told, was that I didn't fit in with their strategy. The initial plan had been to run the ball. That didn't work so they told me to kick. Still we lost and they blamed me, making it known that I didn't fit in 'with their style of play'. I have no doubt I would have stood a better chance of keeping my place had I been an Afrikaner, as 90 per cent of the team were; if for no other reason than I found communicating with the rest of the team very difficult. I was devastated and my confidence dipped alarmingly. Only my brothers kept me from jacking in training.

Perhaps I was over-sensitive; after all I was the fourth fly-half to get the bullet that year in an Eastern Province team which had a reputation for reacting to defeats by dropping players. That year they lost eight of their ten matches. They had also had a reputation for having big-kicking number 10s, and I didn't want to kick. It made me wonder whether I was ever going to get a decent run at top-flight rugby, or whether I was banging my head against a brick wall. I was frustrated and didn't know what to do for the best. I envied Pete who was away in Canada with the South African triathlon team and I despaired of ever getting the chance to follow him into international sport.

I needed something to happen in my life to spark a chance of fortune and it came at my twenty-first birthday party, of all occasions. We had an aeroplane party where each room was themed as a different country, full of the food and drink associated with it. My recollection is that there was more drink than food. We started in France on the champagne, then moved to Russia and got on the vodka. I was just heading into Mexico to start slamming tequilas when the phone rang. It was Pete ringing from Stroud in England where he was visiting our uncle Doug on the way back from Canada.

'Mate, get yourself over to England. It's a fantastic place. You'll love it.'

I returned to my tequila and then moved into the South African room where I spent the rest of the evening necking Castle beers and soaking up a fraction of the alcohol I had put away with braaivleis and biltong. But even in my significantly inebriated state, Pete's words kept repeating in my head. I was out of the Eastern Province team, there was no suggestion that I would get my place back any time soon. What the hell?

The following Monday I talked it through with Carmen, my girlfriend at the time, and we agreed I should grasp the opportunity.

It was only a holiday, I told myself; to spend some time with Pete and meet my uncle and grandparents. And Carmen could always come over and join me. It wasn't as though I would be leaving Port Elizabeth for ever. After all, my South African passport had a visa limiting my stay to four months.

I didn't tell mum and dad until two days before I was due to leave, when the tickets arrived, partly because I thought there was a chance dad might say no. Three weeks earlier I had been offered the chance to go and play in Australia for Wollongong with one of my younger brother's friends, but dad had vetoed it and I'd thrown a proper tantrum. It was the first time I ever swore at him.

I need not have worried. We had family in England and mum was particularly excited that I would be visiting her country and her brother and parents, not to mention Pete. She said it was a great opportunity to see a bit of the outside world and experience life away from the Eastern Cape. Dad was slightly more reserved, though only because it meant me leaving my job. But my mind was made up. I was going to England.

2
ON MY OWN

Heathrow Airport, 27 September 1992

I had had enough. I was lost, I was alone and I was thousands of miles from home. What ever had persuaded me to leave everything I knew and loved to come to England with only a rucksack for company? I was in bits. And I had been on foreign soil for less than an hour.

Heathrow can be pretty daunting at the best of times. People queuing, people pushing, nobody looking where they are going. I had only ever been to a small airport in my life and here I was deposited in the biggest and busiest airport in the world. I wanted to jump straight back on the plane and go home. There was no one to meet me and I was badly hung over because the boys had got me so pissed the night before I left.

I reached into my rucksack to pull out the contact details for where I was to go, which I had scrawled on a bit of paper the previous day. Nothing. The pocket was zipped up but inside there was nothing but a wedge of Rand notes. Typically I hadn't done my homework and so knew nothing at all of the geography of England. I thought Heathrow was slap bang in the middle of the country. I knew Jack and Pam, my mum's parents, lived somewhere in the south, not a million miles from an airport called Gatwick, but where exactly that was I didn't have a clue.

I panicked. There were no long slow deep breaths, no let's-think-about-this-calmly sort of reaction. Bugger, bugger, bugger! It was very overwhelming. I hadn't exchanged any money and so had no means of phoning home. I had 4,000 Rand on me, about £350. I found a bureau de change but couldn't find an exchange rate for South African currency. First the woman behind the counter couldn't understand what I was saying due to my thick accent, then she had to go and get the information I needed from someone else.

Eventually I got my hands on enough 50-pence coins to get me a couple of minutes long-distance to Port Elizabeth, only no one was at home. Mum was at work, as was dad. I had no other telephone numbers with me. A lady at the information desk suggested I looked for my grandparents in the phone book and handed me this enormous tome. By chance it covered the Sussex area and I found a J. Crowther listed in Eastbourne.

Again nobody answered but, thinking I now knew where I was going, I took a coach to Gatwick, then headed off on a train I thought was bound for the south coast, only for it to terminate in Tonbridge. Depressed and in a state of panic, I booked into a nearby bed and breakfast and lay awake all night wondering what the hell I was up to. The next morning I finally got through to gran and she drove in from the coast to pick me up.

I stayed a week in Eastbourne, which I spent sightseeing. But the attraction of walking the tourist trail with a couple of seventy-five-year-olds soon wore off and uncle Doug answered my SOS to come and fetch me. Just as well, mind, as if it had been left to me to find a village called Bussage in the West Country I'd still be looking.

Pete was already there when I arrived, along with Doug's girl-friend Kathy and his two daughters Fiona and Jayne. They are northern girls and were very welcoming. I received a kiss from each before I had even introduced myself. This is more like it, I thought.

Pete and I worked with the two girls and Jayne's then boyfriend Greg, who was a landscape gardener. It was the middle of winter and we were building stone walls right at the bottom of a valley. For two weeks Greg would pick us up at seven o'clock in the morning and take us down the valley where it was still dark at eleven o'clock. I would then spend the rest of the day getting my fingers caught underneath boulders. It was cold, no, bloody freezing. Not quite the same as my early starts in Port Elizabeth.

Because it only left the pitch-black evenings in which to train, Pete and I only lasted a fortnight before deciding we needed to find some other job which would allow us more training time. Problem was we didn't find anything and instead just dossed about until my uncle had a day off, saw us lying idle around the house and told us we couldn't continue like that.

Other than the two girls and Greg we didn't know a soul and I was feeling pretty homesick. The weather was cold and miserable and I longed to be back in the sunshine of Port Elizabeth. From being with my mates every day for so many years at home, I now had no mates at all. I was not loving England quite as much as Pete had thought I would.

My mood wasn't improved by a night out my brother and I had at a club in Stroud. We then went into town with the girls and ended up in a club called Egypt Mill. It was a horrible atmosphere full stop, the like of which I had never experienced in South Africa. There were a lot of blokes getting lary, looking for a scrap. My brother is quite a feisty bugger and we were lucky to get out in one piece.

The lack of friends was getting me down and I talked it through with my uncle. Between us we came to the conclusion that the best way of me making mates was through rugby, and my uncle offered to find me a club to play for. He mentioned Sevenoaks, a Kent club that he had played for, but we agreed that it was too far to travel. Stroud was convenient but my uncle reckoned that as I had played for Eastern Province I could do better.

'Let's give Gloucester a call,' he said.

I knew nothing whatsoever about English club rugby and nodded in agreement, whilst making no move towards the phone. I had never heard of Gloucester.

Then a fateful thing happened. Doug dialled the number for Kingsholm and the phone rang out. Nobody answered. He let it ring some more. Still nothing.

'Right, I'll try Bath instead,' he said.

Whatever, I thought, little knowing at the time how significant that turn of events was to be. I didn't know if I was up to their standard for the simple reason that I didn't know what their standard was. It was only subsequently that I watched *Rugby Special* with my uncle and the commentator reeled off all the trophies Bath had won that I realised what a prestigious club it was.

The secretary at Bath picked up, my uncle explained the situation and he was put on to Gareth Chilcott who said I would be welcome to come down for a run around at the Lambridge training ground and they would see what sort of standard I was. It was only when I got there that I realised how big a deal it was. While I knew nothing about Bath or English club rugby, Five Nations matches were screened in South Africa and England's star players were well known to me. But to find that the likes of Jeremy Guscott, Richard Hill, Stuart Barnes, Phil de Glanville, Jon Webb and John Hall all played for Bath came as a major shock.

With my new boots, bought earlier that day in Stroud, and my black and red striped Eastern Province rugby shirt, I arrived at Lambridge feeling like a new boy on the first day of school, unsure if I was doing the right thing. But within minutes Chilcott, known to all as Coach, had welcomed me and I was immediately struck by a feeling that it didn't matter to anyone where I came from or what accent I had. The days of being discriminated against because I was not Afrikaaner were over. Respect at Bath Rugby Club would be earned purely by how I played rugby.

The flip side of that was that nobody, particularly Jerry Guscott, would give you any respect you until you earned your stripes on the pitch. With Jerry, if you were a good player he would talk to you. If you weren't he wouldn't. But that was fine by me. Brian Ashton, the Bath backs coach, suggested I join in with the team run around the pitch. There was Nigel Redman, Ben Clarke, Tony Swift, Jon Webb, Victor Ubogu, Andy Robinson, Dave Egerton and Jon Callard, all of whom I recognised from England games I had tuned in to watch back in Port Elizabeth. Bloody hell, I thought, do England pick players from any other club? I couldn't wait to get back to my uncle's to phone dad and tell him who I had been training with.

As we jogged, Sean O'Leary, a giant of a second row, made a point of introducing himself to me and we chatted, helping to settle my nerves as we went. At the end of the warm-up Chilcott asked me to go and continue training with the second and third XV team players on the other pitch and at the end of the session I was told that they intended to start me at fly-half for the Thirds against Plymouth Albion at the weekend. I was absolutely buzzing.

The goal kickers stayed out practising at the end of the session and I stood behind the posts watching. Stuart Barnes kicked one near to where I was standing and I caught it and returned it with interest, catching it a little too well and sending the ball spiralling over his head and way beyond him. Barnes looked at me as if to say who the hell is this guy?

I felt a bit embarrassed as he turned round and set off to retrieve the ball. Yet at no time in those early days at the club did I feel out of my depth. Although I was naturally shy, the rugby field was my stage, that was where I could express myself, purely by playing. I didn't have to open my mouth and do other things.

That is not to say it was not a demanding place to play your rugby. The head coach was Jack Rowell and if a guy didn't make the grade Jack would eff and blind. A number of players came and went pretty sharply, guys who either weren't good enough or simply couldn't handle the criticism Jack dished out. His style of management was to test players, physically and mentally, and see how far he could push them. His theory was always that his confrontational approach bred competitiveness. It was definitely not to everybody's liking. A fair few simply walked off the pitch, not prepared to be shown up in front of the rest of the squad any longer. Good old Jack.

I put up with it largely because I was able to swear at him in

Afrikaans and he didn't have a clue what I was saying, but also because I was keen as mustard to make it at Bath. So keen, in fact, I moved out of my uncle's house and into Bath, even though I had little money and nowhere to stay. I spent the first two weeks living out of my backpack and staying in the youth hostel halfway up Bathwick Hill.

Life took a turn for the better when I found a two-bedroom flat on London Road near to the training ground, or so I thought. My girlfriend Carmen was due to come over from Port Elizabeth with my pal Kerry Bosch and the three of us were going to split the cost. There were only two problems with that. The first was that I thought the monthly rent was 390 Rand when in fact it was £390, a hugely significant difference. The second was that Carmen and Kerry then decided not to come.

To compound my misery I didn't know how to work the central heating system in the flat and would spend each night on my own, lying in the lounge wrapped up in a sleeping bag. There was no telly, nothing. My only company was a guitar and with nothing else to do I spent hours trying to teach myself to play the damned thing.

For three months I bled my savings accounts dry paying for the place, with no job or other income to pay the bills. Only money my gran had been paying into an account for me since the day I was born kept me afloat. I didn't have any transport either and we trained at Bath University, a three-mile run uphill from where I was staying. Every morning I would get up at 5.45 a.m. and set off up the hill. After a while some of the lads with cars realised what I was doing and would stop and give me a lift, which is how I got to know John Mallett, Iestyn Lewis and Ian Sanders in particular.

At the end of my lease John, Iestyn, Gareth Adams and myself moved into a flat in Pulteney Street and my days of loneliness came to an abrupt end. Let's just say it was a good student flat and that some of what went on there was a massive eye-opener for me. I was very conservative and had only had one girlfriend in my life. I couldn't believe how open English girls were about sex. We would wake up on a Sunday morning not knowing who was in the flat because everybody used to just crash there. It was a complete mess and I had a tiny little room, but at least I could work the heating.

But rugby remained my focus and with no job to occupy my week I spent a lot of time training at the university. An early morning gym session would be followed by breakfast and then we would do speed work or plyometrics or watch videos of recent Bath and England matches; whatever it took to improve us as players and bring forward the day when we would get a chance in the first team.

Mine came in December 1992 in a friendly against Nottingham up at their place, but I made my first impact at the club on my second appearance the following month, when I scored two tries from fly-half in a convincing win over London Irish at the Rec, Bath's home ground. Stuart Barnes returned after that game, having been away captaining the South & South-West to the Divisional Championship, and I was relegated to the second XV, but three weeks later Jack gave me my Courage League debut, away at Gloucester of all places.

This was a big deal for me and we won the game 20–0, thanks to a try by Tony Swift and five penalties kicked by Jon Webb. Jack went ape in the changing room afterwards, ripping into all but myself and Ian Sanders. We were the new boys and Jack decided to spare us on this occasion. My time would come. And with a vengeance.

In my first season I never really understood this guy, both his methods and actually what he was saying. Jack is six foot six and would spend every training session screaming and shouting in his north-east accent. I just tried to keep my head down and get on with training and playing but, after we played Gloucester in Jon Webb's final appearance for the club, Jack went for me.

We had lost the game, a friendly, 17–16 after I conceded a late try attempting a little chip in our 22 which was picked off and run back. Jack was furious. The door into the Bath changing room opens from right to left and I was sitting on the bench nearest the door. As Jack walked through the door he whacked me across my head.

'If you ever play like that again, you'll never play football for us,' he raged. 'You might play like that for Eastern Province, but you're not going to play like that here in Bath.'

I was totally shocked, I couldn't believe what he had done and I wasn't about to accept it.

'Fuck off, you wanker,' I yelled in front of all the boys. 'How dare you fucking do that to me!'

It was purely an instinctive reaction to what he had done to me but it didn't go down at all well. Everyone stopped what they were doing and looked up. Our confrontation had been unusual for the simple reason that the more experienced players would have belted Jack back. I had chosen to use expletives rather than violence. I vented my fury, then sat back down and put my head in my hands.

Jack didn't say anything. I don't think he could believe that someone had spoken like that to him. He addressed the team and our collective failings in the game. Then he walked out of the changing room. All eyes turned to me. Seconds later he came back in and called me out into the massage room next door.

'Don't you ever belittle me in front of those players again.'

I felt bad. I mean really bad. It was my first season at Bath and this was a guy who was not only head coach but had also suggested to me that I might get a game for England's Under-21 team later that season, an international honour which wouldn't jeopardise my chances of playing for the Springboks. He said he had spoken to the 21s coach, John Elliott.

But I was also convinced that he was in the wrong. So when he demanded that I go back into the changing room and apologise to him in front of the other players, I refused. 'I'm sorry, Jack, but you can't go around hitting people.'

'Enough!' he barked. 'Don't you ever say that again.' With that he stormed out.

I sought out Gareth Chilcott and asked him what I should do. Typical of the man he replied: 'Don't worry about it, Catty. He'll respect you for standing up to him, and if he does it again I'll shove his watch up his arse.'

I appreciated his support and that of other players, particularly Martin Haag, who had taken me under his wing from the start, and assured me that it wouldn't be a problem, 'so don't make it a problem'. I didn't feel I needed to apologise to Jack. I didn't think I had done anything wrong – other, obviously, than to have gifted Gloucester the winning try, which of course I regretted. But three days after our spat I had heard nothing further from Jack and I turned up for training more than a little apprehensive. This guy wielded all the power at the club.

Midway through the session, as Jack went from drill to drill, he walked up to me and, without ceremony, said, 'I apologise.' It caught me by surprise. 'Oh, yeah, fine, no worries,' I responded and carried on jogging. It wasn't a sit-down apology and he didn't say it in earshot of anybody else but at least he acknowledged he had been at fault. From that day on I think he changed his opinion of me. I think his respect for me actually grew. I think he thought, fair play, this boy has got some mettle.

But the incident had brought on my homesickness again. My brother was back in South Africa, I had no money, I missed the sunshine and, to cap it all, Carmen had failed one of her exams at university and, because she would have to retake it in February, had decided not to come over but instead wait for me to come home, as scheduled, at the end of that month.

My mind was in a spin. On the one hand I wanted to go home for all the stuff I was missing, and because I felt I had something I wanted to prove to Eastern Province for dropping me and I still had my heart set on winning a Springbok jersey. On the other I had started playing regularly for the Bath first team and was loving the club's brand of rugby. It was instinctive, exactly the way I had grown up playing. I didn't have to change my game in any way. What you saw you did and the players around you reacted to it.

I had a big decision to make, one which was no longer influenced by a visa-enforced time restraint as dad had sorted out a British passport for me which had come through. Of all people to sway me into staying it was Jack. His lobbying of John Elliott had worked and I was picked to play for the England Under-21s against the French

Armed Forces at Twickenham in a curtain-raiser to the Pilkington Cup final.

I had never seriously considered that I would play for England before that point. Why would I, after just nine games for Bath, eight of which were friendlies? When the possibility became reality it suddenly hit me. I started thinking, do I really want to play for England when I have spent my life dreaming of playing for South Africa? What would everyone back home in Port Elizabeth make of it?

I spoke to my family, each and every one of them. I was homesick in a foreign country which now wanted me to represent it. What the hell should I do? Mum, being English, was obviously chuffed to bits. Dad saw it as an opportunity to develop my career. He reminded me of what I already knew; that winning an Under-21 cap for one country did not preclude me from representing another at senior level. But never did he put any pressure on me to play for South Africa. Not once. The reaction of my parents and brothers was exactly what I wanted to hear and made my decision far easier. Now I just needed to convince myself that it was the right thing to do.

What were the implications to my rugby career of going home? Well, I would be an Englishman in an Afrikaaner environment again, and have obstacles placed in my way for that reason alone. Even if I did play I would be in a dogfight every weekend, playing a very physical game at the bottom of the Currie Cup standings and kicking a lot. Club rugby in South Africa resembled a boxing match. How would that develop me as a player?

Okay, I thought, what is the alternative? Stay at Bath, who had just been crowned English champions on points difference ahead of Wasps, play week in week out with so many great players, and win basically everything. All of a sudden it didn't seem quite such a tough call. At school I had always told myself that if an opportunity came up I would take it. I stayed true to that pledge. I didn't see myself as English in any way, but being a part of Bath had enormous appeal.

On 1 May 1993 something changed inside me. It was the day of my England debut and my first appearance at Twickenham and at the end of it I would never again yearn to play for South Africa. Pulling on the white shirt would make up my mind for me. I can't explain it. Up to then all my dreams had revolved around pulling on the green and gold. But I would walk off Twickenham and be struck with this feeling of certainty that I had taken the right path.

All this happened before a capacity crowd of 54,000 had taken their seats to watch Leicester beat Harlequins to win the Pilkington Cup final, with a young second row forward called Martin Johnson scoring the decisive try in a 23–16 victory. Our Under-21 game was a midday kick-off and my team-mates included future England stars Lawrence Dallaglio, Richard Hill, Mark Regan, Simon Shaw, Tony Diprose, Tim Stimpson and Jon Sleightholme.

It was a good day for me in every respect. I scored one of our three tries, converted two and added four penalty goals for 21 points in total. I particularly enjoyed my try. We were awarded a penalty and my body language suggested I was going to go for the posts. The French obviously thought so and dropped their guard. I tapped and went, cutting through two forwards to score.

Because it was lunchtime all but probably 10,000 of the crowd were still troughing in the car parks, but I like to think I made an impression on those who were in the stadium. Only later, however, did I get the recognition that mattered most to me when I was named in the Under-21s squad to tour Australia at the end of the month. I had achieved my ambition. I had become an international sportsman.

3

GOING HOME

Port Elizabeth, 7 June 1994

It was a day I had longed for. The day I returned to Port Elizabeth as England fly-half to play against Eastern Province, the team who told me I was not good enough. On paper it was a dream come true, a triumphant homecoming. In reality it turned out to be an absolute nightmare.

My progress had been swift since the Under-21 tour to Australia a year earlier, on which we beat the Aussies and I scored one of our three tries. Victories don't come any sweeter than that. I then flew off to Canada with Bath on a pre-season tour and, in the absence of Stuart Barnes, made a name for myself at fly-half.

That opened all sorts of doors for me. Not only did I start the season in Bath's first team, due to a long-term injury to Jerry Guscott, I was picked by the South-West, by England 'A' and by Emerging England to play in games against the touring All Blacks. By the end of the season Bath had won the league and cup double, I had been voted Whitbread Most Promising Player of the Year and I had made my full England debut, albeit ingloriously, against Wales in the final match of the Five Nations Championship.

Now here I was back home looking to cap a brilliant season by proving a point to my former team, as well as showing off the city I loved to my England mates. I had told them so much about it. Port Elizabeth was not known as the Friendly City for nothing, I assured them. They would get the warmest of welcomes.

Twenty-eight minutes into the game Jon Callard received his, and it could have cost him the sight in his right eye. Seeing him on the floor at a ruck, Eastern Province lock Elandre van der Bergh stamped on Callard's head, causing a three-inch gash horrifically close to his eye which needed twenty-five stitches to sew together.

It had been bad enough that the year-round sunshine of my youth had been replaced by a howling wind and driving rain; any resort boasting a beach as its number one attraction suffers when the weather turns. The flight down from Johannesburg had also been awful, we had been taken to the wrong hotel and when we eventually found the right one the facilities were distinctly unimpressive.

Now there was less than half an hour on the clock and we were already three men down, Dean Ryan having suffered a broken thumb and Graham Rowntree having been forced off with concussion. It was already the dirtiest, most unpleasant match I had ever played in and it was taking place in my home town.

I had done a deal with Jack for my younger brother Rich to be on the England bench as we were short of a scrum-half following an injury to Dewi Morris the previous weekend. The agreement was that in return for Rich saving the Rugby Football Union the cost of flying out a replacement for the final week of the tour, Steve Bates would come off and Catt the Younger would be given the last five minutes.

But those best laid plans were ruined by the diabolical behaviour of our opponents and the actions of the home referee. The earlier tour matches had suggested strongly to us that South African refs didn't know how to handle big games, were biased in favour of the home sides and allowed violence to go unpunished. Now we felt sure of that.

Tempers reached boiling point when van der Bergh was allowed to stay on the pitch. To make matters worse the ref gave us a penalty, which meant the incident had been dealt with and van der Bergh could not later be cited. Two minutes later the balloon went up when Tim Rodber, on as a replacement for Dean Ryan, reacted to a punch from EP flanker Simon Tremain by unloading a flurry in reply and became the first England player since Mike Burton, nineteen years earlier, to be sent off.

The worst indictment of all is that I was not surprised by what we encountered. I knew from my own experience that that was what club rugby in Port Elizabeth was about. You put boxing gloves on and went out on to the pitch. That was one of the reasons I left. The only thing that shocked me was the intensity of bitterness we encountered. It was almost as though the Eastern Province team were under instruction to do as much damage as possible to England prior to the Second Test in Cape Town that weekend. Against all expectation we had easily won the First Test at altitude in Pretoria, striking a massive blow to the heart of the Afrikaans community, with Rob Andrew helping himself to 27 points in our 32–15 win. South Africa would not accept a 2–0 series defeat.

In all the chaos Rich never made it on to the field, which added to my anger. The game ended in a 30–13 win for us but the result was lost amid the recriminations. Both Rich and I were very upset and almost embarrassed to say we came from Port Elizabeth and had played rugby for Eastern Province. That's how bad it was. These were good rugby players resorting to one tactic: intimidation. This was the town our family called home yet England had been subjected to a torrid experience. The squad wasted no time in walking out of the post-match function. The boys couldn't get to Cape Town fast enough.

I had been away from home for only two years, yet so much seemed to have changed. When I had first arrived in Bath I got very angry with a bloke at the university who laid into me over the apartheid regime in South Africa which he branded a 'total disgrace'. 'It's not at all like that,' I snapped. 'Get your facts right, man.' But as the days passed, more and more evidence to support his assertion was broadcast on the BBC. I would watch the footage with a sense of shocked disbelief and be sufficiently concerned to phone home to make sure everyone was okay. There were some terrible images. Riots, petrol bombings, people getting beaten and stabbed. It could not have been more different from my perception of my country while growing up there.

I had no idea that South Africa had become an international pariah due to apartheid while I lived in the country, nor that it had provoked such anger overseas. Could it really be true that a protestor had attempted to hijack the Springboks' team bus, complete with half the side, from outside their London hotel four hours before they played England at Twickenham in 1969? The only reason I knew of opposition to the 1981 Boks' tour of New Zealand was because South African television was caught on the hop by protestors disrupting the Third and final Test at Eden Park in Auckland by dropping flour bombs on to the pitch from a low-flying aircraft.

Yet after phoning home I was confused as to what to believe. I would speak to my folks and my brothers and they would say that precious little had changed in our neighbourhood from my childhood years, other than one burglary at home in which intruders had beaten our big golden labrador with a broom then ransacked the house. 'What about the footage I'm seeing in the UK?' I would ask. 'We never see any of it,' said mum. I tended to go with what my family told me. They were safe and content and, frankly, that was the top and bottom of it for me.

Returning to South Africa with England, however, I did notice a change. Yes, I was looking for it because of what I had seen and read, and from what my brother Doug had experienced in the riot squads doing National Service. Nonetheless the increase in crime levels was obvious. There was a hell of a lot more violence than before I left. Muggings and car-jacking seemed to have become worryingly routine, certainly in bigger cities like Johannesburg and Cape Town. You certainly didn't want to make a habit of stopping at traffic lights. But people adapted to what they could and could not do. Gated developments sprang up, complete with razor wire and electric fences. Life went on.

It was not all negative. President F. W. de Klerk's government had repealed the last of the apartheid laws in 1990, four months after ending Nelson Mandela's twenty-seven-year stay in prison. Two years later South Africa was re-admitted to international sport. In 1993 de Klerk and Mandela shared the Nobel Peace prize for ending apartheid and, in May of 1994, a month before England arrived on tour and following the first multi-racial democratic elections, Mandela was sworn into office as the country's new president.

On a personal level, I began to sponsor Langa Plaatjies, a young boy who had been brought up by his grandmother, who in turn was a close friend of my childhood nanny. Langa did not have any of the advantages I was fortunate to enjoy, so I paid for him to go through school. Not everyone appeared ready to embrace the changes sweeping South Africa overnight. How exactly that explained the reception we received in Bloemfontein in the first game of the tour I'm not quite sure. Stuart Barnes was one of nine of our squad not involved in the game who were abused in Afrikaans at a pre-match function, and Barnes did not mince his words in his *Daily Telegraph* column: 'countless people informed us that we would lose every game on tour and return to watch South Africa win the World Cup at a canter. At least one or two players had the satisfaction of informing our malignant hosts that they would never see the sun rise on their homegrown Fourth Reich. The saddest fact is that our defeat by Orange Free State convinced them of the superiority of their master race.'

By the time we got to Potchefstoom, and the very same Olen Park where I made my debut for Eastern Province as an eighteen-year-old, Barnes was at the eye of a storm whipped up by his column, in which he also implied that the Afrikaans community had not come to terms with the outcome of the recent elections. I too had to take some stick for dusting down my Afrikaans and laying into some of the locals in no uncertain terms.

In truth, it was not the happiest tour for me. Yes, I got to meet former President de Klerk in the tunnel before the First Test at Loftus Versfeld and was presented to President Mandela on the pitch. And yes, having split with Carmen that spring, I met Debbie, sister of my best mate Carl's girlfriend, and she came back to England with me.

But the trip had ended on a low note when South Africa won the Second Test 27–9 at Newlands, after we tired and they scored 24 points after half-time. I hadn't made the team in either Test and I was not overly happy with my contribution on the playing front. Nobody said anything but I knew. I had not been focused enough and I would need to improve.

Back in Bath it was all change for the new season. Jack Rowell had left at the end of the previous campaign to succeed Geoff Cooke as England manager, with Brian Ashton stepping up to replace him at the Rec. Every bit as significant from my point of view, Stuart Barnes had retired, along with Gareth Chilcott and Richard Hill, and that meant a vacancy at half-back which I hoped had my name written on it.

The only doubt lay with my team-mates, as I had stayed on in South Africa after the tour to see my family and friends and there was concern that I would return in no shape to begin the new season. I was known as Beer Monster at the club for my love of drink and a good party and, having been gone four weeks, it was assumed that my fitness would be shot. They were right that I had been on the sauce, big time, but they need not have worried.

I am a bit of a freak of nature when it comes to fitness. I was one of those kids who just ran and ran, and loved doing it. From the cross-country races I monopolised at school through to becoming Eastern Province Under-21 triathlon champion, I built up a very good fitness base which I still benefit from today. All the way through to the 2003 World Cup I knew that nobody in the England squad could or would beat me over three kilometres.

Sure enough, when I reported back for pre-season with Bath I destroyed all the guys who had a month of training already under their belts. I just had that ability and, particularly in those amateur days when we used to drink a lot of booze, it stood me in good stead. It meant I could get away with being pissed every Saturday night and then on Sunday return to the club to do it all again with the 'wine-tasting' club. We'd bring the cheapest plonk we could buy from the local store, sit in a circle saying, 'Oh, this one is really fruity', and then proceed to get absolutely hammered.

I was having the time of my life, winning games and drinking like a fish. I couldn't live that lifestyle now and play professional rugby, but this was a different era. For a start I was much younger. For another everybody was doing it. When we met up with England on Wednesday nights before an international weekend we would go out and have a few beers at the Sun Inn in Richmond. If we had a Sunday training session at Twickenham we would head to Richmond on the Saturday night and get blitzed, then train the next morning. Even the night before internationals I would share a relaxing bottle of red with Stuart Barnes and Jerry Guscott.

Because we were only training two nights a week with Bath we were not putting our bodies through the massive physical ordeal that the advent of professionalism would demand. A decade later if you went on the piss then tried to train, your body would break down. But at the age of twenty-four and twenty-five I had no problems. I could go on a three-day bender and still have a great game on the Saturday.

My goals had grown rapidly in a year. Whereas the previous season my ambition had been to get a start for the Bath first team, I now had my sights set on another England shirt. My debut at Twickenham against Wales the previous season had whetted my appetite, though if I'm honest it had also caused me some embarrassment. I had been unbelievably nervous when called into action with less than three minutes left to be played after Rob Andrew's back went into spasm. I ran on to the pitch almost paralysed with fear, so much adrenaline was pumping around my body.

This was in an age where replacements were so rarely used, so I was not prepared mentally at all. I went on and immediately had to take a drop out. I couldn't feel my legs, I couldn't release the ball, I couldn't trust myself to execute the action. That's how bad it was. My kick went too long but I was happy just to have put boot to ball. Then I had to take a penalty from the 10-metre line which didn't even make the 22. Then I got into a fight. I was a complete mess. Only once again in my career would I ever feel that way, so completely overwhelmed by adrenaline – when I led England out as captain on to the same Twickenham pitch thirteen years later.

*

I would win a World Cup with Clive Woodward, or Sir Clive as he became. But he was not the most influential head coach I ever worked with. That honour goes to Jack Rowell, a brilliant business-man and a rugby genius.

Jack used peer pressure to bring the best out of the players he coached. And for a decade at Bath his strategy filled the trophy cabinet with four league titles and seven Pilkington Cups. In the amateur days before Leicester and Wasps began their duopoly of professional rugby's silverware, the Bath that Jack built won every-thing. Did I mention three league and cup doubles?

He was always testing us and not in the orthodox way. He would work out what type of character he was dealing with, then have a go to see if he could get a reaction.

I felt from the day that he whacked me across the head and then tried to get me to apologise to him, that he was one of those guys who dishes it out better than he takes it. He had wanted to lay down the law to me but didn't seem to like it at all when I stood up to him. He hated confrontation.

Will Carling tells a story of the time, after Jack became England boss, that he put down his backs coach Les Cusworth in public with a particularly dismissive, 'Don't ask him, he's only an ex-teacher.' To which Les replied: 'Say what you like, Jack. At least I've played for my country. You can only dream about it.' Rowell went absolutely ballistic with Les for having the nerve to answer back.

Jack never courted popularity, his only concern ever was winning. Success is what makes him tick, be it in sport or business. But I felt he couldn't communicate and in my view he was a poor man-manager, succeeding only in putting people on edge. In Argentina on England's tour in 1997, he stood up in front of the squad and named his Test team. He started with the forwards, went onto the scrum-half and fly-half then stopped. 'Les?' he said to coach Cusworth standing next to him. 'Help me out, help me out!' He had only forgotten the names of the centres he had picked.

By then he had been in charge for three years, but none was more memorable than the first of those, which proved a personal triumph for Jack. He spent the first part of the 1994–95 campaign changing England's style of play, with the assistance of Pierre Villepreux, the visionary French coach, and the second part watching it pay pretty spectacular dividends in the form of a Grand Slam and a major challenge for the World Cup.

It was a helluva gutsy call to change tack so close to a World Cup but Jack knew England had a settled side and he figured that, providing he kept the team stable, he could focus his attention on the way we played. The tour to South Africa had convinced him that if we were to be successful at the World Cup on the hard grounds of my homeland we would need to offer more than a set-piece-orientated, relatively static brand of power rugby.

Jack, as I have said, does things his own way, and that is not to everyone's liking. He had inherited a set-up from Geoff Cooke in which Will Carling wielded enormous influence, even having a say in selection. Will had been captain since 1988 and led the team through a golden era of Grand Slams and a World Cup final. But having helped Jack pick the tour party for South Africa, Will suddenly found his influence was on the wane.

Perhaps he perceived Will as a threat to his authority. Whatever the truth, Jack had his own ideas of the way forward for England. The team was, as he put it, 'running out of tries', and he reckoned it needed a fundamental shift in playing philosophy to turn things around. Put simply, he decided England should spend more time seeking space rather than contact.

I loved the idea because it completely tallied with my philosophy for playing rugby and the timing was absolutely perfect for me, given that I was now an established member of the squad. Through the autumn of 1994 we worked at it with Jack and Pierre at Marlow and then we put our progress to the test in two internationals at the end of the year against Romania and Canada.

Once again I was named on the bench, covering fly-half and full-back, and for the third international running did not feature. But I liked what I saw. Not so much in the 54–3 scoreline against an outclassed Romanian side, but in our hunger to move the ball about after Rob Andrew's ever dependable boot had put the result beyond doubt before half-time. In the second half we ran every penalty bar one and ended the game having taken fifteen tapped penalties; surely a record.

Back at Bath, fortunes were not so good, as Brian Ashton's rota system, designed to give everybody in the squad regular game time in a year which would be massively disrupted by international commitments, was impacting on our form. Jack's policy had always been to pick his strongest side. I knew what Brian was trying to achieve, but as a team we were unable to find any rhythm and I'm not sure our supporters saw us play a single decent game at home before April.

By then my mind was firmly into England mode. I had got lucky in the Canada game when Paul Hull lasted only twenty-seven minutes and I came on at full-back. We won 60–19 and I scored two tries and made two more. Unlike on my debut when my call from the bench took me totally by surprise and traumatised me, I had had plenty of time to prepare as Paul Hull kept playing for a good ten minutes after taking the knock, while I warmed up and got my head right. Consequently, by the time I ran on I felt relaxed. All right, maybe not quite relaxed, but certainly not a bundle of nervous anxiety.

It reflected in my performance and in the headlines the following day. 'Catt thrives in Rowell's new order' read the headline on an article written by my old team-mate and drinking partner Stuart Barnes in the *Daily Telegraph*. He wrote:

> Mike Catt produced one of the most incisive attacking perfor-
> mances imaginable from full-back. Within three minutes of being on
> the field he made a break straight through the previously impervious
> Canadian defence.
>
> It is a long time since an English full-back has run such telling
> angles. Most impressive of all, once Catt breached the defence he
> revealed a precocious rugby maturity and vision by slowing down
> and waiting for support – English players usually have a lemming-
> like capacity to run head-first into the nearest tackle. The result was
> a large hand in two of England's tries and a pair for himself. This is
> cruel on Hull, a revelation since his Test debut against South Africa
> in June, but to be a great side, brave and hard decisions are required.
> The inclusion of Catt, at Hull's expense, is such a necessity.

46

Although I had been a full-back growing up in South Africa it was only the third time I had played in the number 15 jersey since arriving in England and I can't say I had spent too much time thinking my future lay there, not when I was regularly turning out at fly-half for Bath. Yet I had felt comfortable in the position, with more time and space to play my natural running game than was available at stand-off, even at club level.

I turned to the *Sunday Times* to check that Stuart had not overdone the praise for an old team-mate. Evidently he had not. 'England were boosted by a splendid performance from Catt, a superb all-round footballer who replaced Hull in the first half,' observed Stephen Jones. The *Guardian* described England's performance as 'one of the most ambitious counter-attacking games seen at Twickenham for years.' That too made me smile as I knew I was firmly implicated in that. So many compliments after a game in which Rob Andrew equalled Didier Camberabero's world record of 30 points by landing twelve out of twelve kicks at goal. The smile on Jack's face spoke volumes. He had wanted us to develop a fifteen-man game of greater flexibility and greater movement of the ball. Albeit against second division opponents, we had done as asked.

Things snowballed from there. England selected me for their warm-weather training camp in Lanzarote over the New Year when a third of the thirty-three-man squad came from Bath. Then I got the call I had dreamed about as I took a train home to Bath from London. Jack had picked me ahead of Hull for the next game. I would start the Five Nations Championship as England full-back.

*

47

Dublin in January was perishingly cold. An icy gale swept across Lansdowne Road, freezing us to the bone and rocking the goalposts. If I tell you that some of the boys actually wore wet-suit tops underneath their jerseys, you will get the idea. It was impossible to kick into the wind, and playing full-back under the high ball was going to be bloody difficult. There were other factors complicating my big day, one which my brother Pete had flown in from Port Elizabeth to share with me.

The occasion was overshadowed by the political situation at the time. Having grown up in South Africa, I didn't understand what was going on. I knew nothing of Anglo-Irish history and, for me personally, ignorance was bliss. What I knew was that it was no joking matter. The National Anthem was not played, we had a helicopter shadowing the team bus and there were personal body-guards for Tim Rodber, Martin Bayfield, Dean Richards and Rory Underwood – each of whom worked for either the police or armed forces – whenever they went anywhere.

Sure enough Ireland welcomed me to the Five Nations brother-hood by immediately putting up a garryowen off the boot of Paul Burke, a former England Schools captain, making his debut in the green number 10 jersey. Simon Geoghegan clattered into me, spilling the ball from my grasp, then Peter Clohessy followed him in and trampled on my back. For a moment my mind flicked back over the pre-match doubt I had heard some express about me being picked out of position and thus being a potentially weak link for Ireland to exploit. I quickly shook it off. You wanted to play in the Five Nations, I joked to myself as play moved away. Don't complain about it now.

For all that, Ireland didn't get a look-in until the fifth minute of injury time when Anthony Foley nicked a consolation try, and a dubious one at that. That, in all honesty, was about the height of it for them. It was very much our day and, in particular, the forwards. Our greater experience told, but also the confidence we had in the game we had developed during the first half of the season. The conditions were a nightmare for our new dynamic approach, but we stuck to our guns, even when Jack gave us the option of reverting to a tighter game. By the end I felt we were excellent value for our 20–8 victory. Not since 1938, when they stuck 36 points on the Irish, had England won a championship match in Dublin by a more convincing scoreline.

We returned home buzzing. We had won well and had a blinding night out in Dublin into the bargain. France were next up at Twickenham a fortnight later and Jack named an unchanged side. This was a fixture the French had grown to hate as they had shown themselves unable to live with the mind games played chiefly by Brian Moore. Moore had turned it into an art form, though I suspect he will forever be remembered for the time he branded them 'fifteen Eric Cantonas' shortly after Cantona had lost the plot and karate-kicked a fan in the crowd during a game for Manchester United at Selhurst Park. Every year Moore laid into them and every year they got so wound up emotionally that they lost their ability to play.

England had strung seven wins together against them dating back to 1989 and, although we wondered whether this time they would be a tougher nut to crack, having won a Test series 2–0 in New Zealand the previous summer, the performance of their big lock forward Olivier Merle a fortnight earlier against Wales had given us a pretty good idea that they still had a finger firmly on the self-destruct button. Just seven minutes into the game Merle head-butted Ricky Evans, the Wales prop, causing him to fall awkwardly and break his leg in two places.

Merle was suspended for our game at Twickenham. In truth, I don't think it would have mattered who they had available on the day, we were that dominant. Two late tries by Tony Underwood for a 31–10 final scoreline might slightly have flattered us, but only slightly. I loved every moment of it, from my first touch which I picked up off my toes to my contribution in the final minute to Tony's second score. It was a training ground move which was called Cat-trick. Brian Moore was convinced it would not work. For once he was totally wrong.

Dean Richards broke off the back of the scrum and fed Kyran Bracken who quickly sent out a flat pass to Tim Rodber. I picked a really hard, short line off him from full-back, took the ball and exploded through the hole in the French cover before realising I was deep in enemy territory with no back-up. I slowed and turned, allowing Tony to run on to a pop-up inside pass and round behind the posts.

It was a career highlight for me and yet my strength in this championship was not in my ability to touch great heights with moments of trickery, rather to do the simple things well. A lesson I learned at a young age is that the difference between a good player and a world class player is how many mistakes he makes. My campaign was hallmarked by consistency. I didn't try too hard to impress or do anything flash. I just did what I had to do. Physically I felt pretty intimidated stepping up from club rugby at Bath to playing

50

against these big international sides. I was pretty small and physically naive. But I could kick a long way, catch a high ball, tackle and pick the odd line in attack and so was of value to the team.

In the opinion of John Mason, correspondent of the *Daily Telegraph*, that made me 'a footballer of uncommon ability'. I was very flattered, but what pleased me even more was that it followed a 23–9 win over Wales at Cardiff Arms Park. Again questions had been asked about how I would handle the aerial bombardment Neil Jenkins was expected to unleash in my direction and Will Carling was sufficiently concerned to take me to one side and assure me he had every confidence in me. How ironic then that, come game time, the one high ball Wales put up all afternoon should be fielded by the captain.

It was certainly not one of my busier afternoons. I remember making a tackle on Wales scrum-half Robert Jones which saved a try, but that's about it. Other than that it was the Rory Underwood show. Of all the grounds in all the world the Arms Park had been one of Rory's unhappier haunts. Until this day. Rory pounced twice for tries in the second half to settle the issue and erase painful personal memories of previous visits in 1989 and 1993. Just how big a win this was for us is confirmed by a glance at the history books. England had won just once in fifteen previous visits to the Welsh capital dating back thirty years. No England three-quarter had scored a try for us there in ten years. Beforehand the Rugby Football Union had felt the need to bring in a psychologist, Austin Swain, to try and remove the Cardiff demons from our heads.

Now our hearts were starting to beat faster. For three games we had concentrated on the next match, the next challenge. It had served us well. Now it was not that simple. The next match had a Grand Slam resting on it. And not only for us. Following Scotland's fantastic victory at Parc des Princes, their first in Paris for twenty-six years, and a less stunning but equally important 26–13 home victory over Wales, they too had a clean sweep in their sights.

All of a sudden the relaxed mood which had been such a feature of the England camp during the campaign gave way to a tense, anxious atmosphere. The country had good reason to feel positive about its chances of celebrating a third Grand Slam in five years, especially as the team had been unchanged throughout the championship. Not so much as once had Jack summoned a replacement from the bench. Yet there was a feeling of unease in the air.

Our skipper Will Carling had set the positive tone for our campaign by demanding a Grand Slam. But even he was feeling negative. He had led the side against Scotland the last time the two nations had gone to war for a Grand Slam and he had the mental scars to show for it. There is unlikely ever to be another Anglo-Scottish clash to compare with that game in 1990. The rivalry that day was fierce and bitter and England blew it, Will was convinced, because they assumed that they would win.

Jack had the utmost confidence in his team, in each player and in the style of rugby we were playing. He said as much to us. But we were so wound up, I think by the fear of history repeating itself, that the previously healthy environment turned into one laced with tension. In one of our training sessions he ripped into me for making a joke at his expense, demanding that I concentrate on my own game. And because I was the new kid on the block, and regarded the senior figures in the side as legends, it left quite a mark.

It is easy to be wise after the event but Will had no cause for concern, not with Rob Andrew in the team. Rob equalled the Five Nations record with 24 points from seven penalty goals and a dropped goal. I have never found goal kicking easy, but with Rob it was like shelling peas. At the end he was chaired off Twickenham by ecstatic supporters, having gone past Jon Webb's points total and become England's record points scorer.

But my abiding memory of the day is not of Rob immersed in a sea of white-shirted fans with his arms aloft in triumph. Nor is it of the relieved look on Will's face, nor even the vital tackle I made on Gavin Hastings to keep the Scots at bay when they threatened to make it a two-point ball game. It is of Brian Moore installing himself as public enemy number one north of the border by branding our opponents 'disgraceful' and accusing them of 'killing the ball and the game at all costs'.

This was not one of his pre-match rants, designed to get under the skin of the opposition, it was a view he aired on national television following the final whistle. I was savouring the moment of becoming a Five Nations champion and Grand Slam winner for the first time and reflecting on the form which would prompt Paul Ackford, writing in the *Sunday Telegraph*, to describe me as 'England's find of the season'. But Brian it seemed was busy trying to wind up the whole Scottish nation and making a pretty good job of it. Gavin Hastings summed up the feelings of his team when he told the *Daily Mail*: 'For someone of his experience to criticise the opposition in the moment of triumph is not on. His comments have made England bad winners.' Scotland coach Dougie Morgan described Moore as 'England's biggest problem'.

It didn't seem that way inside the England changing room though. Yes, Moore had added to the hatred in the air, but I was struck throughout the championship that everybody seemed to hate England. I couldn't understand it at all. It wasn't one way either. The English lads seemed to feel the same about the Welsh and the Scots. But it was all calculated. It got our forwards going and it put them in a corner from where the only course of action was to come out fighting. And at the end of it all we picked up a Grand Slam.

It was a triumph for Jack who had gone in search of more tries by changing the way England played and thought and had been rewarded by an average of three tries a game. It seemed bizarre now to think that only ten months ago Jack had addressed the media in Cape Town and admitted that England had 'lost the knack of scoring tries'. He was right. Two tries in five games was the sum total of England's productivity in 1993–94. This season we ran in twenty-one in six.

In its Five Nations review, *Rothmans*, rugby's equivalent of *Wisden*, said: 'Mike Catt emerged as a strike full-back of the highest order. Every side in the Championship threatened to expose his lack of experience in the position by bombarding him with high kicks. Catt is still waiting.'

Jack was still not happy. He knew that northern hemisphere dominance was one thing, translating that into global superiority would take an altogether mightier effort. That would require us being fitter and stronger than ever before as at the World Cup the southern hemisphere players would just be going into their season. In contrast we were at the end of ours. The 1994 tour to South Africa had been a dress rehearsal and we had been worn out mentally and physically by the time we got there.

Jack decided he had to do something about this but, because he held no sway with the clubs, he chose to put pressure on us. He demanded total dedication from us as an England squad in the same way he had previously done with us as club players when he was running Bath. That inevitably led to tension at our clubs and a feeling of guilt among us England players that we were not pulling our weight on the domestic scene due to our increased commitment to the national team. I don't believe it is any coincidence that Bath failed to win the league this season, although we still gave our fans a day to remember by retaining the Pilkington Cup at Twickenham.

I missed the game due to injury but I was happy enough. How could I feel any different? I was a South African in England yet I felt perfectly at home, embraced by a nation relishing the resurgence of its rugby team.

4

LIVING DOWN LOMU

Cape Town, 18 June 1995

I can still hear his footsteps in my mind. Feel the ground start to shake and my pulse quicken as the collision approaches. He swats away Tony Underwood, strides past Will Carling. Now he has the try-line in his sights. Only one thing stands between Jonah Lomu and his goal. God, how I wish it wasn't me.

It is a beautiful day in Cape Town and it is the biggest game of my life. England are eighty minutes from a World Cup final. We have beaten the holders, Australia, and we fancy this one. Until now. Shit. What was it I said a few days earlier? . . . 'New Zealand aren't anything special and we think we have the ability to beat them.' Can I take that back? Too late.

'. . . *The England midfield defence is good once more, Jeremy Guscott with the tackle. They're trying to swallow this All Blacks pack. But New Zealand have got it again. Bachop . . . not a great pass. Jonah Lomu with a lot of work to do . . .*'

Bachop has peeled left towards the short side, where he has only Walter Little and Lomu to work with. He throws a looping miss pass which sails over everyone and forces Lomu to check his stride and turn out towards the touchline. Tony and Will are covering him. Danger averted.

'. . . *But he's palmed off Underwood . . . Carling can't get him . . .*'

The ground inside our 22 is really shaking now. It's me against Lomu. The night before, Graham Dawe and I had watched a video of New Zealand's quarter-final against Scotland. I hadn't really paid a lot of attention to the All Blacks during the tournament and I didn't fully realise what this Lomu bloke was about. Not until I watched him break clear with only Gavin Hastings to beat. Big Gav as he was known. I'm Little Mike. Bosh! Hastings was left in a heap.

That had me thinking before the game. And now, with barely two minutes gone, it was me and him, David and Goliath. I had time for one thought. Get your body position right . . .

'. . . *Oh, Mike Catt is simply bulldozed out of the way. Look at that. Massive power. Massive strength. Poor old Mike Catt. Stamped over. What a try by Lomu.*'

So much hope, so quickly destroyed. For we had arrived in South Africa a month earlier as Grand Slam champions, undisputed kings of northern hemisphere rugby, a team given a genuine chance of ending the southern hemisphere monopoly of the World Cup.

Not that you would have known it from our reception when we landed at Jan Smuts Airport in Johannesburg in late May. There was no welcome when we touched down, as we were directed to a transit lounge and then on to a domestic flight down to Durban. There it was no better. A bus met us on the runway and whisked us away from the airport and the waiting England supporters to our hotel.

The country I thought I knew had changed again. Crime levels were significantly up, even on our last visit a year earlier, and no risks were being taken by the organisers. On the flight over I had read an article in *Rugby World* magazine entitled *Danger Zone?* which warned those travelling to the World Cup of criminal activity sweeping South Africa. The piece claimed that the country was 'engulfed in a crime wave verging on anarchy' and said that foreign visitors to the main cities would be 'prime and easy targets for the most ruthless and barbaric robbers and murderers'. Johannesburg, it concluded, was the murder capital of the world.

Bloody hell, I thought, as we checked into our hotel on the beautiful beachfront in Durban. It looked pretty much like any other holiday resort, albeit one I knew well from schooldays when I competed for my life-saving club at the national championships and also played rugby for Eastern Province at Under-21 level against Natal. I'm sure back then tourists were not robbed in phone boxes, as one was on the day we arrived.

Not that we intended putting ourselves in harm's way, at least not off the rugby pitch. We really fancied our chances in this tournament. Whereas in 1991 England were effective but predict-able, we now felt we were more mobile and flexible in our thinking, as well as fitter, stronger and better prepared, mentally and physically.

But expectation breeds pressure and, as the days counted down to our opening pool game against Argentina, so the tension inside the camp built. Nobody was allowed to go out on the beers. We would sign balls, it was agreed, but we would not attend lunches nor make personal appearances. Then the team was announced and Kyran

Bracken, so influential in our Grand Slam triumph, found his jersey given to Dewi Morris.

I was sharing a room with Kyran and he was not himself. He was always reading, which his sister told me he never usually did, lying on the beach by himself or around the pool. I don't know if there was a problem because he didn't open up to me. It just added to the tension around the hotel. With three days to go everyone seemed to be in a bad mood. There was no bounce at all in the camp. All the momentum from our Five Nations success seemed to have gone.

The flat feeling extended into the Argentina game, played in the pouring rain at a half-empty King's Park. We just couldn't get going. Nothing clicked, nothing worked. So much for the new all-singing, all-dancing England. All our points came from Rob Andrew's boot, just like the old days. But 24–18 was too close for comfort. The Pumas, too good for us in the forwards, scored the game's two tries. They would have won had they kicked their goals.

The following day Jack let rip, saying that only Steve Ojomoh had played really well and had seemed committed to winning. We were definitely lazy and I reckon it was born of complacency. We expected to win and didn't work to make it happen. We needed to chill, wind down and have a laugh. Martin Johnson gave us a giggle when he went boogie boarding and had to be rescued from the strong current by a lifeguard. Then Phil de Glanville emerged from the waves with a red-raw stomach, having used the board upside down and been given a severe chaffing.

Amazingly, for Durban, it was wet and windy for our second game against Italy in midweek. Another win, another desperately unconvincing performance. At least we crossed the try-line, the Underwood boys each taking a scoring pass from me in our 27–20 victory. But the smile was wiped from my face when I gifted the Italians a try after having a kick charged down off my left foot. Not only did I never kick with my left foot, but my head was down. A poor piece of rugby all round. It was the first real mistake of my international career and I didn't like the feeling one bit.

Looking back it seems an extreme over-reaction to say that it was one of the most demoralising things ever to happen to me. Rob Andrew told me not to worry about it. 'You've got to get on with the game.' Perhaps that was the difference between him and me. I couldn't just put it behind me. I couldn't simply forget it. I had known nothing but success in rugby since moving to England, save for that one blunder against Gloucester which earned me the wrath of Rowell. I hadn't learned to deal with setbacks.

It came as cold comfort that two wins meant we were assured of a quarter-final place against holders, Australia, who had surprisingly lost the opening game of the tournament to the hosts. We knew we would not even get close to the Wallabies playing the way we were. We had one game left to find a spark and, with Rob injured, Jack said he wanted me to make things happen at fly-half. After my Italian blunder I was only too eager to oblige.

We needed to draw a line under the first two games and make a statement about what England were capable of, if only to give the Wallabies something to think about. It was easier said than done because Jack had drafted in a number of fringe players for our last pool game against Western Samoa and the heat was on us from the press. Against Argentina we had been branded 'gormless', against Italy 'pedestrian', a team stuck 'on the road to nowhere'. It was hard to disagree and I was determined to personally do something about it.

The signs were good in training for the match. We were completely committed to the sessions, which were so different to the ones before the first two games. They were a lot sharper, with a low error rate, which is what we were looking for, and we then translated that to the game. Playing at fly-half allowed me to get more rhythm to my game and I felt I put some zip into the back line. Rory scored two tries and there was a first for England from a young Neil Back. With Jon Callard landing eight of his nine kicks at goal, it all added up to a resounding 44–22 scoreline.

Spirits were lifted right across the squad. At last we had fired a shot in this World Cup. At last we had given our supporters something to write home about. Western Samoa might not be one of the game's superpowers, but they are no mugs and had made lighter work of Italy than we did. They had also overturned a 26–13 deficit in the last ten minutes to beat Argentina 32–26. Still, that did not make them Australia and as we flew up to Johannesburg, our allocated home for the knockout phase, we knew we still had it all to do.

England had lost the 1991 World Cup final to the Aussies at Twickenham and there had been bad blood ever since, always stirred up by David Campese. What Brian Moore is to Anglo-French and Anglo-Scottish relations, Campo is to this fixture. He never missed an opportunity to run England down and to tell them how boring their brand of rugby is. I suspect it was his words which psyched England into changing their playing style for that final, abandoning the tight game – which played to their forward strength and had got them to Twickenham – for a running game which played into the hands of the opposition. England should never have lost that final.

Four years on and we had a team psychologist to make sure those demons remained in the past. And on the eve of our Sunday quarter-final Austin Swain handed every member of the squad a sheet of paper, with slips numbered 1 to 21, and asked each of us to fill in comments anonymously about every other player involved in the matchday squad. Only positive stuff, he reminded us. Now was not the time for jokes. The results were then collected up, put in personalised envelopes and posted under the door of each player's hotel room in Cape Town, where the match was to be played.

'Catty, you're one of the best players I've ever played alongside,' was one message. 'What an honour it is to play with you,' read another. 'When you're firing, mate, nobody can touch you.'

It might have been contrived, but still to get compliments like that from team-mates, many of whom I regarded as legends, further boosted my confidence which was already high after the Western Samoa game. All the same, I had never before played in a game of this magnitude and, as the hours ticked down to the midday kick-off, the nerves kicked in. I had a cup of coffee and promptly threw it up.

It was a cold, wet and windy day at Newlands. Dad was in the stands to watch me play a full international for first time. My oldest brother Doug had flown down too. Before the game even started we had struck the first blow. Austin, our psychologist, had noted down Australia's strike moves and defensive patterns. By the time we took to the field we felt pretty sure that there were no surprises in store for us.

But we had one for them and Rob Andrew delivered it deep in injury-time with the scores locked at 22–22. We had led early through a long-range try by Tony Underwood, after Guscott pounced on a Michael Lynagh handling error on halfway. But our 13–6 half-time lead had been whittled away, first when Damian Smith jumped high to beat me and Tony to a high ball at the start of the new half, then through Lynagh's sharp shooting.

The try apart, I had done everything asked of me. Solid under countless high balls, assured in possession. Yet with five minutes left the Aussies led 22–19 and we were going out. I missed a drop-goal chance with a horrible flat and wayward attempt, but we didn't fold under the pressure, we refused to lie down and Rob came to our rescue, nailing his fifth penalty of the afternoon. Into injury-time and both sides were resigned to an extra period of play when we won a penalty just inside our own half. Rob wanted to have a crack but Will decided it was too far out and instead instructed me to find touch.

Dean Richards, being a Leicester man, knows a driving maul opportunity when he sees one and he spotted this immediately, even though we were still thirty-five metres out. Rob agreed that a drive off the line-out would give him a chance to drop for the posts and back the ball duly came. Rob caught it on Australia's 10-metre line, to the left of centre and a long way out for such an attempt at such a crucial time in such a massive match. Head down, he swung his boot, powering through the ball in text-book fashion. I was too far back to know for sure whether the kick was good, so looked at Rob's body language for a sign. He bounced on his feet as the ball approached its target. 'Go on, go on . . .' Then raised both arms triumphantly as it split the posts. 'You beauty!'

How we felt for Campese at that moment! Australia with their exciting rugby were heading home and 'boring old England' were bound for the semi-finals after what I rated one of England's greatest ever performances. In the changing room we decided on a sing-song. Leaving the door ajar so that the Aussies could hear, we blasted out the words 'I'm leaving on a jet plane, don't know when I'll be back again.' To top off a fabulous day a disconsolate Campese left the stadium and climbed on to the bus heading back to the Wallabies hotel. At least he thought he had. It was actually the transport laid on for our wives and girlfriends. And didn't they let him know it.

Having put out the holders I really thought we would beat New Zealand. It was not a matter of hope. I genuinely expected us to. So sure was I, in fact, that my diary entry for Wednesday 14 June went as follows: 'We're feeling confident now. New Zealand aren't anything special and we think we have the ability to beat them.' Twenty-four hours later I added; 'I suspect Jonah Lomu won't get the chance to run at me because we'll have him under so much pressure that he won't get a look-in. And we know that there are big chinks in his defensive game.'

That looked pretty stupid after Lomu had turned in the single most devastating performance in World Cup history: four tries in a 45–29 New Zealand victory. Never before had England conceded so many points in a match. Yet the fact remained that if we had closed down his space and got in his face, denying him time and room to get going, Lomu wouldn't really have been able to go anywhere. It was when he got up a head of steam that he just killed us. Absolutely crucified us.

Had we stopped them in the first quarter I think it would have been a different game. But that's easily said. A bit like the captain of the *Titanic* saying had he not hit the iceberg it would have been a different journey. New Zealand were absolutely phenomenal. Lomu, who had won only two caps prior to the tournament, was super-human, Josh Kronfeld sensational and others very good. But every ball bounced their way and we made a lot of silly errors which they cashed in on.

In hindsight beating Australia was our World Cup final. It was such a massive victory for us it left us mentally drained and physically heavy-legged. But we didn't help ourselves either in the game or, especially, the build-up. What were we doing going to Sun City for a three-day piss-up in semi-final week? The All Blacks would never have done that, England under Clive Woodward would certainly not have done. Though I had a ball at the time, it now makes me cringe to think about it.

The trip was ill-conceived and it was arrogant on our part. It broke our concentration and we never regained the mental edge which had carried us past the Wallabies. But that England team was full of arrogance, self-confidence, whatever you want to call it. That is just the way the guys were. The likes of Guscott, Carling and Moore had enjoyed years as kingpins in the northern hemisphere, winning Grand Slams and reaching a World Cup final. Now we had put out the holders in a World Cup quarter-final. The feeling was that we could do no wrong. Then the game kicked off at Newlands.

Within two minutes Lomu was heading my way. New Zealand had caught us off guard from the start, with Andrew Mehrtens switching the direction of his kick-off away from his forwards and towards a twenty-year-old dubbed a 'human rhino' by Gareth Chilcott. They had apparently planned the move six months earlier, reckoning that we would be their semi-final opponents. They deliberately broke up our pattern of play, taking the ball away from our forward strength. They caught us with our pants down.

Will Carling and Tony Underwood collided and between them fumbled the kick-off. New Zealand pounced on it and attacked first right, then left. Graeme Bachop, their scrum-half, tossed out a loose pass vaguely in Lomu's direction. Too quickly he readjusted, gathered the ball and began to motor. We had to take him now, before he built up a head of steam.

Tony tried first, thirty metres out, but was handed off. Next came Will, as Lomu accelerated again, diving at his ankles on the edge of the 22. In fairness he managed to make contact but it did more harm than good. Jonah stumbled and lurched towards me. He was now six paces away but his body was at such an angle that I thought I only had to go low and he would crash to earth.

I first felt his left knee, knocking me backwards off my feet. Next came his right and I went from my backside on to my back with the force of the collision. I grasped for something to hold on to, my arms flailing. But he was over the top of me, those tree-trunk legs pumping like pistons. And then it was over. He hadn't fallen at all. In fact he had regained his balance. Three more strides and he dived across the try-line.

In homes, rugby clubs and bars around the UK the voice of ITV commentator Mark Robson rang out, accompanied by a sharp intake of breath from all who witnessed the mismatch. '. . . *Mike Catt is simply bulldozed out of the way. Look at that. Massive power. Massive strength. Poor old Mike Catt. Stamped over. What a try by Lomu.*'

I lay sprawled on the Newlands turf, shell-shocked at what had just happened. Lomu was an irresistible force the like of which I had never experienced. Not even those big, physically intimidating Afrikaner farmers from my youth had even remotely prepared me. Had Carling not ankle tapped him Lomu would still have got past me. He would just have run around me, like he did two times after that to score, when he had so much space and I couldn't get near him. But on that occasion he simply steamrollered me. I barely amounted to a speed bump in his path.

As I clambered to my feet another All Black was in my face. This time it was Frank Bunce. 'Have some of that then,' he roared. Minutes later England's first attack broke down on the New Zealand 22, Guscott missed Little and Kronfeld scored at the end of an eighty-metre attack. 'Have some fucking more of that, then,' Ian Jones, the All Blacks second row, screamed at me. It was later suggested that Tony winking at Lomu during the Haka had enraged the big winger. I'm actually not so sure it changed anything. As a team they were clearly on a mission to completely humiliate England to avenge their Twickenham loss two years before and they made a helluva good job of it.

'New Zealand played with a great deal of movement, the like of which we do not see in the northern hemisphere,' said Jack Rowell. 'I have not seen any international team play with the ease, the power and the pace that they did. We planned that there would always be someone right up on Lomu before he got into his stride. But it did not work. We allowed him too much room.'

It is impossible to argue that the All Blacks got their gameplan just right. In fact they got it perfect. They hit us hard early on, took our breath away, and did not kick to touch which might have given us a chance from the line-outs, one of our strengths. Without the ball we could not put them under pressure and we quickly lost our pattern, our shape and our confidence.

We shipped four tries in the first quarter of an hour and within twenty-five minutes trailed 25–0. Their pace and power simply overwhelmed us. 'Whatever happened to the running game, chicken-shit?' Sean Fitzpatrick shouted at me after I had got my hands on the ball for the first time in the game and kicked it into touch. People always go on about England being arrogant, particularly New Zealanders. Well let me say this. That day the All Blacks were as arrogant as you can get.

They taunted us throughout the game, in our face all the time, smashing us with big hits then screaming, shouting and laughing at us.

The onslaught continued. Lomu completed his hat-trick, then added a fourth, side-stepping me on the inside. And when their number eight, Zinzan Brooke, dropped a goal from about the halfway line we knew it was just not our day. We did manage to restore some pride in the second half as New Zealand sat back. We put some good stuff together and Rory and Will bagged two tries each to bring the scoreline back towards respectability. But the 16-point margin was misleading. Our World Cup dream had died in the first fifteen minutes.

And yet I look back on that day with great fondness. People may think it strange after such a chastening experience but I regard it as one of the best games I have been involved in. Sure, the memory of Lomu running over me is indelibly etched on my mind, but I have never had a single nightmare about it. Why? There was nothing I could do about it so why get distraught about it? Tim Rodber and Martin Johnson couldn't stop him, neither could Gavin Hastings and many other hall-of-famers before and after my experience at Newlands, so I don't think there is any shame in me not being able to. I defy anyone to have made that tackle.

In his autobiography Jonah said he felt sorry for me because 'we both have to live with that try. I get sick of seeing it replayed year after year, I can't imagine how he feels.' It is true, I do get a lot of stick about it because the footage was shown time and time again and continues to be, every time the World Cup comes around. But I really don't have a problem with that. I love talking about it. I love telling the story.

Which is why, 12 years later, when New Zealand television featured the big man on *This Is Your Life*, I was more than happy to send Jonah a video tribute. It was the least I could do. He well and truly put me on the international rugby map.

5
JEERS FOR SOUVENIRS

Richmond, 24 November 1997

From my room in the Petersham Hotel I looked down Richmond Hill and out across the bend in the Thames. It is one of the most sought-after views in London but I didn't appreciate its beauty. My gaze passed over the river and up to the horizon where the roof of Twickenham Stadium met the grey sky. The sight made me feel ill.

I turned away from the window and back to the room. The bed was made, a training top and shorts lay in a muddy heap beside the half opened bathroom door. On the floor by the writing desk was a used towel and my boot bag. Next to that my England holdall, unzipped but still packed, save for a couple of garments I had pulled out that morning.

'That's it,' I thought. 'I can't do this any more.'

I grabbed the shoulder strap, hoisted the kitbag on to the bed to close it and picked up my car keys, unsure what I was doing but convinced that anywhere had to be better than here waiting for another ordeal in the name of the Rose and for me, inevitably, another hammering from the press.

There is so much down time during international weeks to think about things and the negativity which had been coming my way over the past year was now killing me. My goal kicking had gone from bad to worse. I was being scapegoated for the failure of the England team and I couldn't take it any more. 'I'm not bloody Rob Andrew and I'm never going to be!' I cursed to myself. 'This ends now.'

To the left of the bed the telephone rang. I dropped the bag off my shoulder on to the floor and reached for the handset.

'Yeah,' I said, sounding irritated.

'Mike?' came the voice. 'It's Webby. Jon Webb.'

I had not spoken to Jonathan Webb, doctor and former Bath and England full-back, since before the 1995 World Cup, which had ended on such a low note for us, with the tamest of defeats to France in the third place play-off. A year of being unbeaten with England and thinking I could do no wrong, then suddenly I was hit by two losses in the space of four days, while the country of my birth beat New Zealand to be crowned world champions.

Up until then life had been rosy. I was a South African playing for England but that had been okay because I was part of a Grand Slam team and I was not kicking for goal. How quickly everything changed. Rob Andrew came home from South Africa and retired from international rugby, vacating the number 10 jersey and the kicking tee and leaving an impossible act to follow. I was the man chosen to do the impossible.

For the next two years I lived a nightmare. I had seemingly gone from being England's great hope to public enemy number one, culminating in my last game, an horrendous goal kicking experience playing against the All Blacks at Old Trafford. Now I was at my lowest point, rock bottom, and my old friend Jon Webb had picked this day of all days to phone me.

He said that he had seen the New Zealand game and read the press comment and just wanted to tell me to hang in there. He said that he had a fair idea of what I was going through because he had been through similar experiences when he was goal kicking for England in the early nineties.

'Mate, I can't do this any more,' I told him in a defeated voice. 'There is just a continual negative backlash towards me. It doesn't matter how well I play individually, I am judged purely on my goal kicking. I'm never going to get away from this. I can live with being run over by Jonah Lomu, because there's no shame in being unable to stop a guy that nobody else can. But being singled out as the cause of England's problems purely because of goal kicking is driving me mad.'

There was silence on the line.

'This has been going on for about two years', I continued. 'It's not a sudden thing. I have felt a frustration build slowly inside of me each time I play for England until now it feels as if I'm battling against the whole world. I have gone from being upset by the odd comment to being downright depressed. I can't shake this negativity out of my system, I continually dwell on all the bad things. I think about how it affected me in my last game and how it is, inevitably, going to affect me in the next one. How I will be interviewed after the game, and asked about missing a goal kick to win the game in the twentieth minute or something ridiculous like that. Mate, I can't see any way out of this. I'm at my wits' end.'

Again Jon Webb didn't speak, as if giving me the opportunity to get it all off my chest. That was how I responded anyway, and for the next ten minutes unloaded two years of frustration on him. From the day I had returned to the UK after the World Cup, my mind was made up – I only wanted to be considered as a full-back from now on, and I said as much to Phil de Glanville, my captain at Bath.

'Sure, Catty, you can play full-back,' Phil said. 'But it will be for the second team. We're not about to drop Jon Callard. He does an excellent job for us at 15 and he's a fantastic goal kicker. You know that.'

I nodded, though only in partial agreement. I felt that I was a better runner than Callard and, because I was working with top goal kicking coach Dave Alred at the time, that I would soon be able to kick like him too. Then Rob Andrew announced he was stepping down from international duty and Jack Rowell offered me the fly-half slot for the season opener against the now world champion Springboks.

Of course I took it. My form at 10 for Bath was good so it was not as if I didn't warrant selection. The only problem was that I wasn't getting any goal kicking opportunities at Bath because Jon Callard was there. I considered it to be a minor issue. I could not have been more wrong, and Jack has to take a share of the blame. At Bath I did not have to worry about goal kicking and was able to relish playing my natural game, but that was not what England were looking for. They needed someone at fly-half who could kick goals consistently.

The alarm bells started to ring in the very first game against the Boks, a Test into which I went feeling added pressure having talked myself into trouble by saying that François Pienaar, South Africa's World Cup-winning captain and a national icon, was an 'average' player. I can't believe I actually said that. What I meant was that I felt in South Africa there were better players in his position, but that Pienaar was the best captain. It obviously came out wrong and it was blown up into something I really didn't intend it to be.

England lost the game 24–14 and fingers were pointed at me. Although Will Carling made a point of defending me against criticism of England's failing behind the scrum – 'You can't blame individuals . . . It was collective . . . It was not Mike Catt's fault' – the fact was that I was a complete maverick in the role. I wanted to run absolutely everything in a side which for the past ten years had not played that way. Here was a team full of old heads who wanted to play the way that England played when Rob had been there. I didn't know how to play that way. It wasn't in my nature.

I felt I had some great backs outside me and all I wanted to do was release them. That seemed the logical thing to do. It was what I did week in week out at Bath with great success. But the situations were different. At Bath it was very easy because there were so many great players around me that wanted to play the same way as I did. But with England the guys wanted something different – basically, Rob Andrew – and I found it very difficult to adjust.

As it turned out I didn't have to, because the following month I was switched to full-back for the game against Western Samoa, ironically knocking Jon Callard out of the side (something I couldn't manage at Bath). I had not been dropped but that was exactly how it felt, especially as Kyran Bracken, my half-back partner, had been. In our places at half-back came the uncapped Northampton pair of Paul

Grayson and Matt Dawson, who had impressed in the Midlands' midweek defeat of the touring Samoans.

Grayson had a reputation as a kicking fly-half far more in the Andrew mould than I could ever be. I shrugged my shoulders, did not spend too much time reflecting on the selection and focused on the next challenge in front of me. If I was honest, Grayson coming in took a bit of pressure off me and I welcomed that. I could get on with enjoying my game and leave the press to worry about someone else's goal kicking and tactical strategy.

It was only later, when I looked back on the pattern of my selections, that I realised that all this chopping and changing had done me no favours. But at the time, because I could not handle the press and their negative attitudes all the time, I saw no problem with it. As I saw it I could go away to Bath and thoroughly enjoy myself at 10, then come back and play at 15 for England.

England beat Western Samoa 27–9 but we were branded dull and conservative afterwards. Grayson was booed when he lined up penalty kicks at goal, presumably because the Twickenham crowd felt England should be running a small Pacific island ragged. Of course this particular island nation had reached the quarter-finals of the last two World Cups. Only late tries by Lawrence Dallaglio and Rory Underwood spared us almighty grief.

Will Carling had been re-appointed captain at the start of the season by Jack but from the beginning they didn't seem to click as a partnership. They didn't communicate as you would expect a coach and captain to do. Will didn't seem to understand what Jack wanted and Jack wasn't about to give Will a free rein. Whether it was a clash of egos I'm not sure, but it certainly made life more difficult than it needed to be. From a playing point of view it impacted on me as well. With Jerry Guscott a fixture at outside centre, Will being captain meant that Phil de Glanville lost out.

I got along with Will very well. He was good to me in the England set-up and, off the pitch, he took me under his wing pretty early. I had no issue with him but I felt Jack didn't have the balls to make the big decision and leave him out. I knew from playing with Phil at Bath that from a helping-the-10 point of view he was streets ahead of Will. From taking pressure off the fly-half and telling him how to do things Phil was the best in the business. So when Will got the nod over Phil I had mixed feelings. Phil would have encouraged me to run and express myself. Will wanted me to kick the ball.

Phil thought about players around him. The old school – the likes of Guscott, Carling and Rory Underwood – played for themselves. They just did what they were good at. There was also a phenomenal amount of egos in the England side at this time. The youngsters coming in needed help but some of the experienced guys on the team just expected us to be able to fit in.

As a 10, involved in absolutely every decision, that was tough, especially as there was an air of conservatism in the squad, perhaps a subconscious reaction to the pasting we had been given by Lomu and his mates in Cape Town. It led to surely the dullest Five Nations campaign in English rugby history, in 1996. The stats certainly support that claim. England scored three tries in four games, the least of all the participating countries. Yet extraordinarily, bizarrely, disturbingly, England ended up winning the thing. No champion had ever been so miserly in its try output.

It began in Paris where we lost 15–12 to a late dropped goal by

Thomas Castaignède who popped the ball between the posts, then stuck his tongue out and danced on the spot. I had a late chance to win it, but Rory threw an overhead pass to my feet rather than my hands and the opportunity was lost. It was not a good feeling to be a part of the first England team to lose in Paris for eight years. But the real crime had been committed in that World Cup third place play-off when we didn't turn up and allowed the French to get the monkey off their back without breaking sweat.

Next we hosted Wales at Twickenham and again failed to fire. I gave a scoring pass to Rory Underwood for our first try and his fiftieth, and we ran out 21–15 winners, but it was unimpressive stuff and the pressure cranked up a notch on Jack, who was accused of inconsistency of selection, of not knowing what his best team was and of making it up as he went along. The *Daily Telegraph* ran a mock apology to its readers. 'In previous editions of this newspaper we reported England's intention to play a sharper and more expansive game in keeping with the lessons of the World Cup. We acknowledge unreservedly that there was no truth in these suggestions and would like to apologise for any embarrassment or distress caused.'

But I was out of the firing line at full-back and criticism of others barely registered with me. That was their problem, not mine. My focus was on the next game against a Scotland side eighty minutes away from a Grand Slam. Having experienced an almost unbelievable level of hostility in the fixture when we won a Grand Slam against them twelve months earlier, I knew it would be a fasten-your-seatbelts job. But the real fireworks came after a game in which Dean Richards, recalled by Jack to give us more control up front, denied the Scots almost singlehandedly by throttling the life out of them from start to finish in a 18–9 victory. For the second game in three we hadn't crossed the try-line and the press went to war on us.

We were hammered for, in the opinion of the *Guardian*, 'reverting to the role of lumbering dinosaur' and for having 'become the most negative side in world rugby'. Fair enough, to be honest. Not only were we not scoring tries, we weren't playing well. It was dreadful. Our play was so sterile. Game by game we were retreating further into our shells.

The team's response against Ireland on the final weekend would normally have been enough to silence the critics. After all, a 28–15 win at Twickenham was easily the best performance of our campaign and, with France surprisingly losing to Wales in Cardiff, it handed us the title. But that success didn't fool anyone. It merely papered over cracks that we all knew were there.

Timing is everything in sport and my selection to start the autumn campaign back at fly-half could not have come at a worst moment. I had been working every day on my goal kicking, desperate to improve. Every morning I would get up at six o'clock and drive across to Bristol and spend ninety minutes working with Dave Alred at the university. But I never got any better. In fact I seemed to get worse.

By the time the first international came around, against Italy at Twickenham, I was not in a happy place at all with my goal kicking. The thing was this: I was naturally gifted, in that I had always been able to put a ball down, not think about it, and kick it through the posts. But now I *was* thinking about it. Dave is very technical in his approach. He would feed me twenty bits of information at one session and it would addle my mind. No question, it was information overload for me. Every time I kicked the ball I was made to think that this was wrong and that was wrong. It completely mucked me up mentally.

I couldn't grasp what Dave was trying to achieve, I just couldn't understand it. I really like him and he backed me massively, even when I'm sure he was pulling his hair out, thinking to himself 'What is this dickhead doing?' And because he also coached Rob Andrew and had turned him into the best goal kicker in the world I believed in him and persevered, convincing myself that I was getting better because I was working my nuts off, when really I was just getting myself into more and more of a state.

I was England's first-choice goal kicker yet each day I went home from our session and crapped myself. I was petrified. Not about playing, just about the goal kicking. But I never admitted my fears to the coach or captain because I wanted to be in the side. The obvious course of action would have been to bring in someone else to do the kicking and leave me to call the shots. But every time I was asked I said I felt really comfortable kicking, because I was working so flipping hard. I was a fool to myself, my own worst enemy. The truth was that I was living in fear of goal kicking.

It might only have been Italy we played first but for me the real battle was not on the pitch but with those demons in my head. It was a contest I had no confidence of winning and my worst fears were realised when I missed one kick from slap bang in front of the posts and then had a conversion charged down. It was classic paralysis by analysis. Rather than just put the ball down and kick it through the posts I took an age to set up, then did the little walk back and various other Alredisms. By the time I got to the ball I had an opponent in my face.

Afterwards I felt that nobody was talking about the rest of my game and the eight kicks which I did land, I had become that paranoid. In reality there was plenty of credit passed the way of myself and new cap Andy Gomarsall for our attempts to speed up England's style; efforts which brought seven tries and a 54–21 win. Jeremy Guscott said I was England's finest player. But the voices in my head told me differently.

A week later the All Blacks, masquerading under the name of the New Zealand Barbarians, were at Twickenham and, while my general play was again okay, my kicking was horrible. *The Times* was not about to let me get away with it. 'That England should have achieved that position [leading 19–13 at half-time] given the number of times the ball was kicked away from half-back was a tribute to the England forwards,' wrote their correspondent, David Hands. 'There are some fundamentals to the game that cannot be ignored – unromantic things like restarts and touchfinding, and Mike Catt, in particular, fell down on them.' The All Blacks, sorry, Barbarians, came back to win 34–19.

But because of the quality of the opposition the post-match inquest was not too intense. Instead pressure was heaped on to our final game of the autumn series against the amateur players of Argentina; a match I will forever recall with horror. Before the match even started I made one of the biggest mistakes of my entire career, hiding from the management the fact that I had a sternum injury. I should never have played but I was so desperate to change my fortunes that I gambled, and lost big. From minute one I struggled with the injury.

I was in pain and I played like a drain. It says everything that my goal kicking was better than my general play.

The low point came when I was meant to hoof the ball down the pitch from our 22 and I ran, sent it wide and we were turned over and conceded a penalty. Will Carling, who had been succeeded as captain by Phil de Glanville at the start of the season, turned to me, furiously pointing his finger downfield, and yelled, 'Would you just kick the fucking thing down there.' Fair enough, I was having a shocker, though, in the same breath, people around me weren't doing what I wanted them to do either. I was doing it my way and nobody was coming with me. I didn't have the experience then to change it.

When the final whistle blew on a 20–18 victory I was desolate. I had taken flak from one of my own team-mates; I could only imagine what the media would make of my afternoon. 'Though missing three kicks, kicking was not the weakness it might have been for Catt. Dave Alred's tuition must have helped,' wrote John Mason in the *Daily Telegraph*. Then the hammer blow. 'The Catt Achilles heel is his all-round play. Capable, versatile player that he is, he is not, repeat not, an international outside-half.'

I'd gone back to Bath after the game and the following day had got very drunk with my flatmates, sensing what was coming the next day in the papers from journalists who, a week later when I played for Bath, I knew would be praising my performance. I hated the inevitability of it all.

That sort of criticism kills you, it absolutely kills you. People are reading this all around the country, I shuddered to myself. Other comment was more sympathetic. Geoff Cooke, who had given me my debut when he was England manager, told the *Mail on Sunday* that he felt sorry for me, that he felt I was a very talented player, but 'the problem is that I can't put a number on his back'.

Geoff was right. When I played at 15 for England we didn't have a 10 or a 12 who distributed the ball as we needed, and as Stuart Barnes did at Bath, and when I played at 10 we didn't really have people around me who wanted to chuck the ball about. More often than not I seemed to be in what I thought was the right place, at the wrong time. Yet because I was pretty inexperienced I kept quiet and got on with it.

My reward was to be dropped again for the start of the 1997 Five Nations and I knew I could have no complaints. After my display against Argentina I thoroughly deserved to be on the bench, or worse. Jack phoned and told me there were certain lessons to be learned, 'but most of all you need to help yourself'. I assured him that I would do that and that I'd be back. But for the time being I was quite content to see Paul Grayson recalled to the number 10 hot seat. It is a shocking admission, I know, but I was relieved to be out of the limelight. At least I was until England came out all guns blazing against Scotland and scored more tries in a 41–13 home win than we had managed throughout the entire '96 championship. England then went to Dublin and blew Ireland away with four tries in the last seven minutes for a record 46–6 victory.

Ten tries in two games and I was suddenly desperate to get in on the act. England, out of the blue, were playing my sort of game, hunting space rather than targets. But it wasn't my time and when England led France 20–6 after an hour at Twickenham next time out I could not see from where my next chance would come. A clue came when the French fought back to steal victory with 17 unanswered

A dream come true as I captain England to our 28–18 win over France – a very emotional moment.

I wanted to grow up to be a Springbok, but fate had other plans for me.

An unconvincing cadet at Grey High School.

Beating the teachers in Grey High's quadrangle race was more my scene.

Playing against my childhood hero, Naas Botha.

Brother Pete in the Bath triathlon. He suggested I come to England, so I did. It was supposed to be just for a holiday.

With Uncle Doug and his girlfriend Kathy. Doug phoned Bath RFC on the off chance they'd give me a try out. The rest is history...

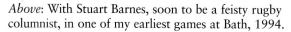

Above: With Stuart Barnes, soon to be a feisty rugby columnist, in one of my earliest games at Bath, 1994.

Right: Jeremy Guscott, world-class team-mate.

Below left: I was Whitbread Most Promising Player of the Year in 1995. Victor Ubogu helped me celebrate.

Below right: Jack Rowell never courted popularity. His only concern was winning, at Bath and with England.

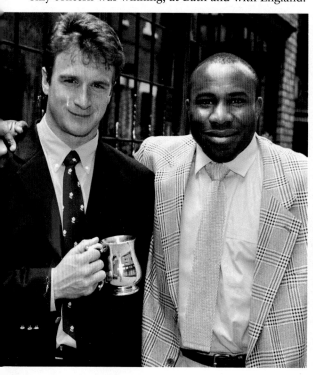

Left: Meeting a living legend on the pitch at Loftus Versfeld.

Above: With Langa, whose schooling I sponsored.

Below: Playing alongside Paul Hull in South Africa. My break for England came when I replaced an injured Hull against Canada.

The Catt-trick worked and Tony Underwood scored under the posts in the final minute of our 1995 Five Nations match against France – one of my career highlights.

Will Carling and Gavin Hastings, rival captains of two sides with scores to settle and long memories in the 1995 Grand Slam decider.

You can tell who won from the champagne, but the Scots branded us bad winners.

In the days before professionalism reduced us to vitamin drinks, there were some wild parties at Bath and my house seemed to be the centre for them. *Above*: John Hall (*left*) and Jerry Guscott (*right*) look fetching in their wigs, and I'm all shook up as The King (*below*).

points in the last quarter. Sure enough, Grayson got the hook for the final game in Cardiff and I was restored to fly-half. It was brilliant news but then I heard that Rob Andrew had been brought out of international retirement to sit on the bench.

How else could I take that other than as a vote of no-confidence in my goal kicking. Of course all the doubts resurfaced in my mind. And when Rob and I practised goal kicking at the Arms Park the day before the match I was absolutely dreadful. The Welsh played with a different make of balls to England and they were terrible to kick. What Rob must have made of my attempts didn't bear thinking about. So of course I did. There wasn't much he could say to me that I didn't know already. It was putting it into practice which was the problem.

I had been given a lift by being named in a British and Irish Lions preliminary squad for the summer tour to South Africa which had controversially omitted Phil de Glanville, Tony Underwood and Jon Sleightholme, so I convinced myself that I had nothing to lose playing for England and so should just give it a rip. My attitude on game day was that I would try and play my game as well as I could and leave it to someone else to judge whether that was good enough for England.

My first kick at goal was from the left-hand corner and I smacked it through the middle from something like forty metres. It was the start of a brilliant game for me. We tore Wales apart. I made two or three great breaks and put Phil de Glanville in for a try from a quick tapped penalty. I picked a line off Austin Healey, playing at scrum-half, and Phil followed me through the hole. I then drew the full-back and popped it up to him. The *Sunday Times* made me Man of the Match, awarding me nine out of ten. 'A superb return,' they said. 'Clever, cool and in control.' Music to my ears.

It had been an awful season for me from an international perspective, yet I had emerged feeling a million dollars. It was a feeling which continued for three weeks until the squad for the Lions tour to South Africa was named and I wasn't in it. I had taken for granted that I would be touring and when I missed out it hit me like a thunderbolt. The memory of that rejection has stayed with me to this day. I was gutted, seriously upset.

The general reaction among the press was that one outstanding display for England did not make an irrefutable case for selection. But there was no shortage of support for me. Naas Botha, a hero of my childhood, said that I was the player he was most shocked to see the Lions ignore.

Stuart Barnes agreed, writing that I 'could and possibly should have been the central cog of the British Lions challenge in South Africa'.

I think Barnes saw himself in me, a maverick talent whom England could not get the best from. His belief was that the Lions would need more than consistency from their fly-half, they would need inspiration. He felt I was the best man to offer that and cited my early season display for Bath against Leicester and my performance for England against Wales as two examples to back up his view. It was good to read but it didn't change anything.

'You've got to look at the positives, mate,' said Jon Webb down the phone, bringing me back to the present. 'You've had a great summer. Bloody hell, every time I looked your name seemed to be up in headlines.'

He was right. It had turned out well for me. Snubbed by the Lions, I had gone to Argentina with England and we had had the most fantastic trip, one of the best I have ever been on. All eyes were on the Lions, which allowed me to relax and banish many of my awful memories from the Pumas' visit to Twickenham seven months earlier. I don't know why, but I never stopped believing that I would join the Lions tour at some point and so I flew to Buenos Aires in a really positive frame of mind, along with three or four others who felt the same way I did. Knowing how incredibly physical South African rugby is, I felt sure the Lions were going to need reinforcements.

What I needed to be, though, was in form, so that if and when an SOS went out it would come my way. I made sure I hit the ground running, scoring 18 points in the first game against Cordoba, including a chip and gather try which I was especially pleased with. I added another in a 50-point thrashing of Argentina's second string and then had a blinder, if I say it myself, in the First Test, scoring a try and landing seven kicks as England thrashed the Pumas 46–20.

My confidence was such that I publicly declared that I wanted the England number 10 shirt for the long term. 'I don't see why I can't have it for the next five years,' I told the *Express*. 'Jack has given us the freedom of the pitch to do what we want and there is a positive atmosphere among the squad.'

That very day, on another continent, Paul Grayson crashed out of the Lions tour. The phone call Jack Rowell had dreaded, but I had secretly longed for, followed before the night was out. Nigel Redman was also summoned. Fran Cotton, manager of the Lions, said he needed the pair of us and the Lions took precedence.

Jack was desperate for me to stay. 'You can go after the Test match on Saturday,' he told me. I replied, 'Look, Jack, I'm sorry, but I can't do that. This is a once in a lifetime opportunity.' A Lions tour is still the ultimate for any player. The senior players all agreed I was doing the right thing and that they would do the same if asked.

Nevertheless I felt bad. England had never won a series in Argentina and we thought we had a great chance. What I know was galling for Jack was that the following weekend, while England without us were being hammered 33–13, neither Nigel nor I featured in the Lions defeat against Northern Transvaal.

Instead I had to wait until the following midweek to start, in the game at Ellis Park against Gauteng Lions which will forever be remembered for John Bentley's superb seventy-metre scoring run. Thank God for that, too. Otherwise we would have lost and I would have been nailed back on the cross for missing five goal kicks out of six. Bentley dug me out of a big hole that day.

Happily, the tour went uphill from there. I was named on the bench for the first two Tests, which the Lions won, much to the disbelief of all of South Africa, and in between those games I went to Bloemfontein and dusted down my Afrikaans. We were sitting in the coffee shop at the airport waiting to fly down to Durban and these two Afrikaners, sitting on the next door table, told us to piss off home in their native tongue. None of the boys could understand what they were saying and so these guys revved it up, calling us every name under the sun. I sat there and laughed to myself for a little bit and then when we got up to leave, I turned round and, in my best Afrikaans, introduced myself and politely told them that they really should be careful what they say in future. You should have seen their jaws drop.

It was good to smile again because it had been a traumatic day, with Will Greenwood coming frighteningly close to dying when he was knocked unconscious by a heavy tackle from Free State back rower, Jaco Coetzee. Will had taken a switch ball from me and been caught by the top of his jersey and swung round. His sleeve was caught in the tackle so he couldn't put his hands out to cushion his fall. His head landed at right-angles to his neck and he lay there sparko.

I didn't realise how serious it was, that Will had stopped breathing. Thankfully, Austin Healey reacted quickly, getting to him, rolling him over and removing his gumshield. Will's mum was hysterical as she ran from the touchline into the changing room. According to Ian McGeechan it was a close run thing.

It was certainly a bad scene, and it took Will a good year and a half to get over it. It also put some of my so-called problems into perspective. Alongside Will's, of course, I had none. I was in the squad for the Second Test, we would win that and I would get to start at fly-half in the third dead rubber in Johannesburg. Dad would fly up from Port Elizabeth for the match and seeing him close to tears with pride is a memory I will always cherish.

I would return home feeling as though I was back on top of the world and, when Jack Rowell resigned and was succeeded as England coach by Clive Woodward, I would find my name in the starting line-up, this time at inside-centre, for his opening game at Twickenham against Australia. Forty-eight hours before kick-off, Alex King, picked at fly-half, would drop out and I would revert to the number 10 shirt. But I would be fine. New coach, new captain in Lawrence Dallaglio, new era.

But the same old problems resurfaced for me, not helped one little bit by a gameplan devised by Clive, which involved us kicking the ball to keep it in play. When I say 'us', of course I predominantly mean me, as I was fly-half. I did as ordered, even from our 22, but to the outside world it looked as though I was having a shocker. The crowd booed because I kept 'missing' touch.

It was a poor Aussie side, yet going into injury-time we trailed 12–15. I went for broke, cutting upfield and chipping the ball over full-back, Steve Larkham. His reaction was to take me out, late and high, and he got a yellow card for it. After the earlier jeers I had a chance to be England's saviour from the penalty spot and I took it – my fifth success – only to then get an even later opportunity, this time to win the match.

The offence was three metres inside our own half and I remember looking at Lawrence, who asked: 'Can you make it?' I replied that I didn't know but would give it my best shot. I knew I didn't have the distance but we weren't going to win the game any other way, not least because there were no other goal kickers in the side. My attempt fell way short and I got a negative reaction from the crowd, just like the bad old days.

'That was a week ago, Webby,' I was back on the phone, pouring my heart out, 'and you saw what happened against the All Blacks at Old Trafford last weekend. Brilliant day, brilliant crowd and from a game perspective I thought I played pretty well. But as a goal kicker I completely lost the plot, mate. I missed five from five and you saw them, they were literally on the 22, right in front of the posts. I couldn't hit a barn door.'

An arena used to seeing goals scored, not missed, got on my back and although I kept going till the end I knew what was coming. Paul

Ackford, in the *Sunday Telegraph*, remarked that I had kicked 'like a plonker'. No mention of my general play. And while the *Sunday Times* did at least credit me for trying 'to make things happen', they concluded that I failed to stamp myself on the occasion 'because the quality of his kicking was simply not up to it'. Horrendous, was the word used by the *Sunday Times*.

'Webby, I'm sick and tired of the press purely basing their judgment of me on my goal kicks. There's a lot more to rugby than fucking goal kicking. Defence, attack, so much more. But nobody picks up on that. I know we are a team not scoring tries so of course the focus is going to be on the kicker. But, Christ, this is doing my head in. I can't do it any more.'

'Sure you can,' he replied. 'Listen, do you remember those days at Bath when you and I first kicked together?'

'Sure.'

'What did you do?'

'I put the ball on the tee and I kicked it through the posts.'

'Mate, go and do exactly that on Saturday. Stuff everyone else. You are thinking far too much about it.'

Easier said than done, I thought. But I said I would try. We chatted some more, then he rang off. I threw my car keys on to the chair and sat down on the bed. No longer was my mind full of bitterness and twisted resentment. I thought about Jon Webb's calming tone and for the first time realised that there was somebody out there, outside my family, who understood how I felt and who was concerned for me. Somebody who had been in that situation before and totally understood what it is like. For him to take time out of his medical schedule to phone me and say what he did was like a gift from God.

I was just so much more relaxed afterwards. I thought, fine, I'm going to give it another go. Things are going to be different.

Five days later I produced the best forty minutes of my England career. Inspired by my friend, I was on fire. My first kick at goal from forty metres went straight through the middle. I then nailed a second from a similar distance. England was 6–0 inside ten minutes. I then noticed that Springboks full-back Percy Montgomery was out of position and kicked to the corner where the ball was fumbled and Nick Greenstock dotted down for 11–0. I felt in complete control of the game and Twickenham seemed to be loving it. Then wham! It was all over. I was knocked unconscious.

My long, emotional road back to a positive frame of mind ended in concussion. In my absence South Africa came back to win the game. The following week I could only watch as England produced a stunning backs-to-the-wall performance its draw 26-26 with a New Zealand side rated as among the best ever. The boys were back in the nation's good books, and I had missed out again.

6

AGAINST ALL ODDS

Bordeaux, 31 January 1998

Deep breath. Eyes closed. Focus. Sit quietly for a moment and think clearly. Right. People say we're out of our depth, let's show them. People have been laughing at us, let's silence them. They want to know what this Bath team is really about? The truth, not what they've seen on that bloody TV documentary. Then keep watching. We can do this. We're going to do this.

'Time, lads.'

Right, that's the ref calling us. Into a huddle. Pull together. C'mon, guys, tighter! I'm feeling loose, that's good. I'm buzzing, I want to get out there.

'Who are we?'

'Bath!'

'Who are we?'

'Bath!!'

'Who are we?'

'Bath!!!'

Okay, here goes. Out of the changing room, down the tunnel. I can see the pitch now. Christ, that's some noise. How many people does this place hold? Stay loose. Out into the sunshine. Here we go . . .

Nobody saw this coming. No one believed that Bath would make it to play Brive in the final of the Heineken Cup. Not in this season of all seasons. We had suffered a club record defeat at Saracens just a month earlier. Our coach Andy Robinson, revered at the Rec during his playing days, had been booed by those same supporters. These were strange, turbulent times for Bath and, frankly, the club had brought them on itself.

A fly-on-the-wall television documentary about the day-to-day running of Bath Rugby Club had made us a laughing stock and was a massive error of judgment by whoever agreed to it. Four hours of footage, screened in six parts on BBC2, showed Bath wash more dirty linen in public than Pauline Fowler managed in over a decade of *EastEnders*. More damaging still, the club had been embroiled in the biggest scandal to hit English rugby in years. An opposition player had had part of his ear bitten off during a match at the Rec.

All that happened in the 1997–8 season. The previous one had been notorious for being the first in which Bath had failed to win a major trophy since 1988. A season in which Andrew Brownsword, a local multi-millionaire businessman, bought the club for £2.5 million, Jason Robinson and Henry Paul were brought over from rugby league on short-term contracts, coach Brian Ashton resigned and director of rugby John Hall was sacked.

Less than two years after winning a fourth league and cup double in seven seasons Bath had been plunged into turmoil. Clive Wood-ward had come and gone, joining us in the spring of 1997 when Andy Robinson took over following John Hall's departure, then leaving to take the England job at the start of the new season – this season, the one which had brought us to Stade Lescure for the biggest day in the club's history.

Our European challenge had begun across the Severn Bridge with a win at Pontypridd, who would be caught up in one hell of a ruck with Brive soon after; one which began on the pitch and continued in a bar in the French town post-match. Three Brive players needed hospital treatment, three Ponty boys faced charges of violence and criminal damage.

It caused an international incident and we capitalised on Brive's flustered state, winning 27–25 at the Rec the following week. At the time we could not know how distracting it had been for them, caught in the eye of a media storm, but we soon would, when London Scottish came to Bath, three weeks before the Heineken Cup final, for a fourth round tie in the Tetley's Bitter Cup.

Having won ten of the previous fourteen finals this was a competition the club took very seriously. But not so seriously that opposition flanker Simon Fenn should have paid for his side coming within a Jon Callard injury-time penalty winner of putting us out by having part of his left ear lobe bitten off.

I had no idea what had gone on and I was standing pretty close to the scrum where the incident took place. The scrum went down and I heard an 'aagh' sort of cry. That was it. I assumed someone had been stood on. Referee Ashley Rowden stopped play and told our captain Andy Nicol that Fenn had been bitten but the message was not relayed to the rest of us. And in the changing room afterwards, honest to God, nothing was mentioned that I heard about any bite. I left the ground genuinely still thinking it had been a boot to the head.

It was only the next day that I realised someone had actually bitten a chunk off the guy's ear, because it was all over the press. Two days after that our prop Kevin Yates, who had put himself on the international rugby map for all the right reasons seven months earlier when he was capped by England in Argentina, was suspended by the club on full pay.

Yates, who has always denied that he was responsible, was a good pal of mine and had come back to my house directly after the game. Nothing unusual there. Often he'd come back after matches and we'd drop our bags and go out on the lash. Like me Yates loved the booze. But that night he put his feet up on the sofa and just lay there. We didn't go out at all. He seemed very depressed, his behaviour like a pet dog who has done something wrong.

Which is not to say that he had. He says he didn't and who am I to argue. All I will say is that if I had been wrongly accused of such a disgusting offence and been given a six-month ban, as he later was, I would have gone berserk. I would have taken the fight to clear my name to the end of the earth. Instead, of the Bath front row cited en bloc by London Scottish in an attempt to root out the man responsible, only Victor Ubogu and Federico Mendez reacted in that way.

I have never seen Victor as angry as he was the day he was accused in connection with the crime. He went ballistic and rightly so, as it could never have been him. He told the *Daily Mirror*: 'Nothing will

94

ever be adequate compensation for having my face splashed across newspapers worldwide, suspected of barbaric cannibalism, when I am completely innocent.' That's what I would have said. 'Worse still,' he added, 'I cannot believe one of my team-mates hasn't had the courage to hold up his hand and come clean about it.'

But nobody did. Kevin Yates was interviewed three times by Bath and three times he denied being the guilty man. As the days passed, so the pressure cranked up on the club. The story was everywhere. Across all the papers, on all the national news bulletins on radio and TV. It gave Bath such a bad name and Brownsword absolutely hated it. Eventually Yates was called to a disciplinary hearing by the Rugby Football Union and, a full month after the offence had been committed, he was convicted and suspended for six months.

He went into his shell after that. We went from being really good friends to not really speaking. I would say 'You all right, mate?' He would reply, 'Yeah, fine' and that would be the height of it. He never once talked to me about the case, either to say he did or didn't do it. That didn't stop the banter flying about among the squad. 'Here comes the ear-muncher,' someone would say when Kevin came into the room. Or, 'Is anybody hungry?' He would just laugh it off. We were not a stupid group of people by any means, but because we didn't know the truth categorically we left it at that.

Yates left soon after, packed his bags and headed off to New Zealand, I guess to try and make a fresh start. He had spent a fortune on legal fees and his career appeared in ruins. As a friend, I sympathised enormously with his plight, but my view on the crime, whoever committed it, remains to this day that biting is unacceptable. Worse even than eye-gouging. I ask myself what has to happen on a rugby pitch for you to do something like that? Answer, nothing. Because there's nothing that can justify biting someone's ear off. By all means throw a little punch if somebody has stood on you or given you a cheap shot. Let them know you are not at all happy about it. But there has to be something seriously wrong with a person who resorts to biting an ear. It is an unspeakably bad thing to do.

I have seen some bad injuries deliberately inflicted in my time. I was playing alongside Phil de Glanville for the South-West Division against the 1993 All Blacks when he was raked by a New Zealand boot at Redruth and needed fifteen stitches to a very nasty eye wound. I was in the same England team as Jon Callard that night in my home town of Port Elizabeth in 1994 when he was stamped on by an Eastern Province forward. I would also witness a shocking eleven-punch attack by New South Wales full-back Duncan McRae on a defenceless Ronan O'Gara in Sydney during the 2001 Lions tour. But none of those compared to what was done to Simon Fenn's ear that January day at the Rec.

It was a disturbing time for Bath as our Heineken Cup quarter-final against Cardiff at the Rec was also marred by an assault, this time on French referee Didier Mene by a visiting fan angry at the manner of his team's elimination. Fortunately Jon Callard and Ieuan Evans ran to the ref's aid and diffused what could have been a really ugly scene. We then reached the final at the expense of Pau, the French club who had a massive suspended fine hanging over their heads for their part in a brawl with Llanelli during the pool stages. Jon Callard kicked five penalties that day as we edged home 20–14.

By this stage of his career Callard was dividing his time between playing and coaching and with Matt Perry, our twenty-year-old full-back, having broken into the England team earlier in the season, Andy Robinson had a big decision to make over who to play in the final. Helpful as always, I made his mind up for him with my kicking performance against Richmond in the next round of the Tetley's *Biter* Cup – as it had become known – seven days before the final in Bordeaux.

I missed a number of shots which contributed to us losing the game and Robinson, quite rightly, decided that if we were to stand any chance of going to France and beating the champions of Europe we could not afford to miss our kicks. That meant only one thing and poor old Matt didn't need to be told. Jon Callard and his trusty right boot got the nod.

I felt bad for Perry, who is Bath born and bred, and I would feel even worse less than a fortnight later when he lost his place at full-back in the England team – to me. Clive Woodward wanted me back in the side for the start of the Five Nations but was not about to drop Paul Grayson after his superb game at Twickenham, where he played really flat to the line in a 26–26 draw against New Zealand. It was the game I missed due to the concussion I suffered against South Africa.

No British club had won the European Cup. Cardiff had reached the first final in 1996 and lost to Toulouse. Leicester had reached the 1997 final but been wiped out by Brive. And that was in front of thousands upon thousands of their own fans down in Cardiff. Nobody was betting against a French hat-trick this time.

Not only were we up against the holders, the match was played in Bordeaux, a short drive west from Brive. We had 5,000 fans in Stade Lescure but you would not have known it. The 37,000-capacity arena was jam-packed and decked out in the black and white colours of our opponents.

We were told we had no chance and there was plenty of evidence to support that. We might have squeezed past Brive at our place when they had Pontypridd very much on their minds, but they easily beat us 29–12 back at theirs in the return. We had also not trained all week with Phil de Glanville, a key man in our back line, because he had needed to be with his wife, who was pregnant.

Nonetheless we had some fantastic players at the club, guys boasting a helluva lot of big game experience. Jerry Guscott, Ieuan Evans, Jon Callard and Andy Nicol in the backs; Victor Ubogu, Martin Haag, Nigel Redman and Dan Lyle up front. We knew we were capable of winning games and, with the exception of the away game in Brive, every time we had played in the Heineken Cup we had performed exceptionally well. We had beaten Pontypridd, Brive, Scottish Borders, Cardiff and Pau. We seemed to thrive on cup rugby and, crucially, we believed we were bloody good at it.

Phil joined up with us on the morning of the match. And coming back into the squad after what he had been through had a calming influence on the rest of us. All right, not on Richard Webster, who got pretty aggressive in the changing room beforehand, winding himself up into a frenzy. But Webster apart, the scene was pretty chilled. People were saying the right things at the right time. As kick-off approached there was an understated confidence about the squad. The forwards had been brought to the boil by Andy Robinson and were now quietly simmering. So much so that we all heard referee Jim Fleming's knock on the door.

'Time, lads.'

Andy Nicol, a massively passionate man, called us together. 'Who are we?' shouted our skipper. We replied in unison. He repeated the question again and then once more. The temperature was rising in the room, so too the volume; voices were raised, throats were cleared and twenty-two pairs of boots clattered on the stone floor. And then we were out in the sunshine, ready for the battle.

It was one of those days when I felt we were never going to lose. That must sound strange, given that we trailed Brive from the second minute until the last, but during the game I just never felt it was going to go against us. We were so at ease with everything. When Christophe Lamaison kicked his third penalty to put them 9 points clear after fifteen minutes, when he landed his fifth to send us into half-time trailing 15–6, even when Brive still led 18–16 entering stoppage time.

It is difficult to explain that feeling, given that we lost five line-outs in the first half on our own throw and Brive were then awarded six successive scrums five yards from our line straight after half-time. I guess I just felt that after all the problems the club had been through this was our time. I can't have been alone in thinking that way either, for we survived those scrums, with what Stephen Jones in the *Sunday*

Times described as 'one of the greatest goal-line stands I have ever seen', then went up the other end of the pitch and showed Brive how to turn pressure into points. Dan Lyle drove from a scrum close to their line, Andy Nicol and Jerry Guscott linked up with him and Jon Callard, who was in for his goal kicking, touched down the try.

Alain Penaud, the Brive full-back, responded by dropping a goal to make the score 18–13 but we dug in again, Callard pegged back 3 points with his third penalty and, with time running out on us, we got a crucial break. Penaud missed touch, Ade Adebayo collected the ball, made ground and chipped ahead. How much danger there was to the Brive line it is hard to say but Yvan Manhes, their second row, shoulder-charged Ade and Callard kicked us ahead for the first time. We had played one minute and thirteen seconds of stoppage time.

Cue a manic finale which had me wondering whether the game would produce a climax to match the drama of our last final, when we played Leicester at Twickenham for the 1996 Pilkington Cup and won the game right at the death after being awarded a penalty try. Sure enough, there was again a sting in the tail. From Brive's restart I took the ball under huge pressure from Lamaison, who must have been miles offside, and found touch only a few yards away.

Much to my annoyance Jim Fleming let him get away with it and then, from the resultant line-out, added insult to injury by ruling that we had dragged down the maul. In my view, it was patently the wrong decision but there was nothing we could do about it. Lamaison had a fairly straightforward kick from twenty-five yards out, and probably eight yards in from touch, to win the final.

*

We had blown it, or so we thought. Two months later Lamaison would kick France to a Grand Slam but, representing Brive on the day that mattered most to Bath, his kick to win the European Cup was, almost unbelievably, a horror show. The ball set off right of the posts and dropped short. It should have been a joyous moment, only Andy Nicol fumbled the catch and Brive were awarded a scrum under our posts. The ball came back on their side, Philippe Carbonneau flung it to Lisandro Arbizu and the Argentine international had the straightforward task of dropping a goal from fifteen yards. Only he too missed it. The ball bounced into our in-goal area, Richard Webster got to it first and the final whistle blew.

An initial feeling of disbelief at the way we had been let off the hook gave way to one of total and utter joy. As a squad we had all believed that we could achieve the ultimate goal in club rugby but nobody outside the Bath squad had. For us to succeed after all the flak we had taken was huge. Leicester and Wasps were now the great powerhouses of English club rugby and yet Bath, a club so many thought with its best years behind it, had become the first from England to win the Heineken Cup. In the space of eighty minutes we had turned a disastrous season into a good one.

Our fans were seated at the other end of the stadium and, as one, we turned and sprinted a hundred yards to where they were. The look on the faces of so many people who had come so far to support us matched the way I felt inside. Ecstatic and unbelievably proud. Against all odds we were on top of European rugby. It felt like the good old days were back.

But what should have been a springboard to further success proved nothing of the sort. Seven successive league wins after

Christmas followed by a Heineken Cup triumph might have erased the nightmare of our 50-point stuffing at Saracens in mid-December, but the cheers of Bordeaux turned to jeers back home by late April as we lost six of our last eight matches in the Premiership to finish a distant 12 points behind champions Newcastle.

It only reflected how we had blown the transition from amateurism to professionalism as a club. When rugby went open Bath needed to do what it had done before, only better and in a more professional way. That meant promoting into management former players to maintain and safeguard the ways and traditions of Bath, whilst also driving the club forwards into the new era, as Leicester have always done so successfully. The club's new owner Andrew Brownsword briefly did that, keeping John Hall as director of rugby. But soon Bath as a club lost focus and a very good man ended up losing his job.

Which is not what Bath fans had expected when Brownsword took over and pledged: 'This club is respected across every continent. It is worth supporting a club which enhances the reputation of one of England's finest cities. The club will be thoroughly organised to run on professional lines. Professionalism may well see some casualties but we won't allow that scenario to ensue here.'

Fine words, but John Hall was sacked three days after the club suffered its heaviest defeat in a decade, to Leicester in the Pilkington Cup. Brian Ashton had already left, to become Ireland coach. Andy Robinson took over, pulled things together towards the end of the 1996–97 season and now had guided us to Heineken Cup final glory.

Andy Nicol had begun his reign as captain the previous autumn by saying that winning was all that counted and that finishing second 'is coming last'. Eight months on and we had not even managed second best on the domestic front. We ended up joint third and Brownsword responded by getting rid of a number of players and asking a number of others, including myself and head coach Andy Robinson, to take a pay cut. At a time when I felt we needed to hold our nerve and build on existing foundations, the owner had other ideas. I initially refused, on principle, as I had two years left on a three-year contract. But Brownsword played hardball. He warned that either I agreed or he'd put me up for sale.

Andy had agreed to his pay cut because, he said, Bath meant so much to him and he expected all his players to do the same. I loved the place too but I was having none of it. I said to Brownsword: 'If you were in my situation would you take a pay cut?' He replied: 'Well I'm not in your situation, am I?' He then warned that if I didn't take the cut and show my 'loyalty' to Bath he would stick me on the transfer list. He said I was one of Bath's highest paid players and he was prepared to get rid of me.

His words made me doubt that this bloke really wanted Bath to succeed. He questioned my loyalty and put me in an impossible position. He knew the club meant the world to me. I didn't want to leave and he knew it. Nor did I want to see the club go under financially. But instead of meeting me halfway as an act of goodwill he left me with no choice. If I wanted to stay I had to take a massive pay cut. At a stroke I lost £40,000 a year.

It didn't help that Andy Robinson and Jon Callard were ill at ease with Brownsword. I remember players and coaches once being invited to a Christmas do at Brownsword's house, nothing more than an informal house party. Jon Callard looked unbelievably nervous. He did not feel comfortable at all. You'd have thought we were taking tea with the Queen. If he and Robinson were uncomfortable with Brownsword, the rest of us had no chance.

Even after I had taken the pay cut I didn't feel any more appreciated. Quite the contrary in fact. When Brownsword got rid of some of the big-name forwards, guys such as Martin Haag and John Mallett, I went to see him to protest. 'Andrew, we don't have a pack of forwards. You have to give us one,' I said. 'We can't do anything without a decent pack.' I felt I was wasting my breath. My opinion seemed to count for nothing with him. It was as if he wasn't listening.

7
FINDING MY FEET

Twickenham, 5 February 2000

They came at me hard, forcing me back into a corner. Two in my face, a third and fourth on my blind side. A bright light shone in my eyes and the interrogation began. They were out for a reaction and they were not about to take no for an answer. The next wave closed in, four or five wielding dictafones, two or more clutching radio microphones. More questions. My eyes adjusted to the glare of the spotlight which came from the top of a shoulder-held television camera.

Where so often before there had been stilted conversations and awkward pauses, there were smiles and handshakes offered on the balcony inside Twickenham overlooking the gymnasium and its accompanying slogan: 'Greatness is achieved by the discipline of attention to detail.' This is where the press pack hunts after England internationals and once again it was me fixed in their sights.

Only this time was different from any time before. I had just walked off the pitch to cheers, not jeers, hailed as a hero rather than a villain for my Man of the Match performance against Ireland. It felt like my first cap all over again. A new position, a new team and a 50–18 win for England in the first match of the 2000 Six Nations. I was on cloud nine.

For three years nothing had worked for me from an England perspective. I had been in and out of the side, played at full-back, fly-half, outside-centre, even on the wing. Seven times I had been dropped. Then on the day I won my fortieth cap something finally clicked into place. All of a sudden I found a position in which I not only didn't have the pressures of goal kicking, but had the right players around me to allow me to play my game. You bet I was emotional about it.

Less than three months before it had all been completely different. England were playing Tonga in the World Cup and would win 101–10. Not prime time for the boo boys you would think, only I was on the replacements' bench and was called upon to replace Jeremy Guscott ten minutes into the second half. I stripped off my tracksuit top and walked to the touchline where Jerry's number was shown on the touch judge's board. Jerry had scored two tries that afternoon on what turned out to be his final game of a brilliant international career, though he says so himself. As he left the field the crowd began to boo.

Sensitive though I am, I took it to be the crowd's reaction to one of England's favourite rugby sons leaving the field so early in the game. It did not occur to me at the time that it was their reaction to me coming on. That was how the press saw it; further evidence in their eyes of my unpopularity with the Twickenham set. It was they who reported that I had been jeered when I missed a goal kick which would have beaten Australia a year before, they who were so quick to point out that I experienced more of the same during a warm-up game against Canada prior to the World Cup.

I genuinely don't feel I was booed that day against Tonga. I could be wrong. Perhaps I was so full of adrenaline that I just blanked it out. It certainly didn't faze me or hinder me one little bit. In fact I didn't even think of it. Jerry came off and I went on. But the media's interpretation became fact. And although I started against Fiji five days later and came off the bench in the quarter-final against South Africa, which we lost, my standing in the England order was viewed as precarious to say the least.

Now, twelve weeks later, I stood looking into the eyes of my critics, whilst in the main interview room on the other side of the wall Clive Woodward sang my praises. 'Catt had a fantastic game,' he said. 'It was his best game for England by a mile.' His statement ended with a full stop. There was no comma followed by 'even if his goal kicking was horrendous'. I had outwitted the Irish defence, cut angles, hit the line flat, kicked smartly from hand and generally, I felt, run the show. There had been tries for England new boys Ben Cohen and Mike Tindall and a record score between the countries for the whole team to savour. As for me, for eighty minutes on the Twickenham pitch that afternoon I had been reborn. I had felt that this was the first day of the rest of my life, that a line had been drawn under the past, that after six years and forty caps spent searching for a sense of belonging I had finally found one.

I suppose it began in April 1998 when completely out of the blue Clive Woodward picked me on the left wing for the final match of

what had been a fairly sorry Five Nations campaign for me personally. I had begun it in Paris at full-back in a match that we lost. I was
then dropped to the bench when Wales came to Twickenham and
England won, scoring eight tries and running up 60 points. Next
came Scotland away and another solid England win – again without
me. So I was not exactly expecting too much the day the side was
named to face Ireland at home. Certainly not to be given the number
11 jersey.

'Catt can play anywhere, I don't think he has a position,' Woodward said by way of justification. 'Often players like Mike get left on
the bench. But I'm determined to have this guy in the team as long as
he's playing well.' It was a shot in the arm for me at a time when I
needed one but it was not that I played and scored a try in our 35–17
victory that was notable that afternoon. It was what happened two
minutes from time.

On to the touchline stepped a young guy barely out of school.
There was a break in play and, at the age of eighteen years and 314
days, Jonny Wilkinson came on to replace me. Little did I know it at
that time, but here was a player who would have a profound
influence in the reshaping of my career.

It did not happen overnight. My season ended in the operating
theatre with ankle surgery whilst Jonny went off with England
to the Southern Hemisphere on what, for obvious reasons,
became known as the Tour From Hell. Played 7, Lost 7. The
autumn was equally miserable for the pair of us. Jonny was
omitted from the England squad and I missed *that* kick to beat
Australia and then only lasted an hour playing at fly-half against
South Africa.

But Woodward had come up with a theory that the future belonged to teams playing with two fly-halves. He believed that having two first receivers controlling the game would throw the opposition in defence whilst vastly increase our own attacking threat. Jonny had emerged at Newcastle playing at inside-centre alongside fly-half Rob Andrew. He already had a strong reputation as a goal kicker and so Woodward decided to pick him at 12 and keep me at 10 for the 1999 Championship.

We began with an unconvincing home win over Scotland and injury put me out of the trip to Ireland where, with Paul Grayson at fly-half, England won well. I returned for the next game against France, which we won, but thanks largely to Jonny's goal kicking. He kicked seven penalties and the post-match clamour was for him to be moved to number 10, the shirt I was wearing. Thankfully it was not a debate the management were interested in. Woodward didn't want his players to be defined by the numbers on their backs, but by what they did.

So we kept the same jerseys for the Grand Slam game against Wales and, instead, were defined by the result. Wales won 32–31 and we were labelled 'chokers'. Due to the old Arms Park being knocked down to make way for the Millennium Stadium, the game was staged at Wembley Stadium. It was a game we should never have lost in a million years but we did, beaten by our own indiscipline and the absence of Jerry Guscott. I feel certain that had we had Jerry playing at 13, rather than Barrie-Jon Mather on debut, we would have destroyed Wales. As it was, we still cut them up, but as a team we kept giving away penalties and Neil Jenkins made us pay.

Jenkins was absolutely phenomenal that day but it still shouldn't have been enough. We had absolutely crucified Wales in open play and with only seconds left we were awarded a penalty, leading 31–25. We had the option to go for goal or to put the ball in the corner. Had Jonny gone for goal the contest and with it the title, the Triple Crown and the Grand Slam would have been ours. But in the heat of the moment Lawrence Dallaglio, our captain, instructed him to kick for touch. I was thinking the same way as Lawrence. My view was, come on, we've got these boys, let's go score again. It was only afterwards that I thought, oh my God, that was an opportunity to put the game away.

From the line-out Tim Rodber was penalised, Wales cleared the ball upfield and Scott Gibbs was allowed to run through our defence to score under the posts. Jenkins landed the conversion, his eighth success from eight attempts, and we had lost. We had been seconds from a trophy-winning triumph to sweep us into the World Cup. Instead we were left stunned. In time we would look back on that day as a vital part of our learning, but that evening in north-west London we just wanted the ground to open up and swallow us.

It would be my last game at fly-half as Woodward decided the timing was now right to give Jonny experience of playing 10 in the three months leading into the World Cup. I moved to outside-centre for the summer Test against Australia in Sydney, a game we again should have won but again couldn't close out. I was then dropped to the bench for four pointless warm-up games against USA, Canada and two Premiership XVs. They were too one-sided to prove anything and so I had no meaningful opportunity to press my claim for a recall. The tournament began and I played no part at all. Until, that is, Jerry's number was held up against Tonga and the booing began.

That memory was still fresh in my mind as I sat in the Twickenham changing room waiting to take the field against Ireland in February 2000. It was England's first match since going out of the World Cup at the quarter-final stage, beaten by Jannie de Beer's five dropped goals for South Africa in Paris. There was a fresh feel to the place. Jerry Guscott had retired from the international game, so too had Phil de Glanville and Tim Rodber. Martin Johnson was injured and Woodward had handed the captaincy to Matt Dawson.

It didn't end there. In the back division Clive had picked the uncapped trio of Ben Cohen, Mike Tindall and Iain Balshaw, youngsters unburdened by past disappointments. I couldn't claim that, not by a long chalk, but I benefited from the injection of youth. Woodward wanted a senior man in midfield to pull it all together and for the first time I had been handed the number 12 jersey. He once again believed that two fly-halves was the way forward.

There was plenty of cause for optimism. We had trained unbelievably hard for the World Cup and, while it didn't pay off in the tournament, those of us still involved now felt physically in great nick. Then there was Matt Dawson's captaincy. He had worked tirelessly to foster a new spirit across the squad. Everyone was encouraged to share their views on the way forward. Lastly, and perhaps most significantly of all, Woodward had emerged from the World Cup disappointment with a nothing-to-lose attitude.

His future had been in considerable doubt after England's elimination. He was continuously reminded that he had asked to be judged on the World Cup and I reckon he decided to go for broke ahead of the 2003 tournament. To give his squad a licence to thrill as never before. It was music to my ears and yet as I prepared for my fortieth cap I was a bundle of nerves. This could, I thought, be my final opportunity.

As I walked onto the Twickenham turf the words of Matt Dawson's pre-match speech echoed in my head. 'This is a new era for England,' he had said. 'Draw a line in the sand and move forward.' It was good stuff, again just what I wanted to hear. 'This is our time,' he added. 'Express yourselves out there. Don't come off the field with any regrets.'

By the final whistle my only regret was that the game had to end. I had made a couple of breaks, set up a couple of tries and put some big hits in as well defensively. The voice on the Tannoy announced that I was Man of the Match. And this time I was sure nobody had booed. What excited me most was that Wilko and I had clicked. Woodward's 10–12 dream combination had worked a treat.

'This is hopefully a stepping stone in the right direction,' I told the media. 'I'm happy, but it's only the one game. I need two or three more before I can start shouting about it.' Inside of me, of course, the shouting had already begun. All at once all the jigsaw pieces had fitted into place. When I had played at 15 we didn't have a gameplan or the personnel to bring me into the game. When I was at 10 I could bring the full-back into the game but the players around me wanted me to kick. Now I was a 12 operating with fast ball and with fast men outside me. To cap it all Jonny was more than happy to have the responsibility of goal kicking.

It felt like all my Christmases had come at once. But I kept the lid on my emotions as the tape recorders rolled in front of me. 'There has been a lot of pressure on me and I'm aware I haven't put a couple of good games together,' I added. 'All I will say is I think all the hard work I put in over the World Cup – shutting up and just getting on with it – is paying off now. I wasn't getting selected but I didn't moan and whinge. And now I've got another chance.'

Matt Dawson walked past, behind the press scrum, and gave me a wink. As captain he had accompanied Woodward to the main press conference which by now had finished. He too had been in and out of the England team. He knew exactly how I felt. Later he would tell me that this was the game I had waited my whole career for. I would nod knowingly. In his autobiography, *Nine Lives*, he would describe me as being 'way ahead of my time'. He put his finger on my problem with England:

> With someone like Mike Catt you've got to play to his strengths, put him in certain areas and give him an opportunity to do what he's good at. Instead he was put at 10 and told to play the same as Rob Andrew at times, and then a bit like Stuart Barnes.
>
> It wasn't until Clive Woodward, Andy Robinson and Brian Ashton took charge that they realised he was so much more effective in midfield. By that time he'd been cowed, to an extent, by the reaction of the Twickenham set. The crowd only respond to what they see, and they'd seen a No. 10 who came on and didn't give them what they were used to. Someone who wasn't executing team strategy as well as, say, Rob Andrew did. They were a bit miffed

by it. Most people, I believe, now acknowledge that Catty was being played in the wrong position for too many years.

I certainly felt I had repaid the faith shown in me by Woodward and from that game on I felt I was an intrinsic part of things. Each England game I looked forward to as opposed to dreading. Working with backs coach Brian Ashton was an absolute pleasure and with the 12 on my back I couldn't wait for the next opportunity to come around.

The difference between this period and the mid-1990s under Jack Rowell was like night and day. Jack had wanted us to play in an almost pre-programmed way, as that was what England had done in previous years when they were successful; whereas under Clive and Brian we were told to play what we saw in front of us. It was so refreshing.

The 2000–01 years were awesome. England scored tries for fun and Brian was forever coming up with new ideas. He would come into training and say, 'Right, this is the formation, over to you. What do you think we could do from here?' He would keep us thinking all the time. If one move worked really well he would alter it and say, 'Right, let's hit this runner rather than that runner.' He was always thinking and the sessions were sharp because we were buzzing mentally. I remember once we stacked every single player on the left-hand side at an attacking scrum except for Jason Robinson, who we left alone out on the right. We won the ball, Jonny kicked to Jason and off he went. I would love to have seen Jack's face.

My press commitments complete, I left the media area to meet up with my girlfriend Ali and a thought occurred to me. How different would my career have been had Alex King not been injured shortly before Woodward's first match in charge? He had been chosen at fly-half for that match against Australia in 1997 with me in the number 12 jersey at inside-centre. But Kingy pulled out injured at the last moment and I was switched to 10 and goal kicker.

Then again, the make-up of the team was different then. Phil de Glanville was a great 12 and so was Will Greenwood. I would have been competing against two fantastic players and probably wouldn't have got a look-in. I dismissed the thought. Forget the past, I told myself. This is your time now.

A fortnight later we took our 2000 Six Nations campaign to Paris and produced one of the great defensive performances to beat the World Cup finalists 15–9 at Stade de France, scene of England's quarter-final elimination four months earlier. We had a defensive call, 'hit the beach', which would be yelled every time we had to redouble our efforts on or around our own goal line. There was a lot of beach hit that day, and we had Simon Shaw and Austin Healey sin-binned in a frantic ending, but we won because, unlike most other goal kickers, Jonny Wilkinson rarely missed. Five penalty goals out of six made him the youngest player to reach 200 international points. It was only his sixteenth cap.

Confidence was high for Wales' visit to Twickenham and we smashed them 46–12, scoring five tries to nil. Then we went to Italy and won 59–12, with Austin getting a hat-trick and Benny Cohen two. That gave him five in four games. Not a bad start to an international career.

Where England is involved everything is viewed as either black or white. We are either world-beaters or not to fit to wear the jersey.

There's no middle ground, at least none I can recall. So with only Scotland left to play in the championship, a team propping up the table with three defeats, we were not only about to win the Grand Slam, we were being talked about as genuine World Cup contenders.

Publicly we dismissed it. We pointed out that we had played only four games since being dumped out of the last World Cup from a great height, that we had as yet achieved nothing and that, anyway, Woodward would not allow his England team to think that way as he had instilled in us a philosophy that you don't think beyond the next game. Not if you want to stay in the team.

But those were words easily spoken. I turned up at the team meeting before the game and some guys were playing pool, others were mucking about. We hadn't done that in Paris or Rome, so why now? At that moment I was struck by an uncomfortable feeling that it wasn't going to happen. It was very bizarre. We had spent a week based at Dalmahoy, looking at a golf course by day, dreaming of a Grand Slam by night. Our focus had slipped. We had developed an attitude problem.

How else can I explain how we lost 19–13 and hardly fired a shot? We had racked up 170 points in the previous four games playing superb rugby. We had conceded four tries and scored nineteen. Talk about a mental issue. It couldn't have been anything else. Yes, Martin Johnson wasn't playing, but he hadn't played in any of those other games either. He missed the whole championship. It was just pathetic. We had already been crowned champions and we got ahead of ourselves. We did everything our coaches had taught us not to do. And that was before the game kicked off.

Okay, we got caught out by the sudden change in weather, from spring-like to Arctic in the space of an hour. That was obviously a factor. It was the coldest I'd ever been on a rugby pitch. But that was no excuse for the way we were bullied and beaten up in the forwards, and our terrible kicking game for which I was partially responsible. Scotland got stuck into Garath Archer and Matt Dawson and instructed James McLaren, a big piece of meat at 12, to run straight over the top of me and Jonny. It was such a basic gameplan and yet so effective. Lawrence Dallaglio gave us the lead with an early try but after that nothing went for us. We got what we deserved.

Sure, Scotland over-achieved but they gave us a lesson in focus. They were mentally spot on, we weren't. They had been beaten in every single game and yet they blitzed us. When the chips were really down they refused to lose, just as Bath had in Bordeaux two years before when we beat Brive to win the Heineken Cup final. Andy Nicol was our captain that day. No prizes for guessing who led Scotland.

After everything I had been through I could not quite believe what I was doing. At last a central cog in the England team, albeit an England side that couldn't close out Grand Slams, I was signing a piece of paper which could change everything. I was in the Kensington Room at Pennyhill Park Hotel, the national team's lavish new training base. Seated around me were the rest of the England squad.

'Let's put it to the vote,' said Martin Johnson.

Johnno had returned from injury after the Six Nations and led us back to winning ways; first on tour in South Africa, where we beat the Boks in Bloemfontein, then back home against Australia, where

Dan Luger's last-second try took us past the world champions. The mishap at Murrayfield was forgotten. We were on a roll, unmistakably this time. Yet now we were risking everything.

Our gripe was this. The RFU were making millions per international and the players were hardly seeing any of it. We felt we were being shafted financially, and had been for the previous six or seven years I had been involved with England.

I had been in tight spots before where money was concerned, most notably when I first arrived in England during rugby's strictly amateur era and naively gave an interview to the *Mail on Sunday* in which I admitted to having been paid to play provincial rugby in South Africa. We did get payment, a little brown envelope after every game for Eastern Province. But it was more beer money than anything else, about £40. The rate for club games was nearer £15.

I thought nothing of it and when quizzed about it by the *Mail* journalist I told him straight. It was the norm, it wasn't big money, I certainly couldn't have survived on it. It was my first dealings with the press and it was not a good start. I was young and naive. I was also, I realised that Sunday, foolish. The back page headline read 'Ban Catt?'

The RFU called a disciplinary hearing and the talk was that I could, indeed, be suspended from playing. Fortunately I had the support of my Bath team-mate Richard Hill who took me to the hearing, talked me through everything and helped me get my defence in order. 'That's the way it was in South Africa,' I testified. 'We weren't under contract. There was no win bonus, just a straight fee.'

That day in London the Union were sympathetic to me. They would be less impressed with the single word I had written down on the piece of paper in front of me. To the question, 'Are you in favour of going out on strike?', I had answered 'yes'.

It was something I never thought I'd do, but I believed passionately in the cause, enough even to sacrifice my England career over, were it to come to that. I still hadn't achieved my ultimate goal of winning a World Cup, but I had played in a semi-final and two quarter-finals, won a Grand Slam and done pretty much everything else.

We had tried to reach a deal through negotiation and diplomacy but had got nowhere. We wanted a package which, essentially, guaranteed us a larger slice of the cake. Rugby union is a high-impact collision sport in which injury is an occupational hazard. There is an ever-present danger that your next game will be your last. Not only were we after a pay rise, we wanted a shift in the balance between basic fee and win bonus.

Sixty per cent of our match payment when playing for England was dependent on us winning. How is it fair that you give everything and lose to the last kick of the game and your fee drops from £5,000 to £2,000? Unless, of course, anyone is suggesting that we need financial motivation to win games. That is complete tosh. The previous weekend, against Australia, we had won with the final move of the match. On the say-so of the video ref we more than doubled our money. It was a nonsense.

The RFU dragged their heels for long enough before making us any offer at all. And when they eventually did we felt the balance was still unacceptable. We asked for a £4,000 match fee and a £2,000 win bonus. From a starting point of £2,000 basic and £4,000 bonus, they moved to £4,000 basic and £1,750 bonus. We rejected that and they came back with a final offer of £3,500 basic plus a £2,250 bonus. It was close but not close enough. It had now become a point of principle. We were fed up with being patronised.

A week earlier Woodward had talked us out of embarrassing the Union into coughing up by wearing our training jerseys inside out, so as to deny England's sponsors the visibility they had signed up for. He managed to, only in return for promising to set up a showdown meeting with RFU bosses. But those broke down and led to us being holed up in a hotel conference room half an hour before midnight discussing withdrawing our labour.

The proposal was to strike. Not to train and not to play until agreement had been reached. Martin Johnson, who along with Matt Dawson and Lawrence Dallaglio made up our negotiating panel, stressed to us that whatever decision we reached everyone had to buy into it. Richard Hill and Martin Corry voted against, with Martin refusing to budge as he said it was dead against his principles, which was fine. We respected that. In fact I sympathised with his stance to a great extent. But then I thought, we have been fighting against these guys for so long. We've got to make a stand. We've got to change things.

Everyone else voted in favour of the proposal and Martin Johnson confirmed the verdict. Strange as it may sound, the atmosphere was one almost of excitement. It felt good being rebellious, if a little scary. In truth, I'm not sure anyone fully understood the implications of our action. It was more like a game. They'll never call our bluff, I thought, as Johnno took our decision upstairs to Francis Baron, chief executive of the RFU. Will they?

We got the answer soon enough. When Martin informed Clive

that we would be withdrawing our labour he went spare. Absolutely ape. He had told us that he would stick with us, his squad, come what may. When he first became coach, he had said: 'I want you guys driving around in sports cars. I want you guys having big houses. I want you guys to be financially successful.' Now he was going back on all that. For him to turn around and say, 'No, you can't', was frankly very hard to stomach. At best he should have supported us. At worst he should have stayed neutral.

But sitting on the fence has never been Woodward's style. He demanded that we leave the hotel at first light. Tuesday morning dawned and he had another word. Still irate, he told us he felt betrayed and let down. He then blew his lid, storming out of the room firing a parting shot. If we were not at training at eleven o'clock the following morning we would not be selected for the match against Argentina that weekend.

As I drove away from Pennyhill Park I called Ali to tell her what had happened. When I put the phone down my answering service rang. It was a message from Clive. 'I can't believe you would do this,' he said. 'Whoever's not at training tomorrow will not be selected for England ever again.' There was a click as he put the phone down. 'You have no more messages,' came the automated voice. One was enough. I had been threatened and my heart dropped out the bottom of my backside. Shit, I thought. Have I done the right thing?

I wasn't the only one to be shocked by Woodward's hard line. I'm pretty sure everybody was. I phoned around the guys to check that we were all still united because I felt uncertain that nobody would backtrack after receiving such an ultimatum. Everyone assured me they were standing firm. I took no pleasure from going against the will of Clive. He had stuck by me when others would have lost faith, he had created a team and a brand of rugby which I was loving being a part of, and he was devoting his every waking hour to helping us to become world champions through his incredible attention to detail.

He clearly couldn't believe it was all happening. His dream was being broken apart but he could have diffused the whole thing. Had we had his backing, had he been 100 per cent behind us and believed in our cause, I think it would have been resolved a lot quicker. Had he sat down with Martin and Lawrence and said, 'Right, come on let's get it right together', I don't believe there would ever have been a strike. But he chose to get into bed with the RFU, who were giving him absolutely everything he needed to be a successful coach.

Thankfully, behind the scenes moves were afoot to broker a compromise deal. Peter Wheeler, chief executive of Leicester and a former England captain, met with the RFU and proposed that £50,000 be taken from the bonus we would receive if we won the 2001 Six Nations title and for it to be shared out among the squad in a one-off payment. That way the RFU could avoid increasing their offer before the following season, and we would not lose out. Thirty-four hours after the strike was called, agreement was reached for us to return to work.

The firework show had not quite finished however. That night we were in Martin Johnson's hotel room after coming back from the team meal, when Clive Woodward came in, firing from the lip. He shot first at Jason Leonard. 'Leonard, I can't believe you did this to me. You've been asking me for a job with the RFU.' Then he took aim at Lawrence. 'Lawrence you've been my friend. I supported you, now you're not supporting me.'

It was totally personal stuff that the rest of us didn't want to know about. A couple of lads returned fire and Woodward, who seemed slightly out of control, left the room. Although normal service was resumed the following morning and we went on to beat Argentina and South Africa on the next two weekends, there is no doubt in my mind that the episode left a scar in our relationship with Clive. Had we been greedy I could have understood his point of view, but because we weren't, why did a man who had said he wanted us to become wealthy stand against us?

There were a number of building blocks in the creation of England's World Cup-winning team, but none more crucial, I would say, than the strike. Two reasons: it bound us tightly together as a team and it marked the emergence of Martin Johnson as a truly inspirational leader.

We all knew Johnno was a great rugby captain from the 1997 Lions tour but away from the pitch he had always come across as a quiet guy who never pushed himself to the fore in anything. All that changed with the strike, during which he was brilliant. In fact, magnificent. I didn't know he had that in him to be honest, to stand up and really lead something so completely different to what he does on a rugby pitch. Over that anxious period his resolve never wavered and he gained such respect from everyone. The way he stood his ground – our ground – and didn't care what Woodward said to him. He was adamant. 'This is what I'm doing, I'm going to see it through and you're not going to stop me.' He never flinched. He wasn't intimidated by anyone.

By the time the chapter had been concluded we, as a group of people, were a truly united force, not just on the pitch but off it. As a squad of players we had taken the action on, provoked a major scandal, and reacted to it as one. Equal parties, a single vote each. It didn't matter how many caps you had, or what you had done in your career.

There had been other scandals during my time in the England squad, but they were of a more individual nature. The 'fifty-seven old farts' affair in 1995, for example, extended no further than Will Carling, the then England captain, who said what he did about the RFU Committee and they sacked him, albeit only briefly. It was fundamentally Will's problem, not the squad's. We were not in camp and we never really communicated as a group about it.

There were no meetings or conversations about whether to come out in support of him. Yeah, we stood up for him, and showed solidarity when senior players Dean Richards and Rob Andrew refused to take over the captaincy. But it only affected the rest of us in as much as there was a World Cup on the horizon and we were faced with going to it without our skipper.

Contrast that with November 2000. During that thirty-four hours – the longest day and a half of my life – we were together in meetings, or on the other end of mobile phone lines. And it was all kicking off. We felt passionately that we were going to do the right thing. Woodward was telling each of us that we were never going to play for England again. Only Will's international career was ever under threat when his off-the-record remark was broadcast by Channel 4.

It is no coincidence England went from strength to strength after the strike, though our tour to South Africa's high veldt five months earlier was also significant to the development of the squad. We had dominated the northern hemisphere under Jack Rowell, but what that tour did was to show us that we could compete and win anywhere, even at altitude. We would have won the First Test in Pretoria but for Tim Stimpson having what I saw as a perfectly good try disallowed. But we channelled our disappointment into winning the following week 6,000 feet above sea level in Bloemfontein, where the Springboks had not lost since 1982.

We returned home with a belief that we could beat anyone, anytime any place anywhere. No more were we a team who felt the height of our ambition was to win one-off games against southern hemisphere sides at Twickenham in the English winter when the opposition were at the end of their season.

It was partly the way that tour was handled. We stayed in a beautiful hotel in Johannesburg and after the First Test we didn't train until Wednesday. It was the start of Woodward really getting a handle on how best to look after players and get the most out of them. It was also the return of Martin Johnson as captain, the innovative coaching of Brian Ashton and the brilliance of Jonny Wilkinson, who scored all 27 of our points in Bloem, despite having only just recovered from food poisoning and not having played a game for seven weeks. We flew home on a real high.

'Phenomenal,' said Brian Ashton. 'He controlled the game with his distribution. I've seen Catty play differently but never better.'

It was February 2001, the first game of a new Six Nations campaign, we had just won in Wales and I had enjoyed one of my best games. Will Greenwood had hogged the try scoring, bagging a hat-trick, but I had done the hard work by making two of them – at least that's what I told him – which is presumably why Brian picked me out for special mention. To win 44–15 at the new Millennium Stadium was a fantastic achievement. Six tries to two was emphatic. It confirmed what I already suspected, that we were now a side who believed the sky was the limit. Best of all, however, was that my display meant I would get to play against Italy in the next game. It would be my fiftieth cap. Only nine England players before me had reached the milestone and I would confidently wager that none of those had been dropped nine times. Rory Underwood, Will Carling and Jason Leonard certainly weren't. Nor Wade Dooley, Peter Winterbottom and Brian Moore. Jerry Guscott missed games through injury and went through that season when Jack Rowell left him on the bench in order to play Carling and Phil de Glanville together. Otherwise he was pretty solid. Rob Andrew and Martin Johnson? Somehow I doubt it.

I was proud of myself for never having given up, even if I had been to the very edge once, when Jon Webb talked me out of jumping in the autumn of 1997. That apart, I had rolled with the punches. Sure I got upset with the press at times – a lot of times actually – but rarely with the England management. I never phoned Clive, I never brown-nosed him in any way to try to get into his good books or to fight my corner. Perhaps that made me an easy target, because I didn't bitch or moan when I was dropped. I'd never shout and scream. I'd just go 'Fine', and off I'd go. Whereas, certainly in the Woodward era, a lot of the other guys would really take him to task on it. My view was, he's made his mind up, I can't change it.

Perhaps I would have done better to have stood up for myself more. Who knows? There were certainly occasions when I listened to too much advice and, to a fault, tried to please everyone. I let myself be walked over at times. I switched positions, I changed styles. Maybe I should have stood firm and said, 'This is what I am, this is what I do. Take it or leave it.' Then again, had I done so, would I be sitting on forty-nine caps with the promise of leading out the England side at Twickenham against Italy to mark my fiftieth.

Nobody needed to point out to me that it had taken six or seven years to find my best position and really establish myself in the side, but great international teams do not become so overnight. It is a process of evolution. I was lucky when I first started because I came into an England side that was already developed. It had already won Grand Slams and been to a World Cup final. But Woodward rebuilt pretty much from scratch. Three key foundation stones were already in place – Leonard, Johnson and Dallaglio up front – but the team had still to be constructed around them and that involved trial and error.

The back row was quickly resolved. Neil Back and Richard Hill complemented Lawrence's skills and the trio proved a perfect blend. That apart, players were brought in and out, auditioned in one position then another, experiencing good times and bad, as Woodward searched for the killer combinations. By 2000 he knew he had a core group of immense talent. By 2001 the pieces in the puzzle had been arranged in the right position. Which is why the England team I proudly led out on 17 February felt it could do no wrong.

The one question in my mind was what sort of a reception I would receive from the Twickenham crowd. I wanted to believe I would get a cheer, but I had long since realised that I divided opinion. As Will

Greenwood had put it in the morning papers: 'To the average man in the street he's like Marmite. You either love him or hate him. There's not been a lot of middle ground with Catty. It is difficult to say why he has evoked the reactions he has. I suppose he likes to play rugby and every now and then there were times it didn't come off. It was not always his fault though. Sometimes it was because people weren't reading him.'

I walked out through the home changing room door at the head of the line and took a deep breath. I walked down the tunnel, paused briefly, and then ran out on to the pitch. Smoke from the pre-match fireworks filled the air and obscured my vision. It had the same effect on the crowd as well and for a moment there was no reaction. Nobody saw me. No one could see me. Just typical, I thought, clutching the ball I was holding tighter under my right arm.

You couldn't have made it up. Of course it seemed longer in my mind than it really was, because I was on edge, anticipating a reaction. The smoke cleared, probably within a few seconds, drifting up high enough to reveal the pitch and a solitary player looking around for his team-mates. The Tannoy announcer introduced me to the crowd and a cheer went up, as enthusiastic as I could have hoped for.

For months afterwards I would replay that moment in my mind, along with other highlights from 2001: a spring in which England rewrote the Six Nations record books, a summer in which I was selected to tour Australia with the British and Irish Lions, an autumn in which my girlfriend Ali became pregnant with our first child and a winter in which we were married.

But nothing lasts forever. My perfect world was about to be

shattered. At the start of 2002 I tore a shoulder tendon which ruled me out of England's entire Six Nations campaign. Then one Sunday morning in May I would wake up looking forward to nine holes of golf and notice that my wife's face appeared swollen. She had a headache, she said. A real thumper.

8
HEAVEN TO HELL

Bath, 6 May 2002

It was shortly before 11 o'clock on a Sunday night and I had just arrived home at the end of a particularly stressful day; a day which had begun with Ali complaining of a headache. Our first baby wasn't due for another five weeks and it had been a brilliant pregnancy. Ali wasn't too big, she didn't have any morning sickness, she wasn't overly tired.

But that morning her face had been swollen, her eyes puffed up. She had never been one to complain about pain. If she had a headache she would lie down and go to sleep and wake feeling fine.

I had an early tee time and Ali told me to go. She just needed sleep, she assured me. She would be fine, she insisted.

So I played then hurried back. Ali had slept but she wasn't fine. I could see that. Her head now appeared unbelievably large and everything about her seemed swollen. She couldn't put rings on her fingers, she couldn't pull on her boots.

It was lunchtime and the doorbell rang. We hadn't seen my oldest brother Doug and his wife Catherine for four months but they were in Bath and thought they would pop in. Today of all days.

130

Catherine took one look at Ali and immediately sensed something wasn't right. She asked me where we kept the birth books. There was an urgency to her tone. I fetched them for her and she flicked through the pages looking for any reference to unusual swelling in pregnancy. The advice was short and to the point. We were to telephone the midwife.

I had never heard of pre-eclampsia, a disorder caused by a defect in the placenta, which joins mother and baby and supplies the unborn child with nutrients and oxygen from the mother's blood. I certainly didn't know it was potentially life-threatening to both if allowed to develop. And there was more. Much more. But I was distracted by the midwife telling us to get Ali along to the Royal United Hospital in Bath posthaste.

I snapped shut the book before getting to the section on signs and symptoms which referred to eclamptic convulsions. These, it explained, look no different from epileptic fits. The mother is gripped by synchronised, repetitive and often quite violent spasms involving muscle groups in the eyes, jaw, neck and limbs. These, it continued, lead to temporary loss of consciousness. I hadn't read any of that. I was speeding in the car.

Within half an hour Ali was at the Royal United Hospital in Bath undergoing protein tests. After what seemed an interminable wait the results came back and showed she had a high level of protein in her blood, but that she was all right. It was late so I felt no concern when they said they would keep her in overnight. Ali and I joked that it was probably for the best in case the baby came early. We laughed together.

Forty minutes later, as I threw a toothbrush and face flannel into Ali's washbag, my phone rang. 'Mr Catt?'

'Yes?'

'Congratulations. You're a father.'

'What?'

'You're a father. You have a daughter. But I'm afraid to tell you that your wife is in Intensive Care.'

My head was in a spin. I had only popped home to pack a bag for Ali. I had been told there was no need to rush. Someone had specifically told me that.

My journey back to the hospital passed in a blur. I dumped the car and ran through the main entrance yelling frantically to nobody in particular to tell me where my wife was. I was pointed in the direction of Intensive Care, where I was greeted by a nurse and an explanation which scared me rigid.

Ali had fitted, the baby, traumatised from losing oxygen, had been delivered by emergency Caesarian. But Ali's fits had continued, and brain damage was a real danger. A nurse suggested I go and see my baby daughter.

'I don't want to see my kid,' I snapped back. 'I want to see my wife.'

Ali and I had been married for less than five months but we had been together for almost five years. She was an estate agent who lived on her own in Bath and was always up for a laugh. From the first day we met I felt I would marry her. She quickly became my whole life outside of rugby. She shared my sense of fun, my liking for a party. She was a larger than life character who always seemed to be out on the town enjoying herself.

I had bought a house in 1996 with the proceeds of my first professional contract. I put in a bar in one room complete with optics and, while I didn't quite run to a disco ball, I did have a talking parrot, until somebody shoved it up the chimney and it went missing for two years.

Team-mates would come back to my place after training, friends would visit from South Africa and on Saturday nights everyone would head out of the clubs to party at my place. But Ali said she didn't particularly want to be with a rugby player because she'd heard rumours about what we got up to. One day I phoned to ask her out and she didn't call me back. I thought she was avoiding me so I called again two weeks later and she claimed she had not only lost my number but had had tonsillitis. That was when I knew for sure that she had been avoiding me. But I persisted, suggesting we go out for a drink together. She agreed on condition that we went somewhere outside Bath where nobody would recognise me. We agreed on a small pub five miles away only for it to be packed with regulars, all of whom seemed to have season tickets at Bath!

From there we took it slowly. She would go out with her mates and me with mine. If we met up later in the evening, then brilliant. We really enjoyed each other's company and over the course of six months we spent an increasing amount of time with one another until it made sense to move in together, which we did in 2000. I proposed to Ali in the autumn of 2001, a fortnight after we found out she was pregnant.

But now that very pregnancy was threatening her life. From outside Intensive Care I phoned Ali's mum Christine to tell her what had happened and she raced over from Warminster, half an hour's drive away. Just as she arrived a doctor came over and asked whether Ali had any history of fitting. Chris, like me beside herself with worry, said that no, Ali had never before had a fit.

We were told we would be unable to see her for another couple of hours, and I was again encouraged to go and visit my baby daughter by one of the nurses. This time I did as she suggested, but when I looked down at the little thing I found I had no feeling whatsoever for her. She was just a kid in an incubator. To the best of my knowledge she was fine but at that moment in time I really didn't care. She was not even meant to be in the world yet. Looking back now I feel awful saying that. In fact worse than awful. But at the time I just wanted Ali to be okay. She was my only concern.

Some time in the middle of this awful night word finally came that we could see Ali. I pushed opened the door and there she was. My wife. Tubed up to the hilt and still fitting. After all this time her whole body was still trembling. I bent over to kiss her and for the first time that I could remember started to cry.

Five months earlier the two of us had shared altogether different emotions. We had been married at the Roman Baths in Bath dressed in Georgian costume. I had always wanted a fancy dress wedding; a great party with all my mates and family. I reminded Ali of that on the day that I proposed, after presenting her with the ring which she had designed a couple of years earlier and which I had secretly had made in South Africa during England's summer tour in 2000, then kept hidden in a shoe in my wardrobe for the next eighteen months.

I thought no more about it as I headed off to join up with England for the autumn internationals. But on the Wednesday before the South Africa game, Ali phoned me at the Pennyhill Park Hotel, where we were based, wanting to talk about the wedding. I told her that I was in the middle of an international build-up and didn't particularly want to go into all that now. We had pencilled it in for the following August so there was plenty of time and we had already decided on fancy dress.

The next day she phoned again. This time she was not asking. 'Right, we're going to get married in December.' That was a month away and this was Thursday night, less than 48 hours before I faced South Africa, the land of my birth.

'Ali, honey, do what you have to do,' I said a little sharply, not imagining for one moment that anything would come of it.

Five weeks later, on our wedding day, more than a hundred guests, everyone in period costume, saw me say 'I do' and Ali turn to them, punch the air with her fist and bring the house down by yelling, 'Yesssss!'

Needless to say it was not Lawrence Dallaglio, dressed as King George, Jonny Wilkinson in a wig, Ben Cohen in tights, or Matt Dawson – who looked more like a 1960s schoolboy than a Georgian police inspector – who took the brunt of the mickey-taking. It was me, the bridegroom. 'Catty is not a fashion victim because he does not understand fashion,' explained Kyran Bracken, I suspect speaking for all my team-mates. 'Picking that Georgian theme was the best thing he could have done, otherwise goodness only knows what he would have worn.'

The memory of that day had made me smile as recently as twelve hours ago. But not now. Ali was drugged up to her eyes to combat pre-eclampsia and every now and again she would start to shake. Finally she awoke and I stood up, lent over and kissed her.

'Mother, you've got a beautiful little girl.'

She opened her eyes and looked straight down to her belly. Only then did she realise she had given birth.

'What do you want to name her?'

Her eyelids dropped and for a moment I thought she had slipped back into unconsciousness.

'Evie,' she whispered.

In truth I wasn't remotely worried about the name. I just wanted to know Ali was going to be okay. She had drainage tubes coming out of everywhere. It was a brutal sight. And yet amid the horror of the situation one bizarre thought kept crossing my mind. How lucky I was.

Had it not been for my sister-in-law, who we hadn't seen for four months, turning up that particular day, Ali would have fitted at home and I probably would have lost both her and Evie. Ali would have said, 'Oh, I just need a good night's sleep', we would have gone to bed and in all likelihood she would not have woken up. It would now be three o'clock in the morning and I would be sitting alone at home without a wife or a daughter. Perhaps both.

We spent another two days in Intensive Care, then Ali was moved into the Maternity Ward. Chris went home and my brother Doug came and looked after me. He was brilliant. We'd spend all day at hospital then he'd take me home and make me get some sleep.

The evenings followed a familiar pattern. We chatted, I cried, then fell asleep on the sofa. All the time I lived in fear of getting another call from the hospital. Every time the phone rang my heart would skip a beat. On the fourth night the call duly arrived. It must have been four o'clock in the morning.

'Mike, I was just wondering, can you bring up a razor for me? I need to shave my legs. It's been a while.'

It was Ali, unable to sleep but otherwise sounding great. I knew then she was going to be fine. It was just a matter of time.

Ali was finally given the okay to go and visit Evie for the first time. Up until then she had had to make do with the Polaroid photos I had taken for her and I was concerned whether their physical separation would affect their bonding. I needn't have worried. Despite being pumped full of morphine to keep the pain at bay and having to be pushed in a wheelchair down to the Neonatal Intensive Care Unit, they connected immediately.

I stood by the door and studied the joy in my wife's eyes. I had fifty-six England caps to my name, I had toured twice with the Lions and won a European Cup and countless domestic league and cup honours at club level with Bath. Yet never had I felt so fortunate as I did at that moment.

For the first time in my life rugby was a million miles from my thoughts. The season had ended prematurely for me, due to an operation I had undergone in February on a torn shoulder tendon which I was told would sideline me for between four and six months. The Six Nations had come and gone and there was no possibility of me touring to Argentina with England in June. I was free to devote my attention to my family and to revel in the feeling that all was right with the world.

That feeling of well-being lasted two weeks. Then I received a call on my mobile from Ali as I drove to Eastbourne for the funeral of my grandad, to whom I owed so much for putting me up when I first came to the UK. Ali was at her mum's in Warminster and there was a concerned tone to her voice that I had not heard since she had been out of hospital.

'Evie's looking really blue. I don't know if she's cold, but she's blue around the lips.'

It was a cold day and they had been for a walk, Evie strapped to Ali's front in a papoose. I suggested that maybe she was cold from the walk and that seemed to make sense to Ali. But when I got back to collect them that evening there was a terrible shock awaiting me.

Ali was feeding Evie, with her mum seated across the room on another sofa, when all of a sudden she let out this ear-piercing scream. She had taken Evie off the breast and the little one was absolutely limp.

'She's not breathing!'

Without a second's thought I leapt to my feet, took Evie from her and, with a calm tone which to this day I cannot explain, directed them to ring 999. Ali was screaming, Chris was screaming, I was ice cool. I laid Evie on the sofa and thought to myself, 'You're not good my darling, are you?' I couldn't get a pulse. There was absolutely no sign of life.

I dropped on to my hands and knees and started giving this tiny creature mouth-to-mouth. I had learned life-saving back in South Africa at the age of twelve and I had been taught that with infants you don't blow too hard and you don't compress the heart. It's more of a massage. Of course I'd never actually practised this

138

theory on a baby or indeed any live being. But I was thinking clearly, there wasn't any emotion. It was like, this is what's in front of you, deal with it.

I removed Evie's babygrow and rubbed her heart. I started blowing gently into her mouth but I didn't get anywhere. A minute, maybe a minute and a half passed, and I was becoming frantic. I thought, fuck it, I might as well go for broke here. I took a deep breath and blew really hard.

Ali was beside herself in the kitchen. She couldn't watch. Poor old Chris was on the phone to the emergency services being told what to do. Four or five times I blew firmly into Evie's tiny mouth. Nothing. Then just when I was losing hope she choked and let out a little scream.

'Jesus Christ, thank you. Thank you.'

As Evie started to cry the door flew open and two paramedics burst into the living room, asking me to move to one side as they slipped a mask over my daughter's face and started giving her oxygen. It had been at most three minutes since Evie passed out but there they were. I couldn't believe it.

Ali jumped into an ambulance with Evie. Our two black labradors were in Ali's car from her earlier walk so I belted back to Bath to drop them at home and raced back towards the same hospital where Ali had fought for her life. A day which had begun with my first family funeral had ended with me having to resuscitate my three-week-old daughter.

In actual fact the day hadn't ended. The next nightmare had only just begun as I chased round the departments of the Royal United, trying to locate my wife and daughter. The doctors decided Evie needed to be shifted to Bristol Children's Hospital because they had better equipment there to deal with her.

I found Ali who was talking to a doctor, 'Can you check her heart? There's something wrong with it, I know there is. You've got to check her heart.'

The doctor knelt down in front of Ali, took her hand and said, 'I promise you that there's nothing wrong with your daughter's heart.'

Ali was having none of it. She looked her in the eye and snapped, 'Just check her heart.'

'Ali, stop it,' I interrupted. 'Trust the doctors. It's not her heart my love. They've said it's not her heart.'

Evie was a little bag of wires as they took her down to the ambulance bay and we headed off to Bristol. There, in the small hours, Ali managed to persuade a heart specialist to look at our daughter, and when he had done so he confirmed her suspicion and told us Evie needed to be operated on straight away. The relief we might have felt at knowing something was going to be done for Evie turned to horrified disbelief when he went on, 'The problem is, they began refurbishing the theatre at five this morning and we're unable to operate here.'

The alternatives were Great Ormond Street in London or the Diana, Princess of Wales Children's Hospital in Birmingham. Birmingham had a bed available, so the hospital suggested Ali and I went ahead because they would have a couple of doctors looking after Evie in the ambulance. Ali didn't want to leave her, but I convinced her that on this the doctor was right. I drove us home to pick up a change of clothes and on the way I phoned Phil de Glanville and his wife Yolande. We needed to hear a friendly voice. Phil dropped everything he was doing and said he would drive us to Birmingham.

An hour later we were halfway up the M5, north of Worcester, when my mobile rang.

'Mr Catt? I'm sorry to tell you that your daughter is not well enough to travel.'

I didn't know what to say or do. We were driving away from our daughter, wasting precious minutes that could be the last she would know. A sign for the NEC and Birmingham Airport passed overhead as we headed towards the first available junction and a swift U-turn.

The phone went again. It was the hospital in Bristol. Evie had stabilised and they had begun moving her from IC down to the ambulance bay. We should definitely continue with our trip as the ambulance would be at Birmingham inside the hour. There would be two police motorcycle outriders leading the way and a patrol car bringing up the rear.

Phil shot me a reassuring look, as if to say, it's going to be all right mate. In truth, he didn't know how seriously ill Evie was until he walked back out through the hospital entrance after dropping us off and encountered the ambulance, blue lights flashing, as she was being stretchered out. They rushed her past him and into the theatre, then a nurse came and found us and explained what the process was. After her a doctor appeared and gave us a completely different diagnosis to the one the guy in Bristol had given us. The only thing on which they seemed to agree was that the odds on Evie surviving were very slim.

'There are no guarantees I'm afraid,' he said. 'I will do my absolute best but you should prepare yourselves for the worst and go and say your final goodbyes.'

We said a goodbye of sorts as Evie was wheeled into theatre, but neither of us allowed ourselves to think that we would not see her alive again.

I phoned Ali's mum to relay the grim news. I mumbled that there was nothing we could do, that it was in the doctors' hands, God's hands, somebody's hands . . . We were then shown to a room where parents can go and stay. There were five or six other couples in there who had sick children and worries of their own. Some of them had kids of two or three years of age who had never been home. We found it mind-blowing. Too much to take.

Somehow, and from somewhere, Ali found a fresh reserve of strength. 'If Evie dies, Mike, it's meant to be. If she has to go she has to go. That's nature.' She was not giving up, she was preparing herself in case we were confronted with a decision in the hours to come over whether or not to turn off a life-support machine. Thankfully the question was never posed. After what seemed an eternity, news reached us that the operation had been successful.

The little girl with the remote survival chance was still alive. The official diagnosis was Total Anomalous Pulmonary Venous Drainage. To you and me that means her heart had been plumbed the wrong way. She had a hole in the bottom left chamber and the blood was being pumped back into the heart rather than around the body. The procedure she underwent involved sealing the hole with a piece of pig's bladder and then rearranging the rest of her plumbing correctly.

She was not out of the woods yet. Not by a long way. We were advised that the next forty-eight hours would be critical.

Four or five hours after she came out of theatre, Ali and I were told we could see her. We didn't know what to prepare ourselves for.

142

Certainly not what we saw. We walked in and there were pipes everywhere. Evie was lying on her back with a sticker across her chest with two words scrawled on it. Chest Open.

It was another massive shock to the system but we were unbelievably grateful that she was alive and reassured by the regular beep of the heart monitor. The doctor came over to us and said that the operation had been a success. He explained that the swelling caused by the surgery to the muscles around the heart meant that they had to keep the sternum open until it all settled down. The next 48 hours, he said, would be critical.

They came and eventually went without major incident and all was going well until four or five days after the operation when it emerged that Evie was starting to have fits. Doctors don't mince their words and I was standing at the reception desk when this Scottish guy, who recognised me as an England rugby player, came over. 'Look, as you know, your daughter is having these fits. They tend to be a sign of brain damage. It doesn't look great but hopefully we can kick it into touch!' I couldn't believe he could say something as inappropriate as that.

Fortunately, there was a Jordanian nurse by the name of Abdullah who had been assigned to look after Evie for twelve hours of each day. This man would become our saviour. Every time we needed anything we went to Abdullah. Every time there was a bit of negative vibe from a doctor, Abdullah would put it in context. Invariably he was spot on.

I turned to him after finishing with Dr Insensitive. 'He's speaking rubbish,' said Abdullah. 'I see this in kids all the time. It's not brain damage. The fitting is just a reaction to certain medicine. Believe me, she's progressing well.' It was the way he said it which reassured us and from that day on we put our trust in his expertise.

Evie made steady progress and she was taken out of Intensive Care. She was still wired up with drainage tubes and the threat of brain damage had not yet been removed. Someone said that girls are better than boys at recovering from trauma, that boys give up a lot more quickly. I had no way of knowing whether that was true, but it was something else to cling to. All we knew for sure was that Evie was alive and, frankly, at that moment that was all that mattered.

We stayed up in Birmingham for two weeks. Every day another kid would arrive. There was an eleven-year-old boy two beds down from us who hadn't regained consciousness after being in a go-kart accident and wasn't expected to make it. There were a lot of very upset relatives around him. Then a four-month-old boy came in with his head as big as a football. He had young parents, not more than nineteen or twenty. He hadn't been strapped in properly to his car seat and they had been in an accident. He wasn't going to make it either.

Relatively speaking, we felt extremely fortunate. Our daughter was only three weeks old and we were being told she would be okay. These poor people had developed relationships with their children and were being told to expect the worst. It was impossible even for us to comprehend what they were going through.

There was so much time to reflect as I sat beside Evie's bed looking at a baby daughter I hardly knew who had undergone heart surgery and had at least twice cheated death. A month ago I was a rugby player whose biggest care was whether I would be selected for the weekend. My life had been turned upside down. For me, sport could never again seem a matter of life and death.

9
GOING TO PIECES

Bath, 10 August 2002

It was the start of pre-season, three months on from Ali's blinding headache, and it was time to go back to work. I had not played since February when I tore my shoulder and underwent surgery. Only my closest friends at Bath knew the extent of the trauma I had been through with my family and I wasn't about to shout it from the rooftops. So I felt it was important to start the new season promptly.

Only my heart wasn't in it. The World Cup, to which I had been counting down with such excitement as England cut loose in the 2001 Six Nations, was now only a year away. I had to be in it to win it, which meant I had to be back playing for Bath, putting pressure on the current England centre pairing of Will Greenwood and Mike Tindall, which had been an ever-present feature of the 2002 Championship in my absence.

I should have taken my time. I should have had another three weeks off to spend time with my family and get my head right. I had been through a life-altering experience, seen things no father would ever wish to see, felt emotions no husband would willingly feel. I was completely drained.

Instead I clocked in for the start of pre-season and my body couldn't handle it. I couldn't do weights because my shoulder was still troubling me. The surgeon had not done a very good job. So I did a lot of running and, to my horror, my hamstring went. I didn't realise that this is what stress does to you. It breaks your body down. You produce hormones that actually break muscle down. I didn't know that.

The initial shock of what happened to Ali and Evie I had handled. Yeah, I cried, but I dealt with what was in front of me. There wasn't time to reflect on what was actually going on. I did what I had to do. I was strong in myself and for others and I gave the support that was needed. But from an emotional point of view I had never experienced anything even remotely similar. We had not had any close experience of death in the family until my grandfather; the most emotional turmoil I had ever been through was when my parents divorced. That was the hardest thing I had ever had to deal with. And that was seventeen years before Evie was born. Suddenly I was suffering this delayed reaction.

I should have been distraught that my hamstring had packed in at such an important stage of the World Cup cycle. I certainly had been in February when I was told I needed an operation on my shoulder. But my priorities had changed. Rugby was no longer my sole obsession. The health of my family had taken precedence. As long as my wife and daughter were safe and sound at home, for the first time in my life I didn't give a toss about a sport which all my life had defined me. I almost felt as if I had won a World Cup and I didn't need to play rugby any more.

I wanted to get to know Evie properly. I had reacted coldly to her

Celebrating Rob Andrew's injury-time drop goal from the Australian 10-metre line that took us to the World Cup semi-final in 1995.

Time out in Durban: me, Bracken, Back and West, pretty impressive surfers – on dry land.

The Jonah Lomu experience and the beginning of the end of our World Cup hopes for 1995.

Castaignède and Dourthe (*above*) celebrate their first win over us in Paris for eight years. But we win the Five Nations championship in 1996 though only when Wales beat France and hand us the trophy. Will Carling and Prince Edward (*below*) put a brave face on, but our success fooled nobody – things needed to change if England were to become world-beaters.

Dave Alred worked with Rob Andrew and Jonny Wilkinson and did his best with me.

Brian Ashton had faith in me at Bath and at national level, and it was he who invited me to captain England.

Jon Webb – a massive support, he helped me out of my crisis of confidence.

My Bath team-mate and close friend Phil de Glanville (*above left*) took over the captaincy for the 1997 England tour to Argentina. I scored a try (*below*) and landed seven kicks in the First Test, but all the time was hoping for phone call from the Lions.

The Springboks took no prisoners on the 1997 Lions tour. Will Greenwood was eighteen months recovering from the tackle that saw him stretchered off against the Free State (*above*). I was luckier. I bounced between Johan Erasmus and Danie van Schalkwyk (*below*).

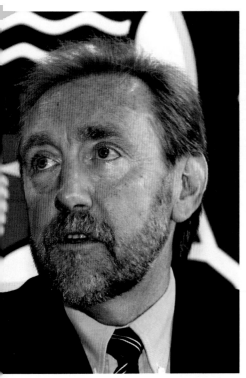

New faces at Bath in the nineties: Andrew Brownsword (*above left*), the millionaire who bought the club; Jason Robinson, (*above right*), an exciting transfer from rugby league.

Mark Regan, Ieuan Evans and I celebrate winning the Heineken Cup after beating Brive in 1998.

A consoling hug (*above*) for my opposite number, Thomas Castaignède, when we beat France in 1999. But despair, (*right*), after losing to Wales and being labelled chokers.

Below: Clive Woodward and Lawrence Dallaglio – new coach, new captain, new era.

birth out of fear that I was about to lose Ali as a consequence. I had responded smartly, but dispassionately, bringing her back to life when she stopped breathing that night in Warminster. I had poured my heart and soul into my wife, but emotionally I had short-changed my daughter. It was time that changed.

We spent an increasing amount of time together and as the weeks passed I came to understand that the love of a child is different from any other. It is totally unconditional. I can say that now because I am an over-the-top doting dad, unable to fathom how any parent cannot love their children. But I didn't get it to start with. It would be another year, on a different continent, before the penny finally dropped.

After my initial emotions settled down, my determination to make the squad bound for Australia returned. The problem was that my hamstring was not responding to treatment down at Bath. With hindsight I should have listened to my body and questioned what the medics were doing. Instead I blindly placed my trust in them and waited for the improvement to happen.

I waited and waited and, in between outings with Evie to the park and to Starbucks my thoughts often flashed back to the England team which had left me behind the previous year. To that Italian game, my fiftieth cap, which we won 80–23, breaking Championship records for size of scoreline and margin of victory, though only after falling behind early on by conceding two sloppy tries. I recalled how, shocked into a response, we unloaded on the Italians, with the entire three-quarter line getting on the scoreboard, except me. But as it was England's eleventh win in twelve matches since I had been switched to inside-centre and made defensive captain I wasn't too upset.

That was the afternoon England welcomed rugby league superstar Jason Robinson into the fold, bringing him off the bench for the last thirty-four minutes. The Twickenham crowd, no longer baying for England's set-piece game of the late 1990s, rose to salute Jason and the team responded by scoring 40 unanswered points. He didn't receive a single pass, however, and post-match debate surrounded whether we had in some way snubbed him.

The very suggestion was a nonsense. The fact of the matter was that gaps opened up in the middle of the field rather than out on his wing and the inside runners were the players to capitalise. Jason didn't seem too upset about it and I certainly wasn't. I knew that in him we had found another strike weapon, another player who lived for running the ball in space and scoring tries. At the end of a memorable day for me personally it was another reason to be cheerful.

Nothing could stop us in 2001, I was convinced of that. We had beaten Scotland by a record 43–3 margin at Twickenham with a display which stunned even Scottish coach Ian McGeechan, and Will Greenwood had notched another try to cap a satisfying day for the two England centres, whom Finlay Calder, the former Scotland and Lions captain, had helpfully termed 'the poorest midfield pair in the Six Nations' in a column he penned for *Scotland on Sunday*. Three games played and the team had already broken the record for tries scored in a Six Nations campaign.

But there was a dark cloud on the horizon, which came out of the countryside and threatened to wreck our Grand Slam dream yet again. An outbreak of foot-and-mouth disease had quickly become an epidemic, sweeping the nation. Terrified by the prospect of it crossing the Irish Sea, Ireland closed her borders and forced the postponement of the country's away game against Wales for fear of travelling fans bringing it back with them.

We had France to worry about but in the back of our minds was a growing concern that our last game, against Ireland in Dublin, would also be postponed. If that happened, what with the season ending early to make room for the 2001 Lions tour to Australia, our campaign would inevitably, it seemed, be stretched into the autumn.

There was nothing we could do about it and we didn't want to make a fuss, not when so many farming communities were seeing their herds of livestock destroyed and their livelihoods ruined. So we focused on France's visit to Twickenham, a match our government was content to let go ahead. More than a month had passed since the Scotland game and we took a while to get going. In fact we trailed at half-time. But such was the confidence in the team that nobody panicked. We could see that the French looked tired after forty minutes, whereas we had barely broken sweat, and it came as no surprise to me that we ran riot in the second period. There were five England tries without reply and none emphasised our self-confidence more than mine, created by Austin's cheeky overhead chip with his back to the posts. With the French defence bewildered, I ran through, caught the ball and touched down.

Another record win, this one 48–19 and France were so shocked that their coach Bernard Laporte demanded that his players follow England's example and professionalise themselves, or be left behind. That was a mighty compliment but he was right. Whilst Clive Woodward had embraced sports science to move us forward,

Laporte admitted that French rugby was still locked in a drinking and smoking culture.

I could not be too holier-than-thou about that, however, as for two weeks every off-season up until 2002, I observed a strange ritual which you won't see in any good health guides. I had a binge, smoking forty cigarettes a day and drinking more than was sensible. I actually hate smoking, but each year I felt my body as well as my mind needed a release from the strict regime professionalism places on it. So I went mad, really let myself go. I developed massive cold sores around my mouth and generally became a right mess. But each morning I would be up early to sweat it out of my system in the gym and by the end of the fortnight my extreme de-tox had flushed out my system ready for another campaign.

Right now in October 2002 such gym work was beyond me. My hamstring was too sore to work the lower body and my tender shoulder meant lifting meaningful weights was out of the question. My life became a cycle of physio sessions at the club and time spent at home with my daughter. I was well aware that the World Cup kicked off in exactly a year. The only consolation I could find was that twelve months earlier now seemed a lifetime away, so much drama and frustration had I packed into it.

It had been in October 2001 that England finally got around to completing its Six Nations campaign in Dublin. Foot-and-mouth had pushed it into the start of the new season and, it turned out, dealt a fatal blow to our Grand Slam ambitions. Our unstoppable momentum of the spring, which left Wales, France, Italy and Scotland screaming for mercy, had been halted by the crisis in the countryside. By the time the Ireland game finally came around many of our squad had lost both focus and form touring Australia with the Lions. I didn't even have the consolation of adding to the Test cap I won on the 1997 tour as my back went before we left Heathrow and I then tore a calf muscle.

In my heart of hearts I never thought I'd be right, despite persuading Lions coach Graham Henry after a week of watching the lads train at Aldershot that my back would come good. I gave it my best shot and I don't regret it. Maybe I was selfish for denying someone else a chance but I would not have forgiven myself had I not tried. I was playing so well for England and the thought of playing in between Brian O'Driscoll and Jonny Wilkinson in a Lions back line was just mindblowing. I was convinced the 2001 Lions were an even stronger squad than their 1997 predecessors and I was so desperate to be a part of it that every morning I woke up at six o'clock and lay in a hot bath for an hour to try and loosen up.

It didn't work. I sat out the first three games and was getting to the stage where I felt almost embarrassed to be there, taking up a place in the squad that could go to someone who was fit. Graham gave me one last chance to prove myself in the game against Australia 'A' at Gosford and before kick-off came over and said, 'You're one of the best 12s in the world, go and show it.' I had not even been able to train that day. And although I thought, right, come on, man, enough of being a gooseberry, I knew I was chasing a lost cause. I didn't get to half-time before breaking down.

My tour was over and I went on a road trip with Dan Luger and Phil Greening, who had also been forced off tour by injury. We started in Brisbane and headed south to Coffs Harbour and Byron

Bay before ending up in Sydney. Every time we stopped we tossed a coin to determine whether we'd stay or move on. We drank and we partied. Lawrence Dallaglio was then forced off tour by injury and he joined us. Of course we were gutted to miss out with the Lions, but it was the end of a hard season so we let our hair down.

To my mind that tour will go down as a massive missed opportunity. And it started from day one. Because that was when we started beasting each other on the training field. Team manager Donal Lenihan had promised us a fun time. He had to be joking, for it was everything but. In '97 we assembled as a tour party, went out for a serious drink, got to know each other and then went about winning the series. In 2001 there was none of that. It was just a grind.

The Spartan regime was in total contrast to the luxury England afforded its players and it was no surprise to me that dissension on tour emanated from the English quarter. We kept saying to Andy Robinson, who was forwards coach for both England and the Lions, 'Robbo, you've got to get them to let us chill out sometimes. It's just too intense.' But nothing changed. And so the guys took matters into their own hands. Matt Dawson wrote a diary in the *Daily Telegraph* which was highly critical of Graham Henry's regime and got him in a load of trouble. Austin Healey used his columns in the *Observer* and the *Guardian* to detail his own dissatisfaction, for which he was found guilty of bringing the Lions into disrepute and fined.

Maybe they should not have spoken out but it was a last resort. Guys were absolutely exhausted, especially the Leicester lads who had come on tour straight from winning a Treble. The players gave everything they had and won the First Test against all expectation with a fantastic display in Brisbane. But non-stop training then caught up with them. I honestly believe that if those first few weeks had been a little bit lighter and a little bit more enjoyable, we would have won that series.

Back home Clive Woodward had only one thing on his mind, England's rearranged match against Ireland in October 2001. While the fallout from the Lions tour spread like wildfire across the media, he tried to ignore it and tap back into the spirit England had generated in springtime. Only that had gone. For a lot of players the Lions was their last reference point. Form had been lost, so too that critical edge of self-belief. Woodward seemed to think he could refocus the group simply by having us back in the England environment. He was so confident that he picked players like Iain Balshaw, who was so out of sorts after failing to win a Lions starting place that he wasn't even getting selected by Bath.

I have no doubt that had we played Ireland when we should have done we would have stuffed them. In our four other Six Nations games our lowest score had been 43 points. We had scored twenty-eight tries in those matches, which were just brilliant to play in. It was a different ball game at Lansdowne Road. We got rattled, we didn't know where we were going or what we were doing. I was furious. I just couldn't believe we were letting another Grand Slam opportunity slip through our grasp, even if we would again pick up the title. Once had been unfortunate, twice careless, but three times . . . When, I thought to myself, are we ever going to learn?

We hadn't seen defeat coming in any of our three Grand Slam games. Neither at Wembley, nor at Murrayfield nor in Dublin had there been any doubt in our minds that we would win. I wouldn't say that was arrogance, rather confidence based on the way we had been playing. But because were so used to winning – and winning by such wide margins – we didn't know how to get ourselves out of a hole. We were still an outstanding team, and we showed that by beating Australia, Romania and South Africa on successive weekends the following month, but Dublin had demonstrated that we were still fallible.

I didn't know it at the time but the game against South Africa in November 2001, and our fifth consecutive win in the fixture, would be my last England appearance at Twickenham for six years. In the space of two months I got married, suffered the trauma of Ali and Evie's fight for life, returned to a struggling Bath team, then lost my England jersey.

When Woodward announced his England team for the 2002 Six Nations opener against Scotland I was dropped to the bench. I had tweaked a knee ligament playing for Bath and Clive, who always insisted that he wanted only 100 per cent fit players, chose Mike Tindall instead. I was gutted as I was convinced I would be fit for the weekend. Save for the game against Romania in November, when Jonny Wilkinson and myself were rested, I had missed only one game at inside-centre since the World Cup.

Instead I returned to Bath and my fortunes went from bad to worse. In a defence session I badly hurt my shoulder making a tackle. A scan revealed that I had torn a tendon and would need surgery. In a matter of days the bottom had fallen out of my season. England lost 20–15 to France in Paris and I could only watch as Jonny was hunted down by the French back row, in particular Serge Betsen. With me unavailable, Woodward had gone against his instinct of playing two first receivers and Jonny had suffered the consequences. It was a lesson he would not forget and which would prove invaluable on a rainy night in Australia some twenty months later.

The Backs coach, Brian Ashton, left midway through the championship, citing personal reasons, and pretty quickly England reverted to playing no expansive rugby whatsoever, just crashing Ben Cohen or Mike Tindall up the middle. Woodward went completely away from the style Ashton had us playing and resorted to pure brute force. The attitude seemed to be, 'Right, we're going through these guys', and that's what England did. Our forwards would dominate and we'd go from there. Jonny had a good platform to work off and he dictated where we went on the pitch. It was good enough to win in Scotland and to beat Ireland and Wales comprehensively at Twickenham, but we had needed a more subtle approach in Paris.

My frustration grew as I watched from the sidelines. At home, Bath slipped further and further down the Premiership table. We had reached the Zurich Championship final the previous season, now we were in dire straits. We hadn't won away all season and with two games remaining we were one of three clubs level on points at the bottom. Only points difference kept us out of the drop zone, above bottom clubs, Harlequins and Leeds. It was a shocking state of affairs for a club with our history and one I was helpless to influence. Although we saved ourselves by beating Leeds at home in our penultimate game, it was no cause for celebration. Bath were a shambles and things needed to change. It was a massive relief to me when Jack Rowell answered an SOS to return as director of rugby at the start of June.

Before the premature arrival of Evie and all the complications that came with her, I had been approached by Leeds and made a very attractive offer to move to Yorkshire. Wasps had also expressed an interest. I was injured, out of the England team and had just turned thirty. My World Cup hopes were diminishing by the day. It was a critical decision for me. Jack called me into his office and I told him my concerns.

He listened intently to what I had to say and, when I finished, he began. He reminisced over the good times we had shared together between 1992 and 1994, when he had left to become England manager and taken us to a Grand Slam and my date with Jonah in the World Cup semi-final. He said that together we could bring those times back. He said that he would not have rejoined had he not believed Bath could be turned around. 'This club is in your blood, Catty, as it is in mine,' he said. 'Come on. What do you say?'

He turned on the flattery and he made a big play of the fact that, as with him, Bath had always been my rugby home and I didn't really want that to change. By the end of our conversation I had agreed to a contract extension which would keep me at the club until the end of the 2004 season. Mike Foley, the former Australia hooker who had succeeded Jon Callard as head coach, echoed Jack's words and gave the impression I was a player who meant the world to the club and would have a large role to play in its future.

The only role I was playing now was that of Sicknote. Each day I would report for duty, not to play or even to be the great leader and wonderful mentor for the younger players that Foley had billed me as. Not at this time. My days were spent getting treatment on a hamstring which didn't seem to want to know. For some reason, which I didn't fully understand, the medics also worked to loosen up my glutes, my pelvis and my back. One day, fresh from being loosened up, I went out to train and my other hamstring went.

By November I was no nearer fitness and the club announced that I was being rested for a month to allow my hamstrings to settle down and for me to work on strength conditioning. Three days later, Foley named me in the team to play Sale. I lasted four minutes. 'It looks like Mike's hamstring is a major issue,' he told the press afterwards. You don't say? 'There's nothing new about his injury,' he added. 'It's just that now it's a lot worse than it originally was.'

The club were becoming increasingly irritated with me for not playing and my frustration had grown to breaking point. I wasn't playing but England were. And winning. On three successive Twickenham weekends they beat New Zealand, Australia and South Africa. England shot to number one in the world rankings. Everyone was talking about how special this team was and what they would achieve in 2003. Nobody mentioned me.

Over Christmas and into the New Year I finally started to become suspicious at the treatment I was receiving. I had joined up with England at a couple of training camps and their physios worked on my hamstrings; specifically on my hamstrings. I then found I was able to train without pain. Inevitably the whispers started at Bath. 'That's right, he's fit for England but not for us.' Then when I came back to the club I'd have my glutes, my pelvis and my back loosened and I would get a negative reaction. I became really really frustrated, embarrassed almost. I was feeling great and wanting to play but I couldn't because of the neural stuff that was going on in my leg.

By late January 2003 I was totally fed up. My hamstrings were sore and my shoulder, a year on from the operation, was still giving me problems to the point that holding almost anything was painful. I asked the doctor to have another look at it and I was sent for a series of scans which revealed that bony spurs were rubbing against my bicep tendon. This, in turn, was causing inflammation and weakening my arm.

It was clear these spurs needed to be removed, which meant another operation and the end of any hope I had of returning to the England set-up in the Six Nations. If I couldn't play in the Championship I would not be able to tour in the summer and if I couldn't make that trip to New Zealand and Australia I wouldn't be able to stake a claim for a place in the World Cup squad. Basically, I thought my international career was over.

I went home very upset, having been booked in for surgery the following Monday. I couldn't believe I had wasted a year because the operation had been botched the first time. I was livid and, thinking I no longer had anything else to lose, made myself available for Bath's Powergen Cup quarter-final with Northampton at the weekend. It would be my last chance of a game of rugby that season, so what the hell?

A minute into the match the inevitable happened. Ben Cohen ran at me, I stretched to tackle him and I felt a twang in my upper arm. I played on, convincing myself that I couldn't make it any worse. I didn't want the Bath fans to see me come off again. If this was to be my last game for some time I would at least see it through. We ended up losing narrowly and I headed to the changing room in considerable discomfort.

Tentatively I started to remove the strapping which before the game I had bound tight around my shoulder to hold it in place. I peeled it off whilst talking to Mike Tindall so I was looking at him rather than my body when he stopped me in mid-sentence. 'Shit, mate. What the hell has happened to your arm?' I looked down. There appeared to be a big hole in my bicep. The top half of it was totally missing. The muscle had dropped to just above the elbow and was hanging loose. My bicep tendon had ruptured.

I didn't know how to react. I was in shock. I had never seen anything like it before. Mike sat me down on the bench and called over one of the physios. This really is it, I cursed to myself. The World Cup is gone. I'm going to be out for God knows how long. Damn it.

Nobody could tell me anything I wanted to hear so I went to shower, keeping the damaged arm bent horizontal at the elbow with my good arm, before being helped into my shirt and heading home. I was hurting, yet a strange thing happened. As the evening wore on the pain lessened. It was still sore from the trauma but there was no great swelling or bruising.

I took a couple of painkillers and went to bed, expecting the worst the following morning; but when I woke I couldn't feel anything. I thought I must be dreaming. Ali confirmed that I wasn't. I flexed the fingers in my hand. No reaction from the bicep but no pain either. I thought maybe I had slept on my arm and it had gone numb. I sat up. No tingling, no numbness, just a bit of tenderness. It was a bloody miracle.

I had heard stories of tendons snapping and people being out for six months or more. Yet I felt as good as gold. It was too good to be true. I half expected when I stood up that some other part of my body would drop off. There was nothing. I grabbed a protein shake and told Ali I was heading to the gym. She thought I was joking. I wasn't, I was excited. My whole body felt different, like it had been in some way liberated.

Once in the gym I stretched thoroughly and then set the weights to the fairly pathetic level I'd had them at all season. I lay on the bench and eased the bar upwards, slowly straightening my arms. No problem. In actual fact it was almost effortless. I increased the weight and tried again. Again no problem. I sat up, carefully rose to my feet and walked across the gym floor. All the pain had gone from my lower back, my hamstring and my shoulder.

The next morning I phoned the club, told them the news, and said I would be in for training later. 'Yes, I *am* sure,' I repeated. I then called my specialist and told him I was now fine and would not need the operation. He said he would be the judge of that and asked me to come in and see him, which I did. He looked at it, confirmed that the short head bicep tendon had snapped but said that by leaving it as it was I would lose only five per cent of the strength in my arm. To this day I haven't repaired it.

Having got his blessing, I drove to Lambridge for training. The rest of the lads were already there, preparing for the big game against Leicester that weekend. I walked on to the pitch and they looked at me as though they'd just seen a ghost. 'It's absolutely unbelievable,' I told a reporter. 'It's like I've been given a new lease of life. I know time is short before the World Cup but I suddenly feel I'm well capable of being in that England squad as I'm probably the fittest I've been for two years.' I started to play again regularly for the club. My confidence returned fairly quickly, despite the Leicester game being only my second full eighty minutes in more than three months. Bath were having another awful season but I had been given a reprieve I didn't expect and I played with a freedom which reflected my devil-may-care attitude. I even started sending the odd 'remember me?' texts to Clive Woodward and then phoned him to say, 'I am really keen to get back involved.'

His reply was always the same. 'I have to see you play more games.' He said that I couldn't just turn up and play an international on a Saturday if I was sitting out training until the Wednesday or Thursday in Test week. 'You have to train right through or else I'm not interested,' Woodward told me. He could afford to play it cool. Will Greenwood was on top of his game at 12 and England were on a roll. Furthermore, Clive was far from convinced that he could rely on me to finish a full game.

It was made clear to me how far off I still was when I turned up one day at Pennyhill Park prior to the start of the 2003 Championship for fitness testing and was met by team doctor Simon Kemp. Rather than welcome me back after so long out he told me in no uncertain terms that unless I went and got my hair cut Woodward wouldn't even consider picking me. I couldn't believe what I was hearing. He was obviously repeating some humorous comment Clive had made, but the timing was all wrong. I was gutted because I could see the way the team was developing in my absence and I felt I was missing the boat. I didn't need to get that sort of grief on top. I was pretty close to giving him a smack.

Successive wins over France, Wales and Italy took England's winning streak to nine and for the umpteenth year the papers were full of Grand Slam talk – or at least Fleet Street was. Doubtless the

Celtic countries were debating how we'd find a way to blow it again. Looking in from the outside there seemed to be a reassuring solidity about England's game, though I could see little cracks in the armour from a kicking and a control point of view which I felt my skills could fill. The back line pyrotechnics of 2000 and 2001 had gone, replaced by a forward platform which was crushing all-comers. And having, in November 2002, put 50 points on the Springboks, who would be the main obstacle between England and the semi-finals come the World Cup, there was a growing belief about the squad that this was going to be our year.

I say 'our' but I was still no nearer a return to the set-up, although I took heart from Woodward reverting to his policy of playing two fly-halves, with Charlie Hodgson picked between Jonny and Will in the 12 shirt against France and Wales. I had read in the press that he was considering resting Jonny from one of the games in the Championship and I wondered whether that might open a door for me. It was wishful thinking, of course, but my chances improved when poor Charlie ruptured an anterior cruciate knee ligament after coming on as a replacement against Italy and was ruled out for the rest of the year.

Two days later Woodward texted me to say he was considering starting me at fly-half against Scotland the following week. Despite Charlie's injury knock-out he was still keen to go ahead with resting Jonny. He had not made a firm decision, he explained, it was just an idea he was exploring. He said he had also short-listed Paul Grayson – who had not worn an England shirt since the 1999 World Cup, though he had toured with England in 2001 as goal kicking coach – and that he would come down to Bath to watch Paul and me play against each other at the weekend.

I didn't get my hopes up, but I must say the prospect of returning to a side unbeaten in its last twenty internationals at Twickenham had my competitive juices flowing in a hurry. The league game was played and ended with no clear winner between myself and Paul Grayson. It turned out to be irrelevant. Woodward decided, after all, to stick with Jonny, explaining that resting such a key player would send out the wrong message both to Scotland and to the other England players. Another mind game perhaps?

Jonny's response was typical. Another silky smooth performance, four tries for his back line and seven out of seven with the boot. England won 40–9, denying the opposition a try for the second time in three games. A week later he was at it again in Dublin as England squared up to Ireland in the Grand Slam decider. England were brilliant, no other word for it. They scored five tries and conceded none. It was not quite the rout the 6–42 scoreline suggests, for only seven points separated the sides at the start of the final quarter. What is in no doubt, however, is that England absolutely deserved to land the Slam.

Of course I was frustrated to miss out, having played in the three Grand Slam defeats of 1999–2001, but these were my mates, many of whom, like me, had come through severe personal trauma in their private lives to finally land the Six Nations holy grail. Will Greenwood, who scored two tries, had lost his prematurely born baby son Freddie the September before; Martin Johnson's mum had died from cancer at around the same time; Ben Cohen's father Peter died following a nightclub attack in 2000. Dan Luger's best pal, Nick Duncombe, who was capped by England at scrum-half in 2002, died suddenly on the eve of the championship.

'When you've been through personal shit it's a game of rugby, nothing more,' Will was quoted as saying. 'Losing a game of rugby doesn't even come close to what some of the boys have been through. We are so much tighter as a group now than even twelve months ago, due to the sad times.' Which made me think. It was now exactly a year since Evie had lain in Intensive Care with that sticker on her heart which read 'Chest Open'.

I wanted to get 'tight' with England again, as it had been eighteen months since my last cap. But I had another battle on my hands, one which was not helping my World Cup chances one bit. Bath, the most famous and successful club of the amateur era, were heading for relegation and possible break-up. Defeat to Bristol at Ashton Gate put us bottom of the league with one game to play, at home to Newcastle.

If there is one thing in my career I could change it is this: I would make sure that Malcolm Pearce bought Bath Rugby Club. Had he done so, Bath would have been where Leicester are now and I would never have left. Not only me either. Mike Tindall, Iain Balshaw, countless others. I have no doubt about that. And all the former players would still be involved in some shape or form, as they are at Leicester. Malcolm is a businessman in the city who is passionate about his rugby and even more so about Bath. When I first came over from South Africa it was he who gave me a job which subsidised my rugby.

I was one of ten Bath players he employed. I was involved in his newspaper business, going into work at two o'clock in the morning and stacking papers for six hours before climbing into a van and going round the city delivering them. Later I was 'promoted' to working behind the till at his newsagents. I had it relatively easy. Ben Clarke worked at Malcolm's dairy and had to go and milk the cows at five o'clock every morning.

Malcolm paid me £8,000 a year at a time when money was hard to come by. He made my life a lot easier at a critical stage of my career. I was able to train and devote myself to rugby, knowing that I had his full support. He gave us all so much time off. He was the heart and soul of Bath, so passionate about the club. For him, everything revolved around Bath RFC and I always thought he would buy it. Yet Andrew Brownsword got in first and Malcolm instead ended up buying arch rivals Bristol. I suspect he did that purely out of spite. Meanwhile Bath has won nothing since the 1998 Heineken Cup.

With Bristol and Bath contesting the one relegation place, Malcolm came up with the idea of merging the two clubs together. With relegation amounting to liquidation in many people's eyes at that time, his thinking was that it was better to save both clubs, even in a condensed form, than to lose one. Malcolm described it as 'an obvious way forward' but it went down like a cup of cold sick.

Going into the Newcastle game we were in dire straits, propping up the table and unsure whether it would be our last ever game for Bath. If Bristol won at London Irish we were doomed, whatever we did against the Falcons. Even if they lost, Bath had to win to stay up. Failure to do that, we were told, would signal the end for Bath Rugby Club as we knew it. There was a lot of anxiety around the squad, knowing that our livelihoods could depend on one game of rugby, and there was a lot of anger about town, much of it directed at Brownsword.

Bath had lost a lot of senior players in a short space of time purely because Brownsword had tried to re-sign them on the cheap. Guys with fourteen years' experience had been offered contracts similar to those the Academy players were on. Purely out of pride they could not accept that. It was just not right.

We held our nerve to beat Newcastle and, with Bristol getting well beaten at London Irish, Bath survived by the width of a cigarette paper. Not just as a Premiership club but as a club in its own right. At the end of a twenty-two-game campaign, Bristol went down because their points difference was twenty-four worse than ours. Afterwards Mike Foley offered to stand down as head coach and took a swipe at 'a number of people here who took success for granted. They took the view that Bath would be successful because they're Bath. Frankly that's bullshit. The only reason you're successful is because you attain certain standards and try to improve upon them each year. You don't just drift from one season to another. This club has slipped from where it was on the basis, I think, of complacency and arrogance more than anything.'

That made me mad, and it still does. What did Foley know about Bath? What did he know about what it meant to play for Bath? So he can blame whoever he wants; the bottom line is that Foley presided over the club's worst ever league campaign.

The threat of relegation averted, talk of a merger ended. Had we gone down Malcolm Pearce would have been able to offer Bath his club's Premiership place in return for the two of us becoming one.

But with Bristol finishing last, Malcolm had nothing that Bath needed. Within two days he had sent an email to the Bristol players and staff informing them that they were free to seek employment elsewhere with immediate effect.

We had dodged the relegation bullet for the second year running and, while I was far from happy with the situation at Bath, I turned my attention towards England once again. There was a tour bound for New Zealand and Australia, with Test matches against the All Blacks and the Wallabies on successive weekends. I was desperate to make the trip, but I was passed over in favour of Paul Grayson and Alex King.

Towards the end of the domestic season at Bath my hamstring had begun to trouble me again and I missed a few games. It was reason enough for Clive Woodward to leave me at home and he told me straight. I tried to argue the toss but he wouldn't listen. He said there was no way I was going to get onto that squad. I cursed him and my bad luck and once again I found myself wondering why I seemed to suffer these neural problems far more when I was with the club than with England.

I tossed it around in my head for a few moments then let it go. There were more important matters to attend to. Woody had said there was no way I was going to get onto that squad. It was pretty devastating news. Yet something inside me kept telling me not to give up. Contrary to everything I was being told, I refused to believe that I wouldn't make the World Cup.

10
CALL TO ARMS

Bath, 7 July 2003

The text alert on my mobile sounded. England were about to go into training camp at Pennyhill Park to prepare for three warm-up games prior to the World Cup squad being announced. I had sent a message to Clive Woodward pretty much pleading to be included in his training squad, from which the teams to play Wales in Cardiff, France in Marseilles, and France at Twickenham, would be picked.

'Hi, will call you later,' read Clive's message. 'Need to know fixtures that you are playing for Bath in August. I'm prepared to play you in warm-up games but I'd need to see you play first. Have not seen you play an international for two years which is a long time between meals. Currently I do not think you will make it but will come and watch you wherever you may be playing. Good luck and text me back dates when you are playing. The squad will be announced this week. You are not in it, or to be honest close to it, until I see you play. Clive.'

I texted him straight back to say we had not got our fixture list yet, but that I was as fit as a fiddle and felt ready to be a world-class player again. 'I'm hungry for it, really raring to go,' I signed off.

'Please be clear that you are not coming into the squad until I see you play,' came Woodward's reply moments later. 'It is very simple. No shortcuts for you or anyone. Let me know when I can see you next and I might try you in the warm-up games. It is very straight-forward. Clive.'

True to his word, the squad came out and my name was nowhere to be found. I looked at some who had been included and it just made me more frustrated. It didn't make sense to me. I had played for England more than fifty times and delivered for them on the big stage. I felt I had proved conclusively that when I played alongside Jonny I brought out the best in him and yet Clive couldn't even find me a place in his training squad. For the life of me I couldn't work out what was going on.

Maybe he was unsure whether my body would hold up to the rigours of the training camp. I *had* had a season blighted by injury. But why didn't he have me in his squad of forty-three so that he could judge my fitness for himself? Ali and I would sit and chat for hours and hours and try to figure out what he was thinking.

'Maybe he's just saving you for the World Cup,' said Ali with a smile.

'Yeah, maybe.'

I was losing my sense of humour. Two months before, while England headed Down Under on the most ambitious mission in their history, I had taken Ali and Evie down to the south of Spain specifically with the aim of getting myself fitter than I had ever been. For five weeks I trained twice a day in the summer sunshine. Every mile I ran, every kilo I lifted, I became more and more convinced that it was fate that I would play in the World Cup. I can't explain why I felt that way because on the face of it, I was training for nothing. But ever since the 1997 Lions, when I was initially omitted but later called up as a replacement, I had grown to understand that opportunities arise even after the initial selection has been made.

Sitting in a bar in Puerto Banus drinking beer with England footballer Steve Stone, I watched England beat the All Blacks 15-13 on television. It was an epic win, made all the more notable by the fact we'd had to defend a scrum on our goal line with only six forwards, as Lawrence Dallaglio and Neil Back were in the sin bin. Maybe England didn't need me after all, I thought as I watched enviously the scenes from Wellington. I dismissed the notion. I couldn't afford to start thinking like that.

A week later the doubt resurfaced. England had been even more impressive in beating Australia 25-14 in Melbourne and there had been tries for both centres, Tindall and Greenwood. It was the first time England had ever won in Oz, seven days after only their second victory ever in New Zealand. The days of blowing Grand Slams, and of me being a key part of the team, suddenly seemed an awful long time ago.

But there was no going back for me now. I had worked so hard to convince myself that I would be going to the World Cup, and on arrival home I took it to the next level. Ali wanted to take Evie to visit her dad in Brisbane, as he had endured the trauma of her birth on the end of a long-distance phone line and had still to meet her.

'The two of you go,' I said. 'And when I get to Oz with England, fly across to Perth and I'll meet you off the plane.'

Bath arranged a midweek pre-season friendly against the Celtic Warriors at Pontypridd and as soon as I got the date I fired it across to Clive Woodward. 'You will be coming?' I texted. 'I said I would, didn't I?' he replied curtly. And so he did. What's more, he brought with him his entire management team: Andy Robinson, Phil Larder and Dave Alred.

From the pitch I could see them all seated together in the stands. It was not the most demanding game I had ever played in but I was satisfied with my performance at fly-half and when the final whistle blew I looked up to Clive for a reaction – a thumbs-up, a smile, a wink even? His seat was empty. Agitated, I hurried to the changing room, kicked off my boots and dug my mobile phone out of my kitbag.

I tapped in five words and fired them into the ether. 'Where did you get to?'

'I left ten minutes from the end.'

'I was at my best in the last ten minutes!'

The following day another Woodward message dropped into my inbox. 'Enjoyed the game,' he wrote. 'All I needed was to see you running about. But thought you did well and looked in good shape. Want to wait and see and compare to what happens this weekend and next. Thanks, Clive.'

On the next two weekends England were due in Cardiff and Marseilles. In the first, what could loosely be described as an

England second team beat what could be fairly accurately described as the best Wales had to offer 43-9 at the Millennium Stadium. But Wales were pretty dismal. Next up was France and what would be a far tougher Test match, a week before England's thirty-man squad was named.

Clive texted me again. 'Hi, still waiting to hear from you as to where you are playing over the next twelve days. Thanks, Clive. PS, Nothing is over till the fat lady sings.'

Nothing is over till the fat lady sings? What the hell was he on about, I wondered. I texted him back to let him know that I would be playing for Bath at Exeter that Saturday down in Devon. My mobile then rang. 'Catty, Clive. I won't be there because our game clashes but I'll watch the tape, I promise you.'

The game came and went and there was no further communication with Woodward. In the Stade Vélodrome, England had lost narrowly, ending their fourteen-game winning streak in the process, but they had one more game before they had to name their squad, against France at Twickenham. I had almost worn a hole in the carpet by the phone, pacing up and down waiting for news.

It finally arrived on the Thursday when Woodward phoned, not a moment too soon. I had just come off a call from Ali, asking if there was any news or whether she should look into arranging flights home from Oz for herself and Evie. Clive said I wouldn't be involved against France but that he wanted me to get myself down to Pennyhill Park for a fitness test with Austin Healey and Andy Gomarsall. He explained that Alex King, the Wasps fly-half earmarked for the third fly-half spot, had injured his knee in training and a scan had revealed that the poor guy required surgery. 'I'll be right there,' I said. I put the phone back on its cradle and smiled. He's been playing silly buggers with me all along, the sod, I thought to myself. I didn't know it but at the other end of the line Clive was smiling too.

He had always planned to take me, he told me later. But he wanted to play a Catt and mouse game to ensure that I arrived at the squad on top of my game. 'If I could convince myself that he would be fit I was always going to take Catty,' he said. 'But I didn't want to tell him that. I wanted to keep him thinking that there was always a chance, which in my head there always was. More than a chance actually. But I didn't want to go over the top with him.

'I always believed that we would need an experienced team to win a World Cup, especially playing down in Australia, so I was very keen to get Catty involved. But my concern was that he was a long way short of physical fitness. I took the decision not to name him in the preliminary World Cup squad, nor in any of the warm-up games. I just believed that what was best for him was to stay at Bath and work non-stop, rather than undergo all the squad sessions with us.

'Catty hadn't done himself any favours the previous season. He played for Bath when he wasn't right physically and that showed in his form. What I told him was to take the whole summer off and go away and get in physically great shape. Then he'd have a chance. I told him that he had nothing to prove to me in terms of his playing ability, so he didn't need to play in those warm-up games. I knew he'd been there and done it.

'I honestly felt it was better for me to leave him at Bath. I think if I'd brought him in he may just have taken his foot off the pedal a bit. You've got to keep everyone guessing to a certain degree. Once you start to nail your colours too close to home too early you can lose a bit with some of these players.

'Was it a gamble? I don't think so. Never was I concerned that Mike would respond the wrong way to not being in the preliminary squad and let himself go, because that's not him. He's never ever let me down, with the media or anybody. As far as I was concerned, the door was always open for him.'

The fitness test was a piece of cake. I blitzed Andy and Austin, as I knew I would, and, while I was still far from assured of selection, I walked around Pennyhill buzzing. My only concern was that while I was fresh and bubbly, had a nice tan and was ready to go, the other guys were absolutely hanging. I had joined a bunch of lads who had been sweating blood and tears all summer and looked dead on their feet. Absolutely dead. The amount of training and rugby that had been drilled into them was just incredible and, believe me, there were not many smiles evident. I only hoped they hadn't crossed the line between working exceptionally hard to be primed for the competition and being overdone on the training paddock.

We would know soon enough as England's final warm-up game was the following day against France at Twickenham. After two games fielding a mixed bag of players Woodward had picked his top dogs. There was a carnival mood amongst a 75,000 crowd, who had come to give England a rousing send-off. We had been installed as World Cup favourites; a staggering achievement considering where the tournament was being staged. But would we be overcooked? Final scoreline: England 45, France 14. I had my answer. I wished I had been on the pitch.

Sunday was spent listening to all the rumours and counter-rumours about who was going to be picked the following day. The view seemed to be that Austin, who had done so well to come back from a knee reconstruction but who I had trashed in the fitness testing, was going to be the unlucky back to miss out – largely because Alex King's injury meant they would need a utility back to cover fly-half and centre and that was my strong suit. But it was all speculation and the following morning I was still none the wiser as I boarded a busy commuter train home from London.

We had left Waterloo and passed through Vauxhall heading towards Wandsworth Town when my phone rang. Half the carriage seemed either to be talking on their mobiles or texting and so my ring tone barely registered with anyone but me. I struggled to fish it out of my pocket without disturbing a guy standing next to me with his head buried in a paper.

'Catty, it's Clive.'

'Hang on a sec, Clive,' I said, dropping my bag to my feet and repositioning the handset so I could hear him more clearly. 'Hi, Clive.'

'Catty, I've picked a squad of thirty and it came down to a choice between you and Austin for the final spot.'

'Right . . .'

'Catty, I'm going to go with you. I was always going to go with you. I'll see you in a couple of days.'

I calmly put the phone back in my pocket and stood staring out of the window in a state of shock as the rooftops passed by. Not because he had picked me, but because he was *always going to go with me*. If he knew he was going to take me why didn't he play me in any of the warm-up games, why didn't he have me involved in the squad, even the forty-three-man preliminary squad? At that moment I should have been doing a conga down the carriage and getting strange looks from fellow passengers. I just shook my head.

I had watched Alex King and Dave Walder and Paul Grayson play those games against Wales and France. I had longed for a go. I had lain awake night after night asking myself how I could convince this bloke that I was fit and healthy? How, when the only games I had to look forward to were pre-season friendlies for Bath against Celtic Warriors and Exeter? And now he tells me that he planned to take me all along.

11

SCALING THE PEAK

Sydney, 22 November 2003

'Do not let these fuckers into the game! Don't let them do anything. Look them in the eye and out-graft them. Right from the start!'

Martin Johnson was not looking at me as he spat out the words. He was not looking at anyone in particular. He was addressing the England team, his England team, inside the changing room at Sydney's Olympic Stadium.

There was a brief pause, followed by another explosion of noise. 'No pain no gain, lads,' roared Neil Back. 'Let's go through that pain together, eh? That's what it's gonna take. No escape for the fuckers. Make them work. No stupid penalties. Don't give them an easy way out.'

There were ten minutes still to go. Ten minutes before a knock on the door would tell us it was time to make our way out on to the pitch to play the biggest match of our lives. Players paced the room anxiously. Throats were cleared, fingers and wrists were strapped. I made my final visit to the toilet.

'Our workrate is key today,' emphasised Lawrence Dallaglio. 'Back three, front five, middle five, everyone!'

'It's all going to come at us. All the tricks,' chipped in Matt Dawson. 'We have to expect it. I want to see where all that weights work has gone, where all the fucking training and fitness has gone.'

'Catch them in the headlights,' demanded Lawrence, working himself into a lather. 'Smash them. Win every confrontation. Trust our defence. Trust the fucking blokes next to you. All that anger over the last six weeks is going to come out today. They've got no respect for any of us. No fucking respect. We get it today. Today we earn their respect!'

The 'they' in question were Australia, across the corridor preparing for the same game of rugby. Not any game. The World Cup final. The countdown clock was now showing five minutes.

In the England dressing room Lawrence still had the floor. 'Let these bastards know by the end of the game who you are, where you're from, what you're about, how good you are, how much better than them you are,' he yelled. 'Make them fucking know by the end of the game.'

Another throat was cleared, more snot and saliva expelled into the middle of the room, joining the empty isotonic drink bottles and off-cuts of strapping that littered the place.

A calming voice piped up. 'Every defensive session, guys. Every bit of technique. Put it in. Let's focus, really drive the legs through the collision. Not one miss all day. Stop them.'

Jonny Wilkinson finished and it was Lawrence again. 'They're going to know who we are by the end of this game. They're going to be sick of the fucking sight of us. They've disrespected us all the time we've been here. Digging us all out. Seven weeks of that shit we've had to put up with. Today we ram it down them. We've done no talking. We do it all on the pitch. That's all we have to do. Win.'

The sound of 'I vow to thee my country' playing outside on the stadium Tannoy drifted into the room. Stirring stuff. Patriotic stuff. Emotions were running high. Two minutes to go. Time for the replacements to head out and leave the starting team to bring itself to the boil.

'Right, come in, into a huddle,' instructed Johnno, his tone measured but firm. 'Everything we've done is for today. All the fucking work. Everything. Your whole life is down to now. Here and now.

'Our country is a long way away and everyone there is watching us. We always produce. Every game we fucking produce. Push them round the field. Make it fast and furious but keep control.

'They're going to have the ball at some stage, they're going to do something with it. Just respond. Don't get out of position. Keep working. Look them in the eye and keep fucking working.

'They think they're going to be inspired tonight. They think that's going to be enough for them. That is not going to be enough for them. We're going to take these boys to the cleaners. Work hard for it and it will come. It will come in that last ten minutes. Okay? Don't think you have to do anything special, but don't get inhibited either. Just play. Go out and enjoy it, but enjoy working hard. No regrets. One massive performance boys.

'You can only live this hour and a half once boys. You can only live it once. Do it right.'

*

Lying on the bed in my hotel room in Perth, England's base for the pool stages, I tried to imagine what it would be like to play in a World Cup final. The nerves, the excitement, the anticipation of an entire nation back home. In seven weeks' time I hoped to find out for real. But for that to happen a lot of things had to go right, both for England and for myself. First and foremost I had to stay fit. I had to train my way into a match-day squad, then take whatever opportunity, however brief, came my way. If I did that I just might get a shot in the starting line-up. If I got that . . .

I smiled to myself. I was getting carried away. I had been the last player selected and had been picked so late that boarding had almost commenced at Heathrow on the British Airways flight bound for Perth via Singapore. I had not played for England in almost two years and I was not in the squad for the opening game against Georgia. Never mind winning the World Cup, getting a game would be some achievement.

Yet I couldn't have been happier. I was on the trip, Ali and Evie were flying in from Brisbane later in the week, and I was not being brought down by the weight of expectation. Flight BA015 was a dream. What a difference flat beds make. Our first two days in Australia weren't bad either, basically spent on the piss. We claimed that it helped counter jetlag, which had got to us, big time. Honest. Two mornings running we turned up for breakfast stinking of alcohol, wearing the same clothes we had been out in the night before. On the second occasion Clive Woodward came and sat next to me. Making sure one hand was strategically placed over my mouth I turned to him and said, 'This jetlag's killing me, Clive.'

Things soon got serious and I voiced my disappointment at

missing out on selection for Georgia. In truth, however, I was somewhat relieved. My fitness wasn't quite right and I needed the first fortnight to sort it. I also needed time to learn all the moves again. It might have been my third World Cup but I was way behind the rest of the squad in terms of team preparation and would have to catch up quickly.

The mood in the camp was relaxed but determined. England had won ten in a row against the Southern Hemisphere superpowers. Completely unprecedented. England expected to be successful. And that was just the team. As a squad we were unflappable, though you might not have guessed it from the newspaper headlines. If you believed what you read we had been wound up by South Africa captain Corne Krige describing Martin Johnson as 'one of the dirtiest captains in world rugby'.

Now it is true that we couldn't believe the front of a bloke who had brought shame on himself and the Springboks at Twickenham a year earlier when head-butting, punching and kicking England players in a shocking display of thuggery. For him to suggest that any other player in world rugby was even a contender for the category of 'dirtiest captain' was laughable.

It is true also that every member of the England set-up had been fired up by South Africa's antics that day in November 2002 when it seemed pretty obvious that some of their players had set out to maim some of ours. But England had dealt with it there and then, sticking 50 points on the Springboks, outmuscling them physically and in so doing delivering a massive blow to their macho psyche. Eleven months on it was Clive Woodward, not the players, who chose to make an issue out of foul play. He suggested England would stay clear of the Boks at the opening ceremony and said that it was asking for trouble for the two teams to come out of the tunnel together when we met in the second game.

This was typical Clive. All the time he looked to play mind games. He loved them and if any coach got the better of him he would get mad. I remember in 2001 when we arrived at the Millennium Stadium in Cardiff the day before a Six Nations game against Wales. We walked into the away dressing room to be confronted by huge cardboard cut-outs of each of the Wales team. Clive's face was a picture. He went loopy. He was gutted that someone had got one over on him.

Contrary to my attitude in the late 1990s, I now didn't give a monkey's what was said in the press. I felt I had reached the summit. Most of us had been to Australia enough times to know that whatever was written would not be complimentary. As a squad we were so experienced that nothing that was said or written could upset us. We knew it would have no bearing on what happened on the pitch. We also knew there was nothing we could do to control it.

Our mindset was to win every game, as basic and as simple as that. We didn't care how we did it. We were totally single-minded and that infuriated the traditional critics of England. They had labelled our forwards Dad's Army during the summer tour of New Zealand and Australia, then been made to eat those words when the 'old boys' stuffed it up them. Now they were back to calling England the most boring team in world rugby.

*

I stood in the domestic terminal at Perth Airport looking up at the Arrivals board. In three days England would play Georgia at Subiaco Oval but this was the day I had circled in my diary. After the best part of two months I would see Ali and Evie again. The last time I had seen my daughter she had been a fourteen-month-old baby crawling around our living room at home.

The doors swung open and the first passengers off the Brisbane flight passed through into the Arrivals Hall. I was distracted when a couple of England supporters recognised me and politely asked for an autograph. I obliged and was acknowledging their thanks when I heard a familiar voice.

'Mike,' said Ali, 'have you seen your daughter?'

I looked at my wife, fully expecting Evie to be in her arms. She was not. The crawling baby I had kissed goodbye in July was walking besides Ali, a beaming smile on her face. She was tanned, had gorgeous blonde hair and looked so healthy and beautiful. I choked. Tears, the works. It was as though someone had flicked a switch. The father-and-daughter connection I had sought and tried to nurture since Evie came out of hospital was suddenly made.

Match 1: Pool C, Perth, 12 October 2003

England 84–6 Georgia
A winning start and twelve tries without reply but victory came at a high price. Kyran Bracken injured his back in the pre-match warm-up and his replacement, Matt Dawson, limped off with medial knee ligament damage. Our one other scrum-half, Andy Gomarsall, came

on to replace Matt and he too picked up a knock. Kyran, who missed the 1999 World Cup due to a back problem, was really struggling afterwards and Martyn Wood was flown out as emergency cover. As if that wasn't enough, Richard Hill pulled a hamstring and Ben Cohen accidentally stood on Danny Grewcock's toe and broke it. Thank heavens for Mark Regan's endless capacity to make us laugh. After scoring his try 'Ronnie' tried to celebrate, tripped over, and crashed slap bang into an upright.

As a build-up to England's biggest game in four years it was less than ideal. Within eighty minutes of the tournament starting we had so many injuries that Clive had to postpone selection of the team to face South Africa by twenty-four hours. Matt was ruled out, then named in the team, then ruled out again. One minute we thought Kyran was going home, the next he was in the starting line-up. Andy Gomarsall, the nearest we had to a fit and healthy 9, and who had expected to start, ended up not even making the bench. Understandably, he was gutted. To be honest, Kyran did not look very comfortable at all. But Clive told him he 'has a go or has to go'. We don't appreciate ultimatums like that. I've played with injuries before and made an absolute fool of myself, notably against Argentina in 1996. I hoped for Kyran's sake that he didn't do the same.

Three days before the game a whole load of South African supporters checked into our hotel. At four o'clock on the Thursday morning one of them knocked on Josh Lewsey's door. Whether it was a legitimate mistake or not was never established. The following morning we trained for two and a half hours. It was absolutely ridiculous, the day before an international, particularly one of this magnitude. We had a forty-five-minute walk-through, as is customary on the eve of a game, but then the coaches had a little bit of a panic and wanted to be sure that they had covered everything. They had.

Having initially welcomed being left out of the team, the frustration was now eating away at me. South Africa was a massive game, one that could set us on a life-changing course. I really believed that if we beat them we had a very good chance of getting to the final and winning the competition, as it would mean we avoided a quarter-final against the All Blacks. Eight players in the squad were yet to get a game, of whom Julian White, Stuart Abbott and I had not even been on the bench. But I vowed to myself that I would grin and bear it, bide my time and wait for my chance. I had done so in the past and come through, I would again.

Match 2: Pool C, Perth, 18 October 2003

England 25–6 South Africa
On the journey to the ground I sat with Matt Dawson who predicted a 15-point England win. I told him that I would take that. By half-time I had changed my mind. A 1-point margin would do, thank you very much. The scores were level at 6-6 and we were lucky not to be 6, or even 9, points down. Jonny really struggled with his kicking game and South Africa had opportunities that they didn't take. They cut us apart a couple of times from turnovers and back in the changing room the boys got a bollocking from assistant coach Andy Robinson for not keeping hold of the ball. 'We know they're going to give away penalties,' he said. 'Play the game in their half.'

Thankfully our homework then paid off. Hours studying tapes of the Springboks had revealed that Louis Koen, their fly-half, took forever to clear the ball to the left touchline off his right boot. Midway through the half we worked South Africa into a position where he had to do exactly that. Lewis Moody was all over him, the ball ricocheted loose and Will Greenwood controlled it fantastically to score the decisive try. The same Will who had experienced a mental aberration in the first half, catching the ball from Koen's third miss at goal and chucking it forward to Jonny for the drop-out without actually touching it down first, so conceding a scrum five metres out from our try-line.

Only later would we realise the state of mind Will was in. All week long he had kept secret from us that his pregnant wife Caro had been admitted into intensive care, at pretty much the same stage that their first child Freddie was born prematurely and did not survive. Will left the squad straight after the game to be with her and my heart went out to him. I felt I had some idea of what he was going through and marvelled at his mental strength. I also had a pretty good idea that England would not win a World Cup without him. In every respect I wished for his speedy return.

By the final whistle South Africa had been well beaten but England's attacking game had been poor and the Aussie press wasted no time in telling us about it. *The Australian* newspaper devoted the entire front page of its sports section to a picture of Jonny kicking for goal below the banner headline, 'Is That All You've Got?' If our attacking game was unacceptable then our defence was sensational. For the first time England achieved world-class standard by making 95 per cent of tackles attempted. That is pretty phenomenal against any side, let alone one of South Africa's calibre and physicality. The back row of Neil Back, Lawrence Dallaglio and Lewis Moody made nineteen apiece and did not miss one.

The other standout performer was my room-mate from the World Cup eight years earlier, Kyran Bracken. I honestly did not think he would start the game, let alone finish it, so much pain had he been in during the week. Yet he was my man of the match. Kyran is one hard bugger. He was snapping at the feet of their number 8, Juan Smith, all evening and outplayed his opposite number, Joost van der Westhuizen, hands down. I was so pleased for him. It is amazing how quickly things can turn around. Matt Dawson was supposed to be first choice scrum-half, but Kyran took his chance and was now the man with the jersey. I was reminded of what Clive Woodward had said after selecting me for the squad at the very last minute. 'Catt has been lucky, but that's what sport is all about. You make your own luck.'

Two games down and I didn't feel quite so lucky. I badly needed to be involved in the next game against Samoa for the sake of my own morale. As I said goodbye to Ali and Evie for a couple of weeks and headed off to Melbourne I sensed it was make-or-break time for my World Cup campaign. It is no fun being outside the match squad. You get your own bus to the game, you're not part of the actual team. During the Friday morning team runs you go and do your own conditioning work.

My chance arrived on the Wednesday when I was named on the bench against the Samoans, as cover for fly-half and inside-centre. At a stroke the world seemed a better place. Julian White and Stuart Abbott were picked to start, which was terrific news for them too. The weather in Melbourne was terrible but I suddenly felt great. All those extra pool sessions, all that stretching and yoga to sort out my back had paid off. Finally, I felt part of the squad. Hopefully within four weeks I would be part of the team.

Woodward picked a very strong side, with Jonny Wilkinson again playing at 10. South Africa had been a high-pressure game for him and nobody had really helped from a kicking point of view. Jonny has very high standards and it was no surprise to me that he wanted to play again quickly. I hoped he would just get the first half and then I would be brought on to show what I could do. Clive said that those on the bench would start against Uruguay in our final pool match, so these two games were going to be critical for me.

By Thursday the nerves had kicked in. I could be stepping into the fly-half slot for the first time in a long, long while, providing Mike Tindall stayed injury-free at centre. If so, I would have to call the shots, run the show. Technically I knew we were a much better side than Samoa, but I also knew that they were very talented individuals and if we gave them a sniff they could trouble us. The general consensus was that they would give us a tough time for the first thirty to forty minutes, then we would overpower them up front. Whatever happened it would be a good test for me and my hamstrings.

The night before the game I went down with a headache and my throat started to feel sore. More than that, my back and my bloody hamstrings did not feel good at all. Were my worst fears coming to pass or was it just anxiety? I knew that the following day I had to prove I was still capable of playing at the top level. I knew how much was at stake. I knew I really needed to get all my communication and calls spot on. Above all, I sensed it was my first and final chance to make a mark on Woodward and the coaches, because the following week's game against Uruguay, with no disrespect to them, would be a non-contest. I reached for the paracetamol and a sleeping tablet, pulled the blanket up over my head and crossed my fingers.

Match day dawned and I blinked open my eyes. I had slept for twelve hours. My headache had gone, the glands in my throat were down. I was still concerned about my hamstrings but I had lived and performed with that worry before. I felt anxious but it was a good feeling, one I had missed in the two years since my last England appearance. The physical intensity of international rugby is completely different from the club game. Your body knows you're going into battle and reacts accordingly. I had been gearing up for this over the past couple of days and now I felt ready to go out and entertain 50,000 people and goodness knows how many watching on TV. It was a massive thing for me to play for England again, especially in such a good team, and I was incredibly excited. I had waited a long time and put in a lot of hard work. It was now time to take my chance, to prove to the management that I was not just here to make up the numbers; that I was once again capable of being one of England's best fifteen players.

Match 3: Pool C, Melbourne, 26 October 2003

England 35–22 Samoa
They gave me the 21 shirt on the day I finally came of age as a player at this World Cup. Collectively we made very hard work of beating

Samoa. Three times we trailed and we needed two tries in the last ten minutes to shut the door on Michael Jones' team. I can smile because I came on in the seventy-first minute for my fifty-seventh cap, provided the scoring pass for Phil Vickery's first-ever England try and generally, I felt, made an impact. Afterwards was the first time the management had smiled at me all trip. It was just a pity I did not get on a bit earlier because the team were really struggling with the calls and the kicking game.

Before the South Africa game all the media focus had been on Jonny Wilkinson and I had worried for him. I knew from painful experience how difficult it is to deal with the pressures of play-making and goal kicking for England, and Jonny was doing it in a team widely expected to win the World Cup. A week on and the level of press scrutiny had cranked up another notch.

Better than anyone I know you should not judge a player on his goal kicking, but when Jonny missed a penalty from right in front of the posts it said to me that something was wrong. He was killing himself inside, trying to do too much himself. Nobody was helping him on the pitch and he needed a rest. That was the goal I set myself when I replaced Stuart Abbott and slotted in alongside Jonny at inside-centre. I felt I achieved it and I was encouraged that Nigel Melville, the former England captain, saw it the same way as I did.

In his column in the *Guardian* he wrote: 'It wasn't until Woodward shuffled the pack and brought on Catt to play alongside Wilkinson in the second half that there was a semblance of improvement. At last the ball started to go wide, away from the big-tackling Samoan midfield. Catt looked good, fit and incisive. It is an

190

open secret that Wilkinson needs a playmaker outside him to be at his best. Is Catt the answer?'

There was no doubt in my mind that I could be, given the opportunity. 'Go back a few years to when Catt stood between Wilkinson and Will Greenwood, England played their most fluent fifteen-man rugby, using Catt's cut-out passes to get the ball wide quickly,' Melville continued, before identifying a potential stumbling block for me. 'England do not play that way any longer. The past eighteen months have seen the attack get narrower and narrower, relying more and more on the power of Johnson and Co. to crush the opposition and pick up the penalties and the points.'

Perhaps, but I was convinced in my own mind that there would still be times when my way would pay dividends. Samoa, I felt, had been a case in point, although the hole we dug for ourselves was also down to attitude. As a squad, I thought we looked very rusty. I felt we had come off the boil. Compared to the South Africa game, which was a must-win for us, our intensity all week had not been great. Martin Johnson had detected it before kick-off, warning that if we did not sort ourselves out mentally we would be 10 points down inside the first ten minutes, which is exactly what we were – and we had not touched the ball. We needed to get a lot wider and we needed to go forward more. Johnno was probably the only forward who managed that against Samoa and had it not been for our fitness and our stamina in the last fifteen we might well have lost. The truth is that for fifty minutes we were outplayed. We would not win a World Cup playing like that.

Martin Johnson was spewing afterwards about how we had

almost thrown it away and how we had to get our heads right if we wanted to progress in the tournament. Yet, personally, I was buzzing. We were into the quarter-finals and I was on a holiday with my family playing rugby in the sunshine. What more could I ask for? I was absolutely in my element. I had felt we needed to play a different type of game really to open up teams and when I came on we had done that. There was just one catch. For thirty-four seconds in stoppage time we briefly had sixteen men on the field due to a mix-up over a substitution, when Mike Tindall cramped up and Dan Luger was sent on to replace him.

Fifth official Steve Walsh would not let us make the change so, with Woodward's voice screaming in his earpiece, England fitness coach Dave Reddin ignored Walsh and sent Dan on, just as Mike Tindall rolled himself back on to the pitch, a good 100 metres away from where the ball was. Referee Jonathan Kaplan blew his whistle, penalised England and sent Dan back to the bench. To complete the farce Mike also went off, leaving England to play out the last minute or two with one man short.

Reddin was always quite fiery on the touchline. In the same game he had a row with England doctor Simon Kemp over who should take the water on. I disapproved and thought it was the wrong time for them to be squabbling. When the game ended Walsh went for him. He called him an 'English loser' and said, 'Learn the rules, you loser.' The heated exchange continued down the tunnel. Walsh, whom I considered to be the top referee in the world, behaved like a little kid, squirting water at Dave and tripping him up. It was pathetic, unbelievable really.

The Aussie press once again went into a feeding frenzy, demanding that England be kicked out of the tournament, and when we were hit by two misconduct charges it all became a bit worrying. There was a very real prospect of losing the match points we had collected for beating Samoa, which would have condemned us to the quarter-final against New Zealand that we had worked so hard to avoid. Having initially laughed it off, it dawned on us that as Poms in Australia, and favourites for the World Cup, this was a gilt-edged chance to knacker us on a technicality.

Fortunately Woodward had added QC Richard Smith to the England party after Josh Lewsey received no justice in New Zealand during the summer when his head was trampled on by All Blacks lock Ali Williams and no action was taken. Richard dominated the disciplinary hearing and restricted the damage to a £10,000 fine and a two-match touchline ban for Dave. Walsh was found guilty of 'inappropriate behaviour' and suspended for three days.

The threat to England's participation lifted, we turned our attention back to business. We had flown to the Gold Coast for a light week ahead of the Uruguay game in Brisbane. It was extremely hot and humid and we did no rugby training, just conditioning work and weights. I hadn't really enjoyed it as I was struggling with a touch of flu and feeling very lethargic. At the same time I was trying to focus on my first start of the tournament, having been picked at inside-centre. I knew there were places up for grabs in the squad for the knock-out phase because Woodward had said so. He made a point of announcing publicly that he did not consider any player to be indispensable.

With Woodward's rocket under us we headed for Suncorp Stadium to take on Uruguay, who had shipped 72 points against South Africa and conceded 60 to Samoa. We were under instruction to talk

193

up the South Americans and stress how well they had played in beating Georgia. I don't like to bullshit, never have. I prefer to be straight up and dead honest with people. I found it hard not to say, 'We're going to put 70-80 points on these chaps, unfortunately, but that's just the way the game has gone.' I had no doubt it would pan out that way. In the event the result was even more lopsided.

Match 4: Pool C, Brisbane, 2 November 2003

England 111–13 Uruguay

Our pre-match orders were to make it fast and unrelenting for eighty minutes, to use the occasion to get our attacking game back on track. An hour and a half later we had run up a century of points and seventeen tries, including two for me. I had not enjoyed playing a game of rugby so much for years. I don't think England had either. What message had we sent to our rivals? Probably none. Uruguay were poorer than even I had expected. But I don't think I did myself any harm at all. I had shown that I was fit and in form. I had got the back line going with my long passes and while Uruguay were extremely poor defensively and there were holes everywhere, we still had to get the ball there. I came off the field at the end convinced that I could really make a contribution in the knock-out stages.

Whether I would get the chance was another matter. Jonny Wilkinson, Mike Tindall and Will Greenwood, happily back in camp after his wife was given the all-clear, had not lost playing together for England in more than a year. It was hard to see any one of them being dropped now.

Playing in the number 12 jersey for England at last and Man of the Match in a comprehensive 50–18 win over Ireland in the 2000 Six Nations.

Impasse between Clive Woodward and Martin Johnson during the players' strike. Johnson emerged from it as a truly inspirational leader.

Thankfully we were soon back in business, beating Argentina 19–0. Will Greenwood and I help Ben Cohen celebrate his try.

With Martin Johnson back as captain we were now a united force on and off the pitch. Here he gives a pre-match talk before we beat the Springboks at Bloemfontein, where South Africa hadn't lost since 1982.

In 2001 I won my fiftieth England cap. *Below*: Acknowledging the cheers of the Twickenham crowd, once they could see me through the smoke of the fireworks.

I always wanted a fancy dress wedding. Happy day – Ali and I (*left*) were married at the Roman Baths in Georgian costume. My brothers and Dad (*below*) entered into the spirit of things.

World Cup 2003: Clive Woodward had programmed in a little relaxation for us towards the end of the pool stage, (*above left*) at the Wet 'n' Wild center and (*above right*) playing golf with Leonard and Dallaglio. Then it was down to serious business when Wales gave us a wake-up call in the first half of the quarter-final. When I came on after the interval Iestyn Harris and Ceri Sweeney tried to see me off (*below*).

A semi-final tackle on Frédéric Michalak (*above*) and a break through the Australian defence in the final (*below*) then that famous drop with which Jonny won us the 2003 World Cup (*right*).

The grins say it all, with Jonny Wilkinson, and Richard Hill at the Telstra Stadium. I only remember these moments through photos – it was such a daze!

The full England squad with the Queen at Buckingham Palace. One of the corgis shows interest in Clive Woodward's ankle.

Mum, Ali and Doug came to see me receive my World Cup MBE.

12

TOP OF THE WORLD

World Cup quarter-final: Brisbane, 9 November 2003

England 28–17 Wales

'Fellas!' yelled Martin Johnson, angry but still remarkably in control of his temper. 'I am not, repeat not, going home tomorrow. We are not, repeat not, going to lose this game.'

It was the quarter-final of the World Cup. We were playing Wales, a nation England had lost to just once in all the years I had been wearing the jersey since my debut at the old Arms Park in 1994. Against a team our second string had wiped out 43-9 in Cardiff less than three months before, we were trailing 10-3 at half-time.

'Fellas!' raged Matt Dawson, 'We have promised ourselves we are going to deliver and fucking throw everything at them. Yet we're calling bullshit calls. We're going to lose this game and we're going to be left with ifs and buts. For God's sake, this is make or break time.'

I was not in the starting line-up, so I was not on the pitch when Stephen Jones scored Wales' first try, after Shane Williams had run back a kick that Mike Tindall had badly skewed straight down his throat. I had been named on the bench, and it was from there I saw

Welsh captain Colin Charvis barge his way over for his side's second try just four minutes later.

In the England changing room the sense of shock was palpable. The team had been so successful for so long that there was a pretty deep-rooted self-belief that no situation was beyond us, but Wales had us on the rack. Our option-taking had been dismal, we had failed utterly to do as we had been told and, most worrying of all, Jonny Wilkinson had spent the entire half hitting rucks.

In the run-up to the game the media had become convinced that the pressure was getting to Jonny. One even put it to him that he was becoming a basket case. Because he missed three goal kicks against Samoa? Oh, please. It is true that he had put a hell of a lot of pressure on himself. He's that type of guy, so intense, an absolute perfectionist. He gets himself into a frenzy about what he has to do and how he has to do it.

But he is no choker. As I saw it, it was the guys around him who were going into hiding. In the first forty minutes against Wales, nobody helped him and, as a consequence, Jonny tried to do absolutely everything himself. He hit rucks, he made cover tackles. His workrate was just unbelievable. But his forwards weren't giving him the right kind of ball and Mike Tindall and Will Greenwood could not play the kicking game England needed either to trouble Wales or to relieve the pressure on Jonny. That is just not their game. They don't do it at club level. So Jonny didn't have any help from a tactical point of view.

As I followed the team off the field at Suncorp Stadium and into the changing room the place was rocking. There were a hell of a lot of England fans in attendance but the Welsh supporters, and the rest of Australia, were going crazy. The top seeds were on the way out. Everyone seemed convinced of it. What I was convinced of, however, was that I was the missing link in England's game, the player capable of putting things right. I returned to my cubicle, popped the top off a Lucozade and supped it while listening to Martin Johnson and Matt Dawson get stuck in.

Back in 2000 and 2001, when I had last played at 12 alongside Jonny, we had worked so well together. Really complemented each other. If Jonny was not at first receiver I would be and he was comfortable with that. The problem was when injury sidelined me Jonny went back to feeling that he had to be at first receiver every time. He was putting too much pressure on himself, and then had the expectation of the media heaped on top of that.

Never have I doubted his ability on a rugby field but during the course of the tournament I had become concerned for him. We never really saw him. He never really came out with us. He'd never go for walks along beaches with any of us or join us for a drink or simply to chill out. More often than not he would go to the team room and then back to his room.

Jonny had achieved a hell of a lot up to that World Cup, don't get me wrong. He was the wonder kid. But I remember being baffled in Perth in the first week when we came out of the gym, each holding a red clip file, which had our own weights programme in, and had to walk through a scrum of waiting photographers. Jason Leonard and Martin Johnson – absolute legends of the game – took no notice but Jonny used his file to shield his face from the cameras.

That troubled me and something similar happened when the squad went to a water park on the Gold Coast before the Uruguay game. The rest of the boys had a whale of a time but Jonny wouldn't allow himself to enjoy it. He hid from the photographers. Nobody else had a care in the world, but Jonny seemed paranoid. I hadn't been with him for two years and in that period his intensity seemed to have grown to an extent that concerned me. I couldn't understand what he was about. You base your opinions on what you would do in the same situation. I find that if I build myself up too much I lose all focus on things.

With ten minutes left of half-time to regroup, I looked around for the coaches, who were conspicuous by their absence. Perhaps they felt guilty for having worked us into the ground under a sweltering Brisbane sun all week, leaving us heavy-legged and lethargic on game day. If they did not they should have done. Never mind Clive Woodward later blaming the distraction of having the media staying in our hotel, over-training was the prime factor.

The next thing I knew Clive was in the room and crouching down in front of me. 'Right Catty, this is your chance,' he said. 'You're on. I'm taking Dan Luger off, moving Tins to the wing and Will to outside-centre. I want you in the 12 slot. Go out and play your usual game.'

Clive had identified a situation that reminded him all too vividly of England's Six Nations game against France in Paris the previous year when Jonny had desperately needed someone alongside to take the heat off him. That day there was no one and England were well beaten. This game was going much the same way. I've heard people talk about Clive being a great facilitator rather than a great coach. But this was his call, based purely on what had happened in the past. He saw history repeating itself and he was determined not to let that happen. It was a brutal decision to haul Dan Luger off like that. To haul off one of your top try scorers in the heat of battle and replace him with a centre who had never played on the wing, and me, who had been a stranger to the squad for two years, was a big call. And a ballsy one.

Dan was not best pleased to be canned in favour of Mike Tindall but took it on the chin without any backchat or stamping of feet. He picked up his tracksuit and walked out of the changing room. As my pulse started to quicken, I poured some water over the back of my head, retied my boot laces and inwardly thanked my lucky stars. Only four days earlier I had thought my World Cup, and possibly my career, was over

England's defensive session on the previous Wednesday had required us to run at tackle shields, something I had done goodness knows how many times in the past without incident. The idea is that a ball-carrier runs toward two tackle pads, shows a bit of footwork, then forces his way between the two, leading with his head. Kyran Bracken and Josh Lewsey were doing the honours for me but, as I went in, Kyran closed the hole and I crashed head-on into his pad. It was like running into a brick wall and I rolled around on the floor, squealing like a pig. 'Fuck. It's gone, it's gone!' I cried out. I honestly thought I had done something serious to my neck. It had made a terrible sound and hurt like hell.

The medics rushed over to me. Seeing I was able to move my hands reassured me and I calmed down. After three minutes or so I was told I was okay to continue. I stood up but had walked no more than fifty metres when I started feeling pains in the back of my head and down my neck. I dropped to my knees then sat down. The physios took another look and had a change of mind. I was put in a neck brace and lifted on to a spinal board before being taken by ambulance to hospital.

As I lay anxiously awaiting the result of my X-ray I felt nauseous. Was so much hard work going to be wiped out by a freak accident? For what seemed like hours I lay there before Simon Kemp, our team doctor, approached me with good news. There was no structural damage, just bruising, and it would be fine with plenty of rest. The problem was that time was not on my side and I worried about what Clive would say. But he was great. Whilst Kyran apologised over and over again in a ridiculous South African accent that sounded closer to German, Clive told me he would give me until the captain's run (i.e. the final training session before the match) on Saturday to prove my fitness.

It was now Sunday evening and time for me to go to work. This was what I had wanted more than anything since Ali and Evie had been given the all clear more than a year earlier. I was on the biggest stage and all eyes were on me. England had a problem and I was perceived to be the solution. I decided immediately to take the game by the scruff of the neck and the first three times the ball came back from the forwards I moved Jonny away from first receiver, took the pass and hoofed it deep into Welsh territory, sixty to seventy metres down the park. For the first time in the game the onus was on Wales to play in their own half and, under pressure, they started making mistakes.

Three minutes into the half they were forced into a hasty clearance and were then too slow to get to the ball. Jason Robinson quickly took the line-out throw to himself on the edge of our 22 and cut up through their disorganised defence on a fantastic angled run. Will Greenwood went with him and when Jason drew the full-back, Gareth Thomas, he popped Will the scoring pass.

We were back level and a surge of adrenaline went through the team. I made a break and had only to slip the pass to Stuart Abbott for the second try, but I tried to take on Thomas and instead knocked on. For a second I thought, shit, I could have just lost us the game, but the thought passed. I was buzzing and so confident my head didn't drop. I was striking the ball sweetly and we were now playing on the front foot in the right areas of the field. This was the true ability of this England team. We assessed what was going wrong, shuffled our resources and instinctively put it right. Jonny was able to relax and his goal kicks started flying over from everywhere. In the space of twenty-two minutes we had racked up 22 unanswered points and the match was won.

Nevertheless the game was a wake-up call for us. And for nobody more than the coaches. You could see the relief in their eyes afterwards. Our view, as players, was that Wales would be tired after pushing New Zealand so hard in their final pool game, before going down 53-37. We felt they shouldn't get anywhere near us because they had had their one big game. Yet the coaches had been more nervous about Wales than any other opponent and, as a consequence, each one wanted his slot. And because they were so anxious the sessions got longer and longer, lasting up to two hours under the Brisbane sun.

The following day I went out with Jason Leonard, Lawrence Dallaglio and Paul Grayson for a few beers and we agreed that something had to be said. 'If we want to win this thing somebody needs to front up and take control,' I think I said, though we'd had a few by then so it might have been one of the other lads. 'There's nothing these coaches are going to tell us or do to us over the next two weeks that's going to make us win a World Cup. We have done all the preparation. It's all in the bag. But, we could lose a game if we don't sort this out.'

Lawrence said he would bring the matter up in the team meeting and, fair play to him, he was true to his word. I then spoke to Clive when the meeting had broken up. 'This is the way the boys are feeling and I totally back Lawrence in what he said,' I told him. I was very calm but there had been a fair bit of anger about. The message took little deciphering. It amounted to, 'Look, guys, you're not going to ruin our dream. I don't care who you are as a group of coaches. We are this close to getting something special. Don't you start coming and changing things and each of you ticking the boxes. We don't want that. We don't need that.'

The message hit home. Our preparation for France, England's semi-final opponents, was spot on – plenty of rest, very little sweating on the training pitch. We had a few much-needed beers on Monday night to chill out, then short, sharp sessions on Tuesday and Wednesday before being given Thursday and Friday off. Mentally we were where we wanted to be, partly because Richard Hill was finally fit, partly because everyone, it seemed, had written England off. France had blown away Scotland and Ireland, playing the most impressive rugby of the tournament, and were installed as favourites.

As the week wore on I sensed it was going to their heads. Tony Marsh, the 'French' centre, declared that he would not swap any player in his team for any one in ours. Aurelien Rougerie then accused England – players and fans alike – of arrogance. It was tedious and predictable stuff, but fuel to our fire. Still we were aware that we would need to raise our game significantly if we were to reach the final, but Martin Johnson set the positive tone when he used his captain's press conference to declare: 'We are in a World Cup semi-final, for God's sake. Let's be upbeat about it.'

Johnno continued: 'We've won all our games and we're sitting here saying, "Oh, we haven't played well." When we win games we don't think we're unbeatable and when we lose games we don't think we're terrible. What we know is that if we get things right, we've got a good chance of beating whoever we play against.'

Behind the scenes Martin was equally impressive. Every time he said something it was word perfect. He didn't need to talk much because there were so many experienced lieutenants around him – Matt Dawson, Jonny Wilkinson, Lawrence Dallaglio and Neil Back – but when he did speak, it was so right. His timing was impeccable. I remember sitting in team meetings thinking this bloke is just unbelievable.

Tuesday morning before the France game and I had spent two nights wondering whether I had done enough to break into the starting line-up. We had flown south from Queensland and moved onto the superb seafront at Manly, where the beach runs for as far as the eye can see and surfers punctuate the ocean swell, bobbing up and down as they patiently await the perfect wave.

I took the lift down from my room to the team meeting where I would learn my fate. The doors opened a floor early and, of all people, Clive Woodward walked in. 'Ah, Catty,' he said. 'The man I wanted to see. I'm going to start with you and Wilko at 12 and 10. My thinking is this: when the two of you last played together against France three years ago, you beat them with your kicking game. I want you to do that again.'

I knew this was Clive's call and sensed he had not consulted with any of the other coaches about picking me because Phil Larder would have said no, from a defensive point of view. I don't know why. I hardly ever missed tackles playing for England. But Phil didn't think I had the physical presence.

The lift doors opened again and Clive strode out. I gave him a head start, then followed him on to the mezzanine level, trying not to smile too much. But inside I was elated, even though I knew my selection meant my great friend Mike Tindall would miss out. I felt very sorry for Mike. He had been playing exceptionally well for two years, his workrate had been massive. But the way I was able to come on and boss Jonny around on Sunday had swung it my way. I had achieved the final goal I had set myself, to make the starting line-up in the knock-out stages, and I had done it after little more than two hours on the park during the tournament.

I was excited yet very relaxed. I felt I warranted my selection, whereas at times in the past, when I was at 10 and goal kicking, I had questioned whether I really deserved to play. My confidence was massively high and I was feeling no pressure. I had found it easy slotting in against Wales. I came on, kicked probably four times, made one break and a couple of tackles. We won the game, the press gave me nine out of ten and suddenly the whole nation was singing my praises. It just shows how fickle sport is. For as long as I could remember everybody had been undecided about my ability, then I perform for forty minutes in a World Cup quarter-final and everybody is won over. Ridiculous really, but I was not about to complain. Fittingly, being where we were, I was on the crest of a wave and hoped the ride would continue.

On the Friday I caught up with some old friends. Stuart Barnes, Jerry Guscott and Rob Andrew, England team-mates of mine in another era, were all thrilled for me. Rob's advice, as Clive Woodward's had been against Wales, was simply to 'go out and play'. I knew what I needed to do: give the French back row of Serge Betsen, Olivier Magne and Imanol Harinordoquy someone else to think about other than Jonny Wilkinson. If I was successful, hopefully it would give Jonny the time and freedom to control the game.

Mike Tindall was obviously disappointed to miss out but he was great about it. As he put it to me, 'It isn't about individuals, it's about England.' It was about us as a group of players winning the World Cup. He even lent me his DVD set of the first season of '24' to occupy my mind. I sensed that the others felt it was the right decision for the team. They all seemed to understand Clive's thinking from a tactical point of view. Clive would later tell me, in that annoying way of his, that he had always planned to play me from the start against France, because of Paris 2002. 'Your name was first on the list for midfield,' he said. 'I was always going to play you. It was just a question of whether I was going to play Tindall or Greenwood outside you.'

Match day dawned in Manly with beautiful sun. I had slept soundly, not a care in the world, but as I opened my eyes I thought to myself, the French are going to like this. This is going to be a tough game. Back in England, we were told, the nation was becoming steadily gripped by World Cup fever, yet for us it felt much like any other Test morning on tour. We were cocooned away from all the hype. We were in Manly, a ferry ride out of town, miles from the World Cup party capital of Sydney, Darling Harbour.

We had been better supported in our games than any other country bar Australia, but until the previous evening there had been no real evidence that our campaign had grabbed England in the way that football habitually does. On TV we had watched the first semi-final between the Wallabies and New Zealand. Just after half-time a bizarre thing happened. A chant started up. It wasn't 'Australia Fair', nor anything to do with the All Blacks. It was 'Swing Low'. The camera panned around the crowd and the whole top tier in Sydney's Olympic Stadium was populated by white England jerseys. Bloody hell, I thought, what's it going to be like tomorrow night?

At first light there was no clue but by the time we got to the stadium it had become clear. The Telstra Stadium reverberated to the sound of 50,000 English voices. I'd never seen anything like it in my life. Better still, literally as our bus arrived the heavens opened. I looked around the boys and I could almost sense we were all thinking the same thing. This is meant to be.

World Cup semi-final: Sydney, 16 November 2003

England 24–7 France

As we emerged from the tunnel the noise was incredible. Ten and a half thousand miles from home and the place was a sea of white. I had played in the 1995 semi-final in Cape Town, an extraordinary occasion in its own right, but this was something else. Martin Johnson called for passion and on four separate occasions beat his fist furiously against heart in the pre-match huddle as the rain hosed down. 'They say that France are favourites but they haven't played anyone,' he said. 'Today they play someone. Let's see how they like it.' Once again his words had stirred us inside and halfway through our anthem Lawrence Dallaglio and Jason Robinson each had tears in his eyes.

My emotion was more one of worry. I had felt good all week but just when I needed it most my body showed signs of letting me down. My back had not enjoyed the eighty-minute bus journey to the stadium and my legs felt exceptionally tired. I put it down to the tension of the occasion and tried to dismiss it from my mind. But however hard I tried I could not change the fact that I felt flat. I didn't have a great game, I made quite a few errors, didn't really nail any of my kicks and, to be honest, was quite disappointed by my performance. But it wasn't about the individual, any individual, it was about the win and we got it, with Jonny Wilkinson kicking all our points.

I didn't give myself much credit afterwards. I had cramped up for the first time all tournament with thirteen minutes to go and been replaced by Mike Tindall. But others felt my presence had been key in relaxing Jonny and enabling him to kick like a king. True enough, I did detect an added bounce in his step, and where earlier in the tournament he had been very serious, there was a smile here and a joke there. And because we complemented each other so well, decisions were spot on, whatever we did.

With the quality of ball provided by the forwards, who ripped into the French from the start and were simply magnificent all evening, it was very easy for Jonny and me to implement the gameplan. With the conditions the way they were, kicking the ball down the pitch for position was the name of the game. Then it came down to penalties. Frédéric Michalak, the tournament's leading points scorer, missed his, Jonny didn't. Jonny lasted the distance, the much-hyped Michalak didn't. That is the sign of a true champion. When the pressure comes on, you deliver.

France scored first, through Serge Betsen, but Michalak's conversion proved to be their last points of the game. Like New Zealand twenty-four hours earlier, their fluid, eye-catching style, which had lit up the World Cup for the past month and more, was blown away when confronted by serious pressure and world-class defence. And then there was Jonny. Five penalties, three dropped-goals. Simply magnificent.

It had passed midnight by the time we arrived back at the hotel and I was in pieces. I had been smashed in the ribs by Tony Marsh inside the first ten minutes of the game and had kept going for another hour at an intensity my body had not known for two years. I fell into bed, battered and bruised and generally physically exhausted. I should have been on the highest high, instead I tossed and turned, unable to sleep for anxiety. Nobody knows my body like

I do and the alarm bells were ringing. They were telling me that I was going to need some sort of miracle to get myself physically right to start the final in six days' time.

With such a quick turnaround, the team was due to be finalised the next day and I knew I had a decision to make, the consequences of which I would have to live with for the rest of my life. I lay there trying to work out how I was going to approach Clive Woodward the following morning, how I was going to tell Clive that I didn't think it would be a good idea for me to start the World Cup final.

It went against every single principle in my life. Everything in my head screamed this is your opportunity, this is your dream, this is the World Cup final. Don't turn it down. But my body was at odds with my head and it swayed my heart, which told me, man, you've got to tell him you're fucked.

No you haven't, came back my head.

Yes, I do.

By morning I felt nauseous. At last it had happened. The fun had gone out of my World Cup. It was almost a panic attack. This was a once in a lifetime opportunity and I knew I couldn't take it. I remembered what Mike Tindall had said to me when I was picked in his place for the semi-final. 'It's not about me, it's about the team.' I could not take the chance of letting down the team. I would not be able to live with myself if it backfired and England lost the World Cup as a result.

I had spent hours on end trying to find a way to phrase it, to make it sound acceptable, so that when I did speak to Clive it didn't sound like I'd had enough and wanted out. Of course that wasn't true. I had no doubt I was capable of playing in a World Cup final when 100 per cent fit. But I was not close to that. In my heart of hearts I knew I wouldn't last eighty minutes. Australia play a very physical game and Mike Tindall, everybody knew, was a very physical player. Defensively, from the physicality side of things, he was the better choice for the team.

At eight o'clock the phone rang. It was Clive Woodward. He wanted to speak to me in the team room downstairs. Here goes, I thought. 'Catty, I've been thinking,' he said. 'I'm going to start with Mike and I still haven't made my mind up between you or Will Greenwood.'

In an instant I felt the weight of the world lift from my shoulders. 'Clive,' I said, 'I'll make your decision a lot easier for you. Go with Will. I'm genuinely fucked. It's going to take me two or three days to get over this. I've done exceptionally well coming off the bench. I'm very happy with coming off the bench and I think I'll be more of an impact player than Will would be. Will has played so well. Go with him.'

Clive thanked me for my honesty, shook my hand and left the room. Years later he recalled our conversation thus: 'I had been up all night pacing around thinking 'this guy played fantastic against France and I've got to leave him out now. How do I explain this to him rationally and logically?' I wouldn't say he made that decision for me because it was already made, but he made it very very easy.

He said to me, 'Clive, I'm not going to last eighty minutes and I don't want to be left tackling Stirling bloody Mortlock all day. This is a no brainer. I'm best to start on the bench. You haven't got to make this a big deal.' I remember him laughing nervously at this point, then adding: 'But if you don't put me on the bench we'll never speak again.'

I had total and utter respect for him for putting the team first before a game of such size. As I say, the decision was already made. Australia would have gone straight for Catty, I'm sure of that. Wilkinson, Greenwood and Tindall were undoubtedly our best defensive three. They had to start. It meant changing a winning team and I spoke to Martin Johnson about it. 'Catty played pretty well against France you know Clive,' Johnno said. 'Yes he did,' I replied. 'But we need him to come on later because Tindall's not got a great record of completing these games.'

Had he been absolutely at the peak of his fitness and been convinced he could go 80 minutes we might have had a different conversation. But he wasn't. He was certainly fit to play, but not to get through 80 minutes against Australia in a World Cup final. At that time in international rugby there was an 85 per cent chance that teams would be separated by no more than one score entering the last half hour. That's what the stats told us. I had a pretty good idea that that would be the case in this game so I knew we needed to have players on the bench capable of making an impact. Catty fitted that category perfectly.

To this day I have never once regretted my decision, though at the time Ali wasn't very happy that I did not stand my ground. She was a little bit upset by the whole thing. But I knew how I felt. I also knew that Tindall and Greenwood had played together in the epic win over the Wallabies in Melbourne in the summer and that it was in England's best interests to throw the young pup in for an hour and then bring the old Cattman on to produce the goods and, who knows, drop the winning goal.

My only concern was for Jonny Wilkinson. With me out of the team the pressure was back on to him. He wouldn't have that assistance from a tactical and kicking point of view. Greenwood and Tindall didn't do that. I was troubled by the thought that I was letting Jonny down in his hour and a half of greatest need and, sure enough, walking out of the team meeting after the side had been announced he looked at me and sort of shook his head. He was gutted for me but also, I think, for himself too. I consoled myself with the thought that if things started to go wrong, as they did against Wales, Clive would get me straight on.

Selection decided, I concentrated on my recovery. I went swimming in the ocean with Trevor Woodman and Ben Kay as the sun was setting and, although my body was still struggling, I didn't miss a training session all week. Given that it was the build-up to the biggest game in any of our lives the mood in the camp remained remarkably relaxed. The first time we were really aware of the tension cranking up was when Clive spoke to us for the first time about our families. He had let our wives, girlfriends and kids stay with us in the hotel, not that a lot of them did. But at the start of the week he said: 'Guys, let's use our heads here. Kids and families do bring illnesses and things that could stop you from performing. I suggest you move them out for the rest of the week, so that there are no distractions whatsoever.' He said it in the nicest possible way but there was no doubt what he meant. Get rid of them.

It was his attention to detail shining through again. Clive had considered absolutely everything that could go wrong. For the first time it hit me that we were on the brink of something life-changing. As the game drew closer so the buzz grew in Manly. Fans were piling off the planes and more and more would jump on the ferry out of Circular Quay to sample the beach life in front of our hotel. We saw them as we strolled along the front but otherwise nobody got too excited about the whole occasion. Not that the likes of Martin Johnson and Jason Leonard would allow anyone's feet to leave the ground. Their attitude was that this was just another game of rugby. So we treated it as a normal week. We worked on the basis that to do anything else would be to go away from what we knew worked.

By the eve of battle, thinking of it as just another game was becoming difficult. The press corps following us was now enormous, there were photographers everywhere, and the supporters camped outside our hotel had increased in number from hundreds to thousands. We had to be dropped off at the back door to escape the media and Jonny was given extra bodyguards, though I person-ally thought that was ridiculous.

The nearer we got the more convinced I was that we were going to win the World Cup. Louis Koen missing his kicks for South Africa against us, Michalak doing the same. And when Australia beat New Zealand, it only strengthened my belief. We had no doubt we could beat the Wallabies, the All Blacks we were less sure about. We also knew, to a man, that if we could get to the back end of the tournament, given the amount of training we had done, we would be stronger, fitter, faster and mentally more attune than any other team.

Twenty-four hours before kick-off we assembled in our team room at the hotel for a final briefing from the management: Clive

Woodward, forwards coach Andy Robinson and defence coach Phil Larder. After two videos of England's best bits set to music, Clive took the floor.

'I want to say a couple of things,' he said. 'This is England against Australia and we are favourites, which is brilliant. But know this: they will try everything possible to play a little bit different. Do not underestimate for one second what is going to happen. They are going to try everything humanly possible to disrupt and to play in a way that's unfamiliar to us. They will try to play at 100 mph. They are going to go wide wide. They believe they can run this team off the pitch. That is what they fundamentally believe. I've got no doubt about it. They're going to run absolutely everything.'

Robbo turned to the forwards. 'We've got to really take their forward pack on in our driving play and our scrummaging, but also in attacking the short side with backs running against their forwards,' he said. 'We've got to work their front five until they can't get back into the game. We have the power and the pace in this team to do that. What we can't do is sit back after fifteen minutes and allow them to get into the game. From start to finish we have got to be on the edge mentally and physically and we've got to dominate their forwards.'

Clive came in again. 'We've got better players than they have, a better forward pack. But we've got to deliver. We've got to smash them. We've won the last four games against them and each time we've gone out and attacked them, attacked them, attacked them, and given them no time. We just pressure, pressure, pressure. We're not sitting back tomorrow, we're going to attack them, because no one has attacked them this whole World Cup, not for eighty minutes. The sheer pace of our game is absolutely crucial.

'We all know the ref, André Watson. We've had a good meeting with him. The key thing I want to stress, and we've had this guy so many times, is that the only two players I want talking to him are Matt Dawson and Martin Johnson. The thing that pisses André off time and time again are people who start whingeing and moaning. It's got to come through Daws or Johnno. We mustn't piss this guy off. We've got to keep this guy onside.

'Build a score. That's what we did last week when Jonny was awesome. Every time you drop a goal, every time you kick a penalty, it's another knife in these guys. Build a score, build a score, build a score. That's what we do best. The pressure will just build and build on them. Nothing changes going into this game.'

Last to speak was Phil Larder. 'It's so important that when they have the ball, we go forward,' he said. 'What I want us to have in our minds tomorrow is that when they have the ball we are attacking them. That's our mindset: they have the ball, we attack. All the time we're going forward. First man in to tackle go low. Second man in go higher, for the ball. If they start pissing about and throwing the ball about in their own 22, they're just playing into our hands. Quick numbers, go forward and absolutely smash them. What we're after is the ball. We must dominate the breakdown. This is not the game to chase lost causes.'

The meeting broke up and I headed to my room. On the table beside the bed was a goodie bag that Clive Woodward and his wife Jayne had given to each of us when we left England. Inside it was, among other items, a small box. I opened it and found a pair of cufflinks bearing the St George's flag motif. Each cufflink had a screw top. I unscrewed the first to find a little piece of the England flag that had flown above Twickenham. Nice touch, I thought. In the other was a tiny folded piece of paper, no larger than a postage stamp. It was from Ali and Evie.

'Good luck, dadda. Can't wait to see you. Special heart means special daughter. Love you. Evie.'

I turned it over to see a picture of a heart bearing the inscription, 'Ali and Evie love dadda.' I smiled to myself, placed the cufflinks back in the box and switched off the light.

World Cup final: Sydney, 22 November 2003

England 20–17 Australia

Before I knew it morning had arrived and the rain was hammering at my window. Again I smiled. We had beaten France in similar conditions last week, whereas Australia had played New Zealand in beautifully dry weather. Advantage England, I thought. Could I really be about to play in a World Cup final? It didn't feel like anything special. I guess I was a bit tense but that was more because I wanted to get the game out of the way, enjoy the celebrations and get home.

An eight o'clock kick-off meant that the day dragged but countless episodes of '24' kept me occupied and twenty minutes before we boarded the bus I still felt calm. Excited but relaxed. When I'm on the bench in any game I never do any analysis, I don't think about the opposition, I don't think about my game, I just enjoy it. This was no different. Only this was the game I'd worked so hard all my life to get to, from school onwards. All the things I learned from the teachers would now be put to the test on the ultimate stage, a World Cup final. None of us play rugby to come second. It's win or nothing for us. So it was down to this last game.

As I picked up my kitbag and headed for the lift I felt good. I knew it could be the last time I played for England but what better way to finish? Who knows, I thought, we could be about to become absolute legends. It's amazing how the next three hours could change my life, financially, emotionally, incredibly. We've got an opportunity that we have to take with both hands. Let's go get it. Let's win the World Cup.

'You can only live this hour and a half once, boys. You can only live it once. Do it right.'

Martin Johnson finished his speech and the team were out the dressing-room door and headed down the tunnel towards the floodlights and flashbulbs. Not much had needed to be said prior to the game. It was about setting the right emotional tone. The air of confidence among the team was just phenomenal. We had the best-ever England team on the pitch. As long as everybody did their jobs, and did them well, we were right in there with a shout.

Clive Woodward had been right. Australia did try to run us off the pitch and for the second week running we conceded an early try. Twice the Wallabies ignored kickable penalties to keep going for the try before their fly-half Stephen Larkham kicked for the left corner and Lote Tuqiri leapt higher than Jason Robinson to catch the ball and touch down. We gathered under the posts but there was no panic. We had trailed to Samoa, Wales and France and turned it around. This would be no different.

Fifteen minutes later England led, Jonny Wilkinson having nailed two penalty goals, and when Ben Kay was presented with a scoring pass on a three-on-one overlap it should have been happy days. But Ben fumbled it and, although Jonny's boot extended our lead to 9-5 shortly afterwards, the scoreline was far closer than the balance of play demanded. Then Lawrence Dallaglio, whose form had been called into question through much of the tournament, made a break and slipped an inside pass to Wilkinson, who found Jason Robinson on the wing. There was still plenty to be done but Jason made light work of it, powering through the gears to win easily a foot race to the line before diving over in the left corner, then jumping to his feet and punching the ball into the crowd.

Leading 14-5 at half-time, the game was England's to lose. But Australia scored first after the restart, through Elton Flatley's penalty goal, and it seemed to knock us out of our stride. Flatley was given another shot at goal, which he missed, then another after Phil Vickery was penalised for hands in a ruck. He stuck it over and the Wallabies were only 3 points adrift. England had not scored a point since half-time and were clearly in a hole.

Still I remained sitting on the bench unable to influence anything. My dream of playing in a World Cup final appeared to be dying. I looked around for a signal but nobody was looking my way. Jonny had missed his second dropped goal of the game and England were clinging on for dear life. Finally, with three minutes to go, Mike Tindall went down and I got the call from fitness coach, Dave Reddin. Normally when there is three minutes left in an international and you get the nod you think, what the flippin' hell are you putting me on for now? This time it didn't even cross my mind. Every second mattered.

I got on just in time to see Flatley force extra-time by levelling the scores with the final kick of regulation play. Referee André Watson had penalised the England scrum for the umpteenth time, provoking fury in Clive Woodward, and the Wallabies centre held his nerve superbly to tie the game. I should have been dismayed. I wasn't. It meant I got to play for another half an hour.

The whistle went and Martin Johnson called us together into a huddle. Clive had left his box in the stand and run across the pitch to join us. As he arrived he started jabbering. Johnson interrupted him and firmly told him that he had it in hand. 'I've got this, Clive,' he barked. 'This is a player thing.' He then turned back to us, as Clive ran off to find Jonny who was practising kicks on his own, and laid down the law as only he could. 'Right,' Martin said. 'Listen up. If we dwell on the past eighty minutes we're going to lose this game. That's gone. We know we have got it in the bag. We're fitter, stronger, wiser and more experienced than these guys. The next twenty minutes is about what we do.'

I looked around at the faces. Sure enough, nobody was blowing. Everyone was composed, focused. There was no frantic chat. It was quite remarkable. 'Right,' finished Johnno, 'let's go and do it.'

I have two recurring rugby nightmares in my life and neither concerns Jonah Lomu. The first is of a dropped goal I attempted while playing for Bath against Brive in the 1998 Heineken Cup final. The ball did not go anywhere near the posts and was caught by

Sebastien Viars, the France wing, who just had to get past Ieuan Evans to score a try that would have decided the game. Ieuan, thank God, got him with an ankle tap.

My second horror moment occurred in the first half of extra-time in the World Cup final. Again I attempted a drop goal, this time I had it charged down by Justin Harrison, the Wallaby lock. We led 17-14 thanks to a fabulous kick by Jonny from the halfway line, but as I turned to look at what had happened to the ball my heart sank. I saw eight gold shirts running at two in white. I am forever indebted to Phil Waugh for knocking on because had Australia scored I would have gone from hero to zero. The headlines would have read 'Catt the Maverick loses it for England' and I would not have been able to return home.

The drama was still not over. A minute from the end of extra-time Lawrence Dallaglio was pinged for handling in a ruck and Flatley did us again. Sixty seconds remained before a drop-goal shoot-out would come into play to decide who took home the World Cup. We had one last ace up our sleeve, a move that we called Zigzag, designed to get us upfield in a hurry and into drop-goal range. It depended on us getting the ball back quickly from the restart.

We knew that Mat Rogers, the Australia full-back, wasn't getting much distance on his touch kicks from the right side. So we kicked that way, they duly passed it back to Rogers, and under pressure from us he found touch but barely made the 10-metre line. It was our throw and Matt Dawson calmly called Zigzag. Steve Thompson hit Lewis Moody with a perfect throw and the ball came back fast to Jonny. Flatley and Larkham guessed that Jonny would give me a short pass and they were right. I was absolutely smoked, but somehow managed to recycle the ball.

Dawson picked it up and the next thing I knew he was twenty metres up the park. Any other 9 would have hit Jonny from fifty metres out and Jonny would have tried the drop goal. But Dawson had the ability, the arrogance and the vision to do what he did. That was Matt Dawson, a big-game player. In an instant he sized up the situation: either I hit Jonny and he's got a monster kick or I take it on myself to get him closer to the posts. Fair play to him for that.

Next it was Martin Johnson's turn to show a cool head. Matt was at the bottom of the next ruck when the ball came back. Johnson knew the pass had to be fast and perfect for Jonny. He also knew that he wasn't the best man to attempt it. So he took it in to give Dawson time to get back to his feet. Jonny dropped back into the pocket, Dawson fizzed him the ball and over it went, off his right foot, his wrong foot, sailing above Phil Waugh's flailing arms.

He had missed three attempts with his left boot during the game but when it mattered most Jonny nailed it. As the ball passed between the posts I turned and saw the countdown clock on the scoreboard show forty seconds left to play. I bolted back to the halfway line to receive the kick-off, painfully aware that Flatley had time to frustrate us once again. He might have done, too, had he not rushed the restart. We were all at sixes and sevens. We didn't have any formation at all and all their guys were still jogging back from the ruck. Flatley did a little dink kick and Trevor Woodman, of all people, caught it.

I honestly feel that had Australia just calmed themselves, the way the refereeing was going, they could quite easily have contested and won that kick-off and maybe squeezed a penalty or at least a fumble out of us and had another go. But they rushed it, Woodman snapped it up and Matt Dawson aimed his pass back to the first receiver.

One pass and one touch kick and the game was won. Oh, that life was so simple. Will Greenwood was the man standing at first receiver. He yelled, 'Fucking hell, I'm not kicking it.' I had to come in from twenty metres away to take the pass. Then all I remember hearing was Greenwood yelling, 'Kick the fucking thing out.' I went, 'Okay mate, keep your knickers on. I'm going to kick it out, don't worry.'

I hoofed it as far as I could but still the agony wasn't over. As the ball headed towards the crowd I turned to the ref, willing him to blow his whistle. Nothing. There must still have been between ten and fifteen seconds left on the clock. I was suddenly gripped by fear. 'He's going to play the line-out!' In my haste to clear the danger I had kicked the ball directly into touch from outside our 22. The throw to Australia would have been on our 10-yard line. Flatley would get his chance. 'Fuck, what have I done?'

Watson blew his whistle.

Matt Dawson and I jumped up and down and hugged each other. Will Greenwood and Jonny Wilkinson did the same, so too Martin Johnson and Neil Back. What happened next passed in a blur. We clapped Australia off. Then we were by the tunnel and I was looking around for my family. My biggest regret was that Dad wasn't there. I would have flown him over and I didn't even think of it. My brother Pete was getting married that weekend in South Africa and my other brothers Rich and Doug had joined Mum and Dad in Port Elizabeth. So there was a good reason for Dad not being there. But I massively regret at least not inviting him to see his son play in a World Cup final.

There are certain things you want your close family to be a part of. The best I could do in the circumstances was to phone him from the pitch. Pete took the call. He was getting married but he was in tears for my achievement. That choked me up. Then I spoke to Dad, who sounded so proud. 'All those early morning starts, Dad,' I said. 'Worth it, eh? Thanks for everything.'

The match had ended only ten minutes earlier but already there were more than a hundred text messages on my phone. I would read them later. It was time to collect our medals. On the rostrum I stood between Jonny and Kyran Bracken who, unlike me, had not got off the bench. I felt for him, but I was lost in the moment, trying desperately to take in sights and sounds that would never be repeated.

Everybody says John Howard, the Australian prime minister, threw the medals at us, as if in a strop that the Wallabies had been beaten. He didn't strike me as rude and if he was it didn't register with me. My head was in the clouds, my only vivid memories those that were captured on film. Photos become your memories – Richard Hill, Jonny Wilkinson and me standing on the podium, bouncing up and down; Matt Dawson and I dancing around insanely after the final whistle had blown; me with a giant Heineken bottle spraying it everywhere; the England fans singing the Oasis classic 'Wonderwall'; me standing in the middle of a team line-up on the rostrum chanting 'Champion-e, champion-e, ole, ole ole'; Clive Woodward walking towards me with a beaming smile and his arms outstretched.

I was sitting down. He shook my hand, I got up, and we hugged each other. 'You know, Catty,' he said. 'It's not over till the fat lady sings.'

It was the text he had sent me from Marseilles three months earlier, when I was outside the squad looking in. The one that so confused me and left me wondering what the hell was going on in his mind with my World Cup dream.

'I guess the old girl has sung,' I smiled.

'She sure has, mate. And boy did she sound good.'

13
BACK TO REALITY

Sydney, 22 November 2003

Jubilant voices echoed around the England dressing room as I finally tore myself away from the celebrations, still in full swing pitchside in the Telstra Stadium.

'Not bad for an old bunch of idiots,' declared Lawrence Dallaglio.

'Boring, Boring England,' Dorian West chanted ironically.

From the showers a voice I couldn't identify triumphantly sang: 'Who do you think you are kidding, Mr Hitler'. England, world champions 2003, had been branded 'Dad's Army' by the Aussie media.

I had the Webb Ellis Cup in my grasp and Martin Corry was firing off a reel of film for me, using the disposable camera I had bought on the promenade in Manly the day before, when we were still wannabes. Ben Kay walked past, the back of his shirt completely ripped to reveal red tracks caused by a set of Wallaby studs, blood leaking from the right side of his face. Will Greenwood had ice strapped to his left shoulder. Richard Hill, at last injury-free, was getting grief for having sat out almost the whole tournament, only to return to the team for the last two matches. 'Fucking showboater,' someone yelled.

Andy Robinson, England's forwards coach, raised his voice. 'Lads,' he yelled, 'I just want to introduce Tessa Jowell, the Minister for Sport and Culture and Media.' We looked up.

'I just want to say congratulations,' she began. 'Everyone's so proud of you. There won't be a single house back home in England not celebrating. Thank you so much for what you've done.' Five or six players applauded, the Leicester quartet of Martin Johnson, Julian White, Lewis Moody and Neil Back posed with her for a photo. In the background, quietly surveying the scene with a beer in one hand, was Clive Woodward.

He could see players with whom he had been through so much, savouring the historic moment, our faces etched with satisfaction at a job well done. The Specials' classic, 'Too Much, Too Young', boomed through the speakers of a CD player. In one corner a whiteboard, its message harking back two hours to a less certain, considerably more anxious time, still proclaimed, 'Keep line, do not over-commit, go forward. Work rate.' The writing belonged to our defence coach, Phil Larder.

Into the room walked John Howard, Prime Minister of Australia, past one of Clive's motivational slogans: 'Winning is why we are here. Nothing else matters.' Talk about kicking a man when he's down. Mr Howard was accompanied by John O'Neill, chief executive of the Australian Rugby Union. Both men would surely have rather been anywhere else at that moment but each was gracious in defeat, which impressed me. They shook hands with Jonny Wilkinson, breaking off from having his photo taken with Will Greenwood by Matt Dawson. Ben Cohen, chewing a chicken drumstick, licked the fingers of his right hand before introducing himself.

Others were still walking about in a daze. Andy Gomarsall was on his mobile, Dave Reddin too. I had my video camera running, the one I had been given by sponsors ntl during the 2001 Lions series against Australia, which the Wallabies had clinched in the decisive Test in this very stadium. Martin Johnson, captain then as he was now, recognised it and walked towards me. 'Here we are Catty,' he said. 'Same changing room where we bawled our eyes out two years ago, happy as Larry.'

There was a bit of commotion behind my back and I turned to see Prince Harry at the door. He had a hug for Ben Cohen, standing to my right, then he turned to me and, before I knew what I was doing, I was embracing him too. It was that sort of a night. Dave Tennison, our kit man, now had my video camera and was pointing it at me. I grabbed the trophy back off Mike Tindall and wrapped my arms around it. 'You're not going anywhere for four years, my old Bill,' I said – Bill being the name by which Australians refer to the World Cup. 'I might retire in that time. My dreams have come true.'

It was finished. The job was done. There was no need to have any more protein shakes, to get up and do recovery. We had achieved the ultimate. It was the weirdest feeling. Where on earth did we go from here? Right then I did not care, as long as there was a cold beer with my name on it. It was for other people to decide what the future would be. We had held up our end of the bargain.

By the time we had been drugs tested, finished our exhaustive press commitments and got to the winners' party it was half past two in the morning and the wives and girlfriends were the worse for wear.

They wanted to go home but we were having none of it. Fair play to Ali, she got on the water. We went to the Cargo Bar and drank and drank. As if we didn't have enough to celebrate, it was Kyran Bracken's birthday.

By the time we made it back to base daylight was waiting for us, along with two or three thousand supporters. The beachfront was awash with colour. And it wasn't Aussie gold. Flags of St George, England shirts, everyone adorned in red and white. I went to my room, sat on the bed, switched my video camera on to record and turned it towards me. People often talk about wanting to bottle moments in life for posterity. This was as close as I could get. Looking back now I can't believe I was so analytical, so measured. I can only think it was because the full impact of our achievement had not hit me.

'Well here we are, mission accomplished,' I began, holding my medal up to the camera. 'How good do I feel? How dramatic was that finish? Still some Australian fans chanted "Boring, boring". Change the record boys, it's about winning and you lost. Anyway, I thought England played a nice expansive game, one of the best you'll ever see in a World Cup final.

'What a surprise that Wilko had the final say. The guy they dared call a basket case, the guy whose frame of mind had been questioned, the guy who it was said would buckle under the pressure. Good on you, mate. You've been a genius in this tournament. Taken us to the top. I said to Jonny afterwards that he now needs to chill out, enjoy himself, have a few glasses of wine. Go and really enjoy his life. He's had five or six years of solid hard graft and he's achieved the ultimate goal. To my mind he's probably the best player in the world. He's got nothing more to prove. Hopefully I will play with him again before my time is up.'

I wandered downstairs and into a room where Will Greenwood was surrounded by media. He was asked if he had any idea of the scale of pandemonium at home when Jonny dropped his goal.

'I can only imagine it was like when David Platt scored the winner in the last minute for England against Belgium at the 1990 football World Cup,' he said. 'I was still at boarding school up at Sedbergh and we were all crammed round a TV. The ball came over Platty's right shoulder and he ripped it. As the ball hit the net, paintings were coming off the wall, chairs were getting smashed up and people were going berserk. That's how I imagine it was back home as Jonny's kick went over. The difference between then and now is that when Platt and England returned from Italia '90, there were something like 30,000 fans waiting at the airport to welcome them home. I can't see us getting that sort of reception somehow.'

Our flight touched down at Heathrow and my head was throbbing. We travelled business class and someone must have spiked my drinks somewhere between Sydney and Singapore. Martin Corry nicked my passport during the stopover in Singapore and I had to blag my way back on to the plane. By the time we landed in London I was a mess.

As we disembarked there was a hold-up. A copper was talking to Clive Woodward, telling him that we would have to exit into the arrivals hall in groups of three or four. He said something about crowd control. I was hungover and tired and wanted to get home. Let's not make this more complicated than it need be, I thought. A few fans aren't going to cause us any problems. The first group were waved through: Clive, Martin Johnson and Neil Back. As the doors opened I couldn't believe my ears. The noise, in my fragile state, was almost literally mindblowing.

I looked at my watch. It was a little after six o'clock in the morning. 'What the . . . ?' I was in probably the third or fourth group. The doors hummed open and I can only compare the sight that greeted me with that scene in the film *Notting Hill* when Julia Roberts opens the blue door and is blinded by hundreds of flash-bulbs. There were people just everywhere. Every window sill, every rafter, every conceivable vantage point was taken. Then, for the first time, it hit home how big a deal it was for England to have won a World Cup.

In the days that followed you couldn't go anywhere for back-slapping and handshakes. But my celebrations weren't too intense. They couldn't be. In the back of my mind I knew I had to play for my club on the Saturday. Bath wanted us back almost literally the moment we got off the plane. Mike Tindall, Iain Balshaw and I popped into the Rec on our way back from Heathrow just to say hello. Then we were in for training the following day. It was Wednesday, Bath wanted us to play three days later, against Leicester of all teams, and we felt obliged to do so.

I didn't have too much of a problem with that at the time. The club had got me to what I had just achieved, I wanted to start repaying them. But somebody should have recognised that it was not a smart move after such a huge emotional comedown to play a massive, intense game away at Welford Road. I lasted twenty-one minutes.

A lot of guys broke down that week or the next because mentally we had done it and our bodies just packed in. With hindsight, there is no way that anyone involved in the World Cup should have been made to play. It was ridiculous. There should have been a compulsory two weeks off during which time players could adjust their bodies and especially their minds. Winning the World Cup is such a big deal. Had I had a couple of weeks off I believe I would have played the rest of the season. But I felt I had to get back to play for my club because Bath had done so much for me.

There were still great times to enjoy. The parade around Trafalgar Square was an unforgettable experience. The press had predicted 250,000 people would turn out to greet us. I took that to be hype. I was wrong. The actual number was closer to a million. Phenomenal. Having been in Bath, where it was all pretty low key, the hysteria took me by surprise. I arrived in London by train on the day of the parade and hailed a taxi to take me to the meeting point. I've always been told that London cabbies are football-mad but mine wound down his window and said, 'Hey, it's Mike Catt. Well done, Catty mate.' I couldn't believe it.

It was the start of my testimonial year. Before the quarter-final, when I was not in the England team and the team was struggling, ticket sales were going slowly. I was club player Mike Catt, who used to play for England. Lawrence Dallaglio had his too and even he was struggling to sell out. But as soon as the Cup was won the tickets went overnight. Lawrence actually had to add an extra night, another thousand seats, so overwhelming was the demand.

In December I had a Christmas lunch at a venue near Paddington. Six or seven of the guys turned up, including Martin Johnson and

Lawrence, Richard Hill and Jason Leonard. We entered the room to a standing ovation and took our places on the top table. The door then opened again and the World Cup was brought in to the sound of the World Cup anthem. Everyone stood up and applauded. There was a standing ovation – for a trophy. The euphoria that day was something else. A jersey signed by Martin went for £17,000. The day was a massive success and I considered myself incredibly lucky. I made sure others shared my good fortune. Sizeable cheques went to the Anthony Nolan Bone Marrow Trust and to the British Heart Foundation, via the Princess Diana Hospital in Birmingham.

Back at Bath I was struggling with my body. Lasting such a short time up at Leicester had come as a shock to me after being injury-free all World Cup. I had not missed a training session in Australia yet in my first game back at the club I broke down. Was there more to it than simply my body having relaxed after the massive high of Sydney? I thought of what I had put it through since the final. I had been a little bit stiff from the twenty-four-hour flight and had been treated by the club physios on the Wednesday, Thursday and Friday before going to Welford Road.

There were various things wrong with my right hamstring, but they loosened up both my hammys as well as my pelvis, glutes and back. The club started getting annoyed with me for being injured, having been fit for two months while I was with England.

Eventually a physio friend of mind suggested that perhaps I should just concentrate on my hamstring. For two or three weeks I gave it a try and the other problems went away. Relief mixed with bitterness as I thought about the playing time I had lost. God, I had almost missed out on a place in the World Cup squad. At the time I had assumed my body was just breaking down, but now I think I should have listened to what my body was telling me and queried the treatment. Looking back, I can't help feeling I was over-treated. The guys at Bath hadn't done anything deliberately wrong and they meant well, but in the same breath, I think they should have known better.

By the time I was fit again it was nearing the end of the season and the Bath management were wary about playing me because they felt I couldn't be trusted, physically, to last eighty minutes. Their attitude angered me beyond belief and my frustration hit a peak when the club made it to the Zurich Premiership final at Twickenham against Wasps and Mike Foley came up to me and said, 'Look, I'm not picking you.'

'You what?'

He repeated that I was neither going to start nor be on the bench as he had decided to go with Spencer Davey, a twenty-one-year-old who I did not think had anything like my ability. In a rage, and for once not prepared to go with the flow, I went to see John Connolly.

'You are being so ridiculous, you have to pick me in that side. This is a Twickenham final against the European champions. You can't leave me out.' In the back of my mind, however, I knew they had reason for doing it.

Game day arrived, Matt Perry broke down in the warm-up and I ended up playing the whole match at full-back. We lost 10-6 and didn't fire a shot in anger for eighty minutes. Nothing at all. Our whole attacking game simply didn't happen. To this day I believe that had I been picked at 10 we would have won that game.

It was a new experience for Bath to lose a final at Twickenham and my disappointment was magnified by the certainty I felt that my days at the club were numbered. My contract was up at the end of the season and it became crystal clear that I wasn't a part of the club's plans. Foley, I felt, wanted me out. He had been as nice as pie with me when he first joined and I had been impressed with him as a coach. He was very good at what he did, technically fantastic and the forwards loved him. But as time went on, being a back at Bath became an increasingly frustrating business. And two incidents polarised opinion towards him one way or another.

The first was a scuffle with Victor Ubogu in a pub in the town early on in his coaching days. All the boys were there and we separated the two of them. Victor stayed inside and Foley left. But rather than go home he stood outside for what must have been an hour and a half waiting for Victor to come out. I went out and said, 'Foles, just go home, mate, go home to your family. You are being ridiculous.' He said he was going to stay and sort it out. I looked at him and shook my head. I couldn't believe that a grown man like him, in a responsible position, was waiting like a pissed-up teenager for a bloke to come out of the pub. Then, when Victor did finally come out, he walked straight past Foley, who did nothing.

The next morning Foley was on the phone to me asking whether I felt he should offer his resignation. I agreed with him that he had been a prat but told him that everyone makes mistakes and to just get on with it. I said that we'd play it down at the club and it wouldn't be a problem. He asked whether I felt he should apologise to the players. I said I did and that an apology would be a good idea. 'But don't go over the top about it,' I said. 'We have all done stupid things.'

That was the end of the matter and for a while he didn't drink with us. Then one Saturday night, some time later, we were all at the club, Foley had a skinful and in front of everybody had a fight with Kevin Maggs. The next morning he was again full of regret and again said that he would resign. Steve Borthwick phoned me at home to say that the senior players needed to discuss what was best for the club. We met for a coffee with Danny Grewcock and Matt Perry and I expressed the view that Foley should go because it was the second time it had happened.

Steve disagreed. He said that if Foley went, he would probably go too. He said that Foley was a world-class forwards coach, technically the best he had ever worked with. Matt was pretty much on my side but Danny agreed with Steve. 'Okay,' I said eventually. 'I'll go along with you guys for the sake of the club. We'll make sure he doesn't go.' First thing Monday morning we went to see Andrew Brownsword, and he asked each of us for our views. Brownsword knew my dislike of Foley and asked me straight, 'Do you want him to stay?'

'Yes,' I said. 'For the sake of the club. I am not going to pretend to be happy about it but some good people might leave if he does.'

I got home and told Ali what had happened. She was not impressed.

'You should have stuck to your guns,' she said. The previous morning, as I headed out to meet the boys for coffee, she had warned, 'You must get rid of him. If you don't, he'll get rid of you.' Never was a truer word spoken. Three months later, I was gone.

Looking back now, I was a guy who just went with the flow. Foley seemed to distrust the older generation at the club, whom he perhaps saw as a threat. If so, he was wrong. But he hated people who questioned him and he was sick of hearing about the Bath of old. It seemed to me that he wanted to build a new regime and surround himself with new yes men. He bugged the life out of me because he wouldn't let us play the way we wanted to. It was very much rugby by numbers, a you-go-there, you-go-there sort of approach. It was not a style I enjoyed at all and I wasn't alone among the backs. Kevin Maggs, Iain Balshaw and Mike Tindall also complained that we were not playing to our strengths. But Bath were winning and the forwards, who were loving a gameplan that started and finished with them, supported Foley.

Since his arrival as forwards coach at the start of 2002 Foley had quickly become powerful within the management set-up. Jon Callard had been removed as head coach and backs coach Brian Smith had also left as Foley stepped up and persuaded Brownsword to recruit John Connolly, his old pal from Queensland, to work alongside him. They were undeniably successful. A year after almost being relegated we ended the regular season 6 points clear at the top of the Premiership. But it was a grim brand of rugby.

The Zurich Premiership final against Wasps was the last game I played for Bath. Before leaving on tour in June with England for New Zealand and Australia I met Brownsword and he made me such a derisory offer to stay that I would have respected him more had he just come out and said, 'We don't want you.' There are those who believe I priced myself out of the club but that could not be further from the truth. My previous contract had amounted to £80,000 a year. Brownsword offered me a new deal worth £20,000. After a dozen years of service he was basically putting me on an Academy wage.

I found it deeply insulting and I told him so. But Brownsword said that I had only played a small number of games for Bath that season and so that was what he felt I was worth to the club. I replied that had I not been away for three months helping England to win the World Cup I would probably have played twenty times or more. I told him he was ruining the club and that he could shove his offer up his arse. The meeting ended abruptly.

And yet still I didn't want to leave the club. That was how much loyalty I felt to Bath. A couple of days later I saw Brownsword again and begged him – I actually begged him – not to let me go. I said I wasn't asking for a lot of money at all and tried to explain the benefits I would bring to the squad off the pitch as well as on it. 'I have so much to offer this club,' I said. 'I can develop the youngsters, guys like Olly Barkley. I am quite willing to share all my experience with these boys. Just come to the table with a fair offer.'

But I don't think he was really interested. Bath supporters need to understand that I desperately wanted to stay. I had just bought a new house in the city and the club was in my blood. I had been there for as long as I had been in England and I felt a massive loyalty towards an organisation that had given me absolutely everything in my career. The last thing I wanted to do was turn my back on it, knowing that I had so much more to give. But Brownsword left me with no choice. He didn't seem to value my experience or my ability and there was no way I was going to let him walk all over me, not least because it wasn't just me who would have to live with the consequences. I now had a young family to support. Was I bitter? Hell, yes.

Strange as it may sound, I have the utmost respect for what the man has achieved in his business career away from rugby, which has made him in the region of £200 million. He clearly gets a buzz from negotiating with people and getting the best deal. That is why he is so successful. I understand that. But that approach I believe was wrong for Bath. It certainly made me want to leave.

It was only when Conor O'Shea, director of rugby at London Irish, phoned me to ask if I would be interested in joining his club on an £80,000 salary that Brownsword responded, raising his offer to £50,000. I had one other offer on the table, a tax-free £120,000 package to go and play in Japan for a club coached by my old mate Brian Smith.

My mind was spinning. I sought the advice of Sir Clive Woodward and he left me in little doubt that my international career would be over if I moved abroad because I would be out of the coaching loop. Brian Ashton, who was then heading up the RFU National Academy based in Bath but who had spent years playing in Italy, said it was a fantastic opportunity and that I would love the experience. But I knew I wanted to play for England again – the World Cup had convinced me that I still had a lot more to give – and so I turned the opportunity down.

That left me with a straight choice between Bath and London Irish, the only Premiership club that actually wanted me. My head said I had to move but my heart remained unconvinced. Yes, Bath had changed out of all recognition from the club I had known, to the extent that none of the old guys went back. But I was old school. It was still my club. I had not made up my mind when one day I was driving up to London for a dinner and my mobile rang.

'Catty, it's Conor. Sorry to do this to you but I need an answer, mate, before five o'clock tonight because I'm looking at other players.'

As coincidence would have it, I was literally driving past Sunbury at that moment. I made a snap decision. I indicated left and turned off the M3 at the upcoming junction, drove into Irish's training ground and put pen to paper then and there. I then called Ali to give her the news.

'Oh . . . right,' she said. 'So where do we go from here?'

At that moment I wasn't actually sure. 'I guess I'll commute to start with,' I replied, before getting a grip of the situation. 'Hon, this *is* the right decision. I'll make sure of it.'

14

THE COMEBACK CAPTAIN

Moran Hotel, Chiswick, 10 March 2007

Darkness had fallen on West London and I popped a sleeping tablet. It was part of my usual pre-match routine. Acupuncture and a snooze at five o'clock on the evening before a game, followed by a tablet to make sure I get a good seven or eight hours. Only there was nothing usual about this match. I was about to captain England for the first time, at Twickenham against France in the Six Nations Championship.

I like to wake up feeling tired. I love that feeling on a game day morning, I don't know why. I get up early, go and have a quick bite to eat, usually cereal and egg, then jump back into bed for a couple of hours. The team normally meets between 10 and 11 o'clock when I grab another snack, usually a piece of toast and a banana. Then I go back to bed to kill the remaining time until we're ready to leave for the game. I put the telly on with the sound down low and close all the curtains. In the darkness, I doze and let my body prepare itself for the battle to come.

Half an hour before we have to leave I get up, have a shower and a shave and pack my stuff into a kitbag. There is a lot of adrenaline swirling around inside me. I go quiet and become twitchy. When I sit down my legs are constantly moving. Never still. It's weird how my whole body seems to brace itself for war time.

This time it was far worse. I was massively nervous. I was entering unknown territory. I had started only four Tests for England since the 2003 World Cup, all of them heavy defeats in Australia and New Zealand on no-hope end-of-season tours. I worried how the crowd would react to me leading out the England team, I fretted over what the rest of the team would make of my place in the side, let alone my appointment. Having not even been in the squad for the first three games of the championship, would they question my right to be skipper?

It was a hugely important game for English rugby. England had suffered a record Six Nations defeat at the hands of Ireland in the previous game and had returned from an historic and intense first visit to Croke Park without a crumb of comfort. We had to bounce back. With the World Cup on the horizon we had to come up with something to make the country believe again.

During the week I tried to ignore the bigger picture and concentrate on the way we were going to approach eighty minutes of rugby against France that Sunday. 'Focus on the process, not the outcome. Worry about the things you can control.' That's what we are always told. It had to be purely about how we, as a group of individuals, were going to gel better. I'm not one for speeches and getting the captaincy didn't change that. It was tactical stuff all through the week, on the pitch and off it. There was no standing up in front of the team purely for the sake of listening to my own voice. That's not the way I do things.

What I did was to put the onus on each individual to perform. I said, 'Guys, you make the choices. You as individuals decide whether you make the tackle, whether you get to the nearest breakdown, whether you help the bloke in the tackle. It's your choice. Whether you get off the ground quick enough, whether you get the defensive line organised. Your choice. Nobody else's.' We then dispersed and headed off to our rooms. The next time we saw each other would be the biggest day of my sporting life.

This was how I had hoped it would be when I came back from the World Cup in Australia with a medal in my bag and pretty much every rugby ambition achieved. I had no plans to retire, I wanted to play on and enjoy the confidence that came from being a world champion. But it hadn't worked out that way. Not for me and certainly not for England. After Trafalgar Square, audiences with the Prime Minister and Her Majesty the Queen, not to mention an MBE for each of us, things went downhill fast.

The English season was in full swing. Emotionally, mentally and physically we needed a break, an opportunity to regroup, but there was none. The clubs, who had helped us individually and England as a team to achieve the ultimate goal, wanted their pound of flesh. Understandably too, but we were caught in the middle, pulled in different directions by conflicting interests. Not surprisingly, half the squad got injured within the first month of getting back, which decimated our Six Nations plans. Ireland won at Twickenham, England's first home defeat since New Zealand in the 1999 World Cup. We then went to France and were badly outplayed. But the boys were hanging, exhausted at the tail end of a season that seemed to have gone on forever.

And it was not over, not by a long chalk. In the infinite wisdom of the RFU, we were dispatched back Down Under for two Tests against New Zealand and one against Australia. We were in pieces while the All Blacks and Wallabies, just starting their new season and out to give the world champions a bloody nose, were as fresh as daisies. In each game we were hammered out of sight and we returned home completely dispirited.

Pretty quickly Clive Woodward, who had been knighted like England's World Cup-winning football manager Sir Alf Ramsey before him, decided he had had enough and quit the sport. Lawrence Dallaglio followed him out of international rugby, joining Martin Johnson, Neil Back, Jason Leonard, Kyran Bracken, Paul Grayson and Dorian West from the triumphant squad. If we were not back at square one it certainly felt like we were.

'The period after the World Cup was confusing in many areas,' Clive admits. 'I was fighting with so many people in English rugby because I couldn't believe everybody was prepared to sit back and carry on with the system that was in place. Everyone was saying it was fantastic and I was saying it wasn't. To be honest I wasn't quite on top of my selections as I always had been, because I was busy concentrating on trying to win these other battles. Catty didn't feature but I never thought the World Cup was his swansong. I just don't think he ever quite got back to being as fit as he'd liked to have been. I played him off the bench in the last two games of the 2004 Six Nations and he came on the summer tour, after which I resigned.'

England paid an almost forensic attention to detail during the

World Cup campaign but afterwards there was no plan at all. Nothing. We can all be smart with hindsight but I believe a big mistake was to continue with exactly the same coaching team. It all felt very stale, the same thing day after day. There was no buzz and I felt Clive's heart had gone out of it, as if he had ticked the box and was ready to move on. On the one hand he was freshening up the squad, on the other he was keeping the coaching staff as it was. New personnel, same old message. Andy Robinson was still forwards coach, Phil Larder was still in charge of defence and Dave Alred the kicking.

Phil had done a fantastic job up until the World Cup but beyond that I felt he knocked down a few players rather than built them up. Many of the new guys coming in I don't think could handle his abrasive style, whereas the older players knew and understood what Phil was about. I remember him telling Charlie Hodgson, 'My ten-year-old son tackles better than you.' Comments like that to guys trying to find their feet in the international arena are no good at all. Dave was probably the only coach who really provided something new.

As for Clive, he wanted to change the whole structure and he put his plan forward to Francis Baron, the chief executive of the Rugby Football Union. Clive knew it would need drastic change for England to go on and win another World Cup. He repeatedly made the point that England had everything in place in 2003 and yet only won the trophy with a drop goal in extra-time. It was that close. Baron rejected Clive's vision for the future and the pair fell out. Disillusioned that the RFU were questioning his judgement and, I guess he thought, wanting to do things on the cheap, Clive decided he would finish the 2004/05 season and then depart. Baron had other ideas. He said he should go immediately.

What Clive left behind was a set-up that had no clear idea about where it was going. England had won the World Cup and its leading players had gone. Now the coach had followed. Into his shoes stepped forwards coach Andy Robinson, who assured Baron he could work within the framework that Clive found unacceptable. It was Robinson's big mistake, as he would admit two turbulent years later, shortly before he was forced from office after England had lost for the eighth time in nine matches. It was a sorry run, equalling the country's worst ever, set across the 1972 and '73 seasons.

I played in only two of those games, both against Australia on tour in 2006, and to be quite honest I wasn't sorry not to play more. I don't enjoy rugby the way Robinson had England playing, with big sixteen-stone men trucking it up the middle. Had they been abso- lutely firing, chucking the ball around, I would have loved to have been a part of it. But they weren't. So I concentrated on settling in at London Irish.

I knew the key was to get fit, because when you go to a new club you gain respect by playing well. What you're like off the pitch means absolutely nothing, it's what you do in game time that counts. Still, after 227 appearances and 64 tries in Bath colours it did initially feel strange pulling on a green shirt. To begin with, Irish played with no width or flair. Like England, everything seemed to go up the middle. I didn't regret joining because I hadn't had any other option, but it was a difficult time for me. We were living in Bath and I was commuting to Sunbury three times a week, which did my back and hamstrings no good at all. Yet because I had abandoned the programme of over-treatment I received at Bath, and had the physios target specific areas, I still managed to play twenty-five games in my first season.

England meanwhile were having a wretched time. Having finished third in the 2004 Six Nations, behind France and Ireland, they lost their first three games in the 2005 championship – which had not happened since 1987. That made it four in a row, as they had also gone down at home to Australia in the final game of the autumn series. They stopped the rot by winning at Twickenham against Italy and Scotland, but the media was turning up the heat on Andy Robinson.

London Irish were not playing the greatest rugby either and it was a welcome surprise when Conor O'Shea came to me one day and, out of the blue, asked for my thoughts on Brian Smith. I told him that Smith was a fantastic backs coach and that if he was available we should get him in. It proved to be a turning point for the club, as within a year Brian had changed the way we played the game, making us one of the most exciting sides to watch in the Guinness Premiership and turning youngsters such as Topsy Ojo and Dylan Armitage into stars.

I had a big part to play in a gameplan that swept the club into the Premiership play-offs for the first time and, at the age of thirty-four, I was named Premiership Player of the Year, ahead of Northampton fly-half Carlos Spencer, Wasps wing Tom Voyce, Sale lock Jason White and Bristol scrum-half Shaun Perry. I was also linked with a coaching move to Leicester, but my heart was still set on playing the game and I accepted London Irish's offer of another year.

England continued to struggle yet I heard nothing from Andy Robinson at all. I can only think he looked at my age and felt the future belonged to younger men. Age has never been relevant to my thinking. I have never thought, Christ, I'm thirty-something, I've hardly got any time left, bloody pick me. Quite the opposite in fact. The older I have got the better I have played and I don't feel the pressure as I did when I was younger. But there was nothing I could do to make him change his mind other than keep performing for the club, which I think I did pretty well. It was then his decision not to pick me. I once texted him to say, 'Look, I can help, even if you just need someone to come off the bench to change a game.' I didn't get a reply. Nothing at all.

Andy Robinson needed help. He needed experience in his England side. I hated to see the team struggle and I couldn't understand why England were trying to play the way they were. We no longer had a massive England back line, it was plain to see that we had to let the ball do the work instead of trying to muscle it up the middle. It was also obvious that England weren't playing to players' strengths at all. What I found so scary was that the coaching staff could not seem to see this.

I had massive sympathy for Charlie Hodgson, who was experiencing the horrible scenario I had in the late nineties when England's only means of scoring was through goal kicks. Like me, his strength lay less in that area than in playing a running game. He was brilliant at running a game for Sale. But England asked him to play a style that was alien to him. Why, I simply don't know. England had the players to play Charlie's way, but they followed another path and, once again, the fly-half was an all-too convenient scapegoat.

Joe Lydon, a legendary figure in rugby league during his playing days, had been appointed attack coach by Sir Clive Woodward shortly before Clive quit the RFU. Joe is a top man and he proved to be immensely popular with the lads, but for his personality rather than his ability as a coach. He seemed to rely on the players to run everything. Things just got worse rather than better – in 2006, for the second consecutive Six Nations, England lost three games in a row, this time the last three, and as in 2005 they finished fourth.

When England lost 31-6 to France in Paris, a record-equalling loss in the fixture, the knives came out in the media but the RFU held firm. Six days later England lost at home to Ireland, this time 24-28, and the patience of the Rugby Football Union finally snapped. A review into the Six Nations performance ended with the coaching team being sacked but, bizarrely, Andy Robinson being retained. For some reason that I still don't understand, lieutenants Larder, Lydon and Alred were fired but the general lived to fight another day.

Robinson's authority was fatally weakened. The RFU appointed Brian Ashton as attack coach, put John Wells in charge of the forwards and gave Mike Ford the responsibility of sorting out England's defence. They then created a new post of Elite Rugby Director with the idea that the successful applicant would have the final say in all England playing matters. Sir Clive Woodward made the short-list but the job went to Rob Andrew, who for years had been an outspoken critic both of Woodward and Robinson.

It was at this point Andy Robinson finally picked up the phone and called to ask if I would come back to play for England. 'Mike is the ideal man to bring the young backs into play. He has a great ability to bring out the best in people around him,' he told the newspapers. There was a two-Test tour of Australia coming up and he said the number 12 jersey was mine. I was captain of London Irish, I had just received my Premiership award and I was bouncing, so I agreed. When you're as confident as that, you want to get to the top level again. You also believe you can make the difference.

I duly played in both Tests but it was not a happy experience. In Sydney, in the very Olympic Stadium where we had beaten the Wallabies and lifted the World Cup, we were hammered 34-3. Good memories replaced by bad. In Melbourne a week later we shipped six tries and lost 43-18. I came home and was promptly dumped from the squad without explanation. Autumn came and the crisis deepened. The All Blacks romped to a 41-20 victory at Twickenham and a week later Argentina, who had never before beaten England, won 25-18 to inflict a seventh straight defeat on the world champions. There was uproar around the country. Robinson again survived but was told he had two matches to save his skin.

Those games were against South Africa over the next two weekends. England nicked the first 23-21, after Phil Vickery came off the bench to score a late try, and the knives were put back in their sheaths. But a week later they were out again and there was blood on the floor at Twickenham when the Springboks rallied from 14-3 down after half an hour to win 25-14. At the final whistle Robinson's image appeared on the big screen and a disenchanted crowd turned on the England coach and vented their displeasure. Three days later he had gone.

It is too easy to pin all the blame for England's demise on Andy Robinson. The RFU have to take some responsibility too. What was the Union thinking by appointing him without a manager to share the work load? Why didn't they help him? I definitely believe

Robinson was let down by the Union and I know a lot of other players believe that too. Andy is a good guy, I like him a lot, and he is passionate about his rugby. He is what I call a rugby pig. But he needed help. The job was too big for him alone.

Not for one minute did I think about the captaincy when Brian Ashton was appointed as the new England head coach in December 2006. I did allow myself to imagine a return to the England fold however. For as long as I had played rugby Brian had been a massive influence on me. My best years at Bath in the mid-1990s were when Brian was there, so too with England in 2000 and 2001 when he had the back division firing on all cylinders. We share the same philosophy as to how the game should be played. Playing in his teams has always been a pleasure.

Sadly, I was unavailable at the start of his reign. I had been injured during a Heineken Cup game against Ulster in Belfast and the opening round of the 2007 Six Nations was too close for me to recover in time. It was immensely frustrating as the first game at home to Scotland felt so much like the dawn of a new era, albeit with some old faces returning to the fold. Phil Vickery was back after overcoming a career-threatening neck condition and was appointed captain. Jonny Wilkinson also re-appeared in an England shirt for the first time since the World Cup final. He had been beset by injuries ever since getting home from Sydney, and England had clearly suffered in his absence.

There was a new energy within the set-up. Andy Robinson appeared to have taken the 'if it ain't broke' view when he succeeded

Sir Clive Woodward. He saw no need to tamper with what had been a winning formula. But Brian had recognised that it was no longer a winning formula and that he needed to change it and put his own personal mark on the way England did things. He immediately earned the players' respect for doing so – for thinking, 'I don't care what the RFU or anybody says, this is the way I'm doing it.' His arrival had everyone buzzing. For the first time in a long while there were smiling faces around the England camp. He gave the boys the freedom of the pitch and basically said that he wanted us to go out and play the game as we saw it. His influence did not end there. He persuaded Jason Robinson to come out of international retirement, and he handed a debut to another rugby league icon.

Andy Farrell had achieved everything in league before deciding, shortly before his thirtieth birthday, that he fancied a crack at union with the target of playing in the World Cup. That in itself was ambitious enough but he was then struck down by a series of freak injuries that delayed his debut in union until the start of the 2006-07 season. Furthermore, he started union life as a blindside flanker and only switched to inside-centre in December. For every person who said he would make it there seemed to be a hundred who disagreed. But Andy was not interested in what other people thought, and neither was Brian Ashton.

When I was not available for the Scotland game, Brian handed the number 12 jersey to Andy. This made sense as I knew England needed to find out what a player with Farrell's rugby reputation could do at international level – and better that it happened now, from my point of view, than any closer to the World Cup. On a day that could have been scripted in Hollywood, Farrell acquitted himself well as England beat the Scots 42-20. But the headlines were dominated by Jonny Wilkinson, who marked his return with 27 points, and Jason Robinson, who grabbed two tries.

The following week was less impressive. England played Italy, again at home, and struggled to win the game 20-7. The boys managed just one try, again by Jason, and relied on the boot of Jonny to see them home. After the hysteria that had greeted the Scotland performance everyone came down to earth with a bump. I had spent the previous night captaining England A to a 32-5 win over Ireland's second string in Belfast and had enjoyed myself greatly playing with two boys I sensed had big futures in front of them, Harlequins wing David Strettle and London Irish fly-half Shane Geraghty. I hoped my performance would be enough to earn me a call-up.

England's next game was a big one and not just because it was against Ireland. It was the first time an English team had been allowed to play at Croke Park, the home of the Gaelic Athletic Association. But my phone did not ring so I took the bull by the horns and called Brian. It was out of character as normally I take the view that selection happens or it doesn't. But I felt passionately that I was on top of my game and could offer something to England, even if it was from the bench.

Brian told me straight that he was not going to change his side and nor was he going to change the bench. 'When the time is right I won't bring you on the bench, I'll put you straight in the team,' he promised. He then explained to me that he needed a goal kicker up his sleeve, which was why Newcastle's Toby Flood was on the bench, and that he wanted to grow the team with Wilkinson at 10 and Farrell alongside him.

Our conversation ended and I went back to preparing for London Irish's game at Sale, which had been brought forward to Friday night as England were playing the following day. I had taken the captain's run on Thursday when Brian Smith called me in and said, 'Ashton wants you in Dublin. Jonny's definitely not going to be fit and they want you to sit on the bench. Can you phone him and clarify where and what time you leave.'

The situation was far from ideal for the club. We had just finished our final training session, the preparations were complete for an important Guinness Premiership game, which was only thirty-six hours away, and Jonny Wilkinson hadn't officially been ruled out. I phoned Brian and asked how much of a doubt Jonny was. 'We've got a game tomorrow night, Brian,' I said. 'I don't particularly want to come across and just sit there and do nothing.'

'I understand that,' he replied. 'But the medical staff say there's a ninety per cent chance Jonny won't play.'

That was all I needed to hear. I was in the car and I went with the club's blessing. Only when I arrived at Twickenham to join the squad did it transpire that Jonny was actually not resigned to missing the game at all. Knowing him as I do, that didn't surprise me. And when I heard that it was his back rather than his hamstring that had caused neural tightening and twitching, I knew his chances of starting the game were an awful lot better than 10 per cent. It was exactly the problem I'd had two or three years before, and so from experience I know how quickly you can recover from that. You feel it one day, the next day you get up feeling fine.

Sure enough when we got to Croke Park on the Friday morning for a lookaround, Jonny had been kicking for an hour already. Ireland coach Eddie O'Sullivan and captain Brian O'Driscoll felt England were playing silly buggers with Jonny's injury and from the outside you could perhaps understand their point of view. But we weren't. On the Thursday Jonny genuinely had been in trouble.

Never before had an England team been beaten as heavily by Ireland as we were the following day when losing 43-13. The boys didn't get it right. We weren't at the races at all. We were dominated in every aspect of the game which, at international level, you very rarely see these days. Our decision-making in the first twenty minutes was poor. We tried all these little chips over the top and Ronan O'Gara, the Ireland fly-half, just drilled us back into the corners. We didn't get any momentum going. It was so disappointing. We knew we had to get a good start and dominate the Irish pack from the first minute, otherwise they were going to get the upper hand. We failed to do so.

Ireland's phase play, which had been mentioned all week, took us apart. Everybody knew exactly where they were going. They were so well organised, they varied the game so well and they were on the front foot every time. At international level, if you are on the front foot, especially with the players at 10, 12 and 13 that Ireland have (O'Gara, Gordon D'Arcy and O'Driscoll), you are laughing. Simon Easterby was phenomenal. He disrupted everything. We couldn't get over the gain line. Everything that had been said in the week that we shouldn't do, we did. Brian's instructions beforehand had been to 'dominate your opposite player then the rest of the team stuff will come'. To be honest nobody did that.

I was left with mixed emotions. On the one hand, when you are on the outside you don't want the guy in your position to play really well. On the other, I felt the criticism that came Andy Farrell's way afterwards was unfair. He was singled out by an awful lot of people for not posing any attacking threat, but pretty much nobody in the team performed. I know what it's like at 12 when you're not getting quality ball. When you're on the back foot chasing shadows all the time it's very hard to control a game, especially if you've had little international experience at that code.

I felt sorry for Andy. International rugby is an unforgiving environment and it had simply asked too much of him to set the world alight after only a handful of club games and two Test matches playing at inside centre. Brian had a decision to make. It was clear that Jonny needed more help from a tactical and decision-making point of view from the man outside him, so should the coach stick with Farrell, put him on the bench, or drop him completely? The debate raged in the media when we got home. People in the street and journalists writing in papers were calling for my return to the team for the next game, against France at Twickenham. It was nice to hear but I knew better than to pay it much heed. The only opinions that counted were those of Ashton and Rob Andrew.

The squad for France was named and I was in it, despite some neural discomfort in my lower back, which meant I sat out training at the start of the week. I sensed from Brian's tone that he intended to ring the changes, so I was as confident as you ever can be that I would get the call. What I didn't expect was the conversation that Brian engaged me in as I wandered round the training pitch at Bath University.

'There's something I want to tell you,' he said. 'You're playing against France on Saturday. One other thing. I'm thinking of making you captain.'

Phil Vickery had been concussed playing for Wasps against Bristol in the Premiership and Brian said to me that this would probably be a one-game deal. That didn't matter a jot to me. My name would be in the record books, added to a roll of honour of the greatest names ever to wear the England shirt. Nobody would be able to take that away from me. At 35 years and 175 days I was about to become the oldest player to lead England into a Five or Six Nations match since Bristol's Sam Tucker in 1931. Never had I even dreamed it could happen.

We headed back into the university sports centre where Brian had a press conference to attend. 'If there's one player in English rugby who knows the way I want England to develop the game, it's got to be Mike Catt,' he said, explaining his decision to make me skipper ahead of Martin Corry and Jason Robinson, who had held the position before. 'I've known Catty for fifteen years and I'm putting my money on him being able to help deliver the sort of game I want England to play.'

They were nice words and the first part was true as well. I did understand the way Brian's rugby mind worked. To put it mildly, our task was not an easy one. Eleven changes, three positional, to the team that lost in Dublin was some shake-up. Young guns Toby Flood, Dave Strettle, Tom Rees, Mat Tait and Shane Geraghty were all given their chance in the twenty-two, and we had just three days to get to know each other and put a gameplan in place. For us to get up to speed with playing the way Brian wanted us to play was a big ask.

Thankfully, it was the week the Brian Ashton of old returned. As recently as three weeks earlier there had been no recognisable Ashton hallmark on the squad, which had shocked me. He had said he wanted to find a starting point, get the basics right. But with the exception of the Scotland game, when the whole team was lifted by Jonny Wilkinson's extraordinary comeback performance, guys had played as they did for their clubs rather than fitting into an England mould.

Jonny was out injured, as was Andy Farrell, but Brian and I agreed that it was as much about changing individual mindsets as personnel. We also recognised that it would be very hard to do it overnight but that we had to give it a good go. Yes, we would lose games along the way, but the way we intended the team to play would potentially get a lot more out of the players and provide far greater excitement both for us and the supporters.

My view on captaincy was that I wanted to be less a dictator, more a facilitator. I have never been a screamer and a shouter. I saw it as my role purely to lead the team out and make a few decisions on the pitch to enable the guys around me to do what they're good at. I did not see it as being to gee people up. As far as I was concerned that is down to the individual at international level. I would make sure we got the tactics right and did the right things at the right time. I would make sure my team had the balls to try things. Above all, I would work my socks off to make sure everybody understood and bought into the way we needed to play to beat France.

When I got back to the team room I went online to gauge reaction to my appointment. On the BBC Sport website my old mate Jeremy Guscott had written a column. 'What you get with Catt is a player who's not afraid to lose, which means he's not afraid to try something,' he wrote. 'You only have to look at the way London Irish have improved in the last couple of seasons to see the impact Catty can have . . . There are very few players in world rugby who know more about the role of inside-centre than Catt. He's never been ultra quick, but he's always been able to spot a gap and run the line accordingly. He also has an excellent kicking game, which can take some of the onus off Toby Flood at fly-half. Having such an experienced head at 12 will help the young Newcastle fly-half no end.'

I woke up on the morning of the game full of anxiety and completely wound up. The week had taken a huge emotional toll on me and I had not even got to the game. I never imagined it would be so hard. I'd captained London Irish in the Premiership and in European Cup games at places such as Toulouse, but this was fifty times more intense. Was it going to work, was it not? Were we going to win, or get stuffed by 50 points? Would I get booed by Twickenham again, would I be cheered? So many conflicting emotions in my mind.

I had some breakfast and headed back to bed. I closed the curtains again and lay in the darkness. Right, come on, you're going to go and play, I told myself. I shut my eyes and drifted, but never far enough to escape those feelings of apprehension. When it was time, I jumped in the shower and stood for longer than usual under the jets of water, trying to find a peaceful place to park my thoughts.

At Twickenham I headed straight into the home changing room and dropped my kitbag on the bench in my cubicle, beneath a silver plaque bearing the Red Rose of England and my name. Every player in the twenty-two has the same. It is a nice touch, a legacy of Sir Clive Woodward's attention to detail. It makes you feel special. I did feel that way but I was also emotional in a way I had not anticipated. I

Moments to savour: (*above left*) Guinness Premiership Player of the Year 2005–06, in what proved to be a good season for London Irish, (*below*) playing for Irish against the Sale Sharks; (*above right*), relishing my England captaincy success against France, with George Chuter (*left*) and Mike Tindall (*right*).

The picture says it all – I'm none too happy to see the Springboks work their way to a 36–0 victory in the pool stage of the 2007 World Cup.

Andy Gomarsall was outstanding all game against Samoa, repeatedly marshalling us to safety.

The Tongans couldn't handle Paul Sackey's pace – his finishing was as good as any from the southern hemisphere teams.

The quarter-final against Australia: (*above left*) talking tactics with Jonny; (*right*) Jason Robinson, one of the old guard from 2003, shows his class; (*below*) we munched them in the scrum – Andrew Sheridan had a magnificent game.

With seventy-eight seconds on the clock Josh Lewsey scores against France in the semi-final.

The French talismanic figure of Sébastien Chabal brought to earth by the England defence.

Déjà vu. The same move we had executed to set Jonny up for the 2003 World Cup winning kick sets the seal on our semi-final 14–9 win against France.

Phil Vickery's inspiring leadership is vindicated. The underdogs are in the World Cup final.

The 2007 World Cup final: (*above left*) might things have gone differently if Cueto's try had been allowed? (*Above right*), Bryan Habana was player of the tournament, but failed to cross the line in this match; (*below*) me, Tait, Wilkinson, Gomarsall and Sheridan – drained and numb.

A chance to thank the fans who had kept faith, with Brian Ashton (*right*) and Evie aloft.

My family. In the end, they are more important than winning or losing, something I had learnt very early on.

was wound as tight as a coil. I put on a determined smile for the pre-match interviews, which go with the job of England captain, and I told the country we were just going to go out and play and enjoy ourselves.

Then it was time to put those words into action. I led the team out for what was my first Test match for England at Twickenham in six years. I looked up into the stand where I knew my wife Ali and daughter Evie were seated. I picked them out immediately. Evie, now five years old, was watching her dad play at Twickenham in a full international for the first time. I hoped it would be a memory she would keep forever. She had been lifted up onto the shoulders of some guy so she could see me better. I looked closer. I recognised the man. It was my father. I had known my brothers were coming to the game but not dad.

My biggest regret when England won the World Cup final had been that dad had not been in the Olympic Stadium in Sydney to share the experience with me. I know he was at my brother Pete's wedding in Port Elizabeth but I was so cross with myself for at least not having gone to the effort of inviting him. Ali knew that and so she had done this for me. She made sure that this time he didn't miss my big day. She flew him in from South Africa and later he would tell me how overwhelmed he felt to have been a part of the whole experience. He didn't cry but I know that inside he was very affected by what he saw one of his sons do.

I, too, was very emotional, welling up a couple of times during the anthems, though still remembering to flick my ear as the camera passed me on its way along the line. It is a little ritual I perform before matches, my way of acknowledging my family for all their support in getting me to where I am, which on this day was the pitch at Twickenham, in front of 82,000 fans, about to lead my country against an unbeaten France. Jesus! I had said beforehand that the job of a captain these days was simply to lead the team out onto the pitch. Already I had found it was much more than that. You become, in a funny sort of way, the emotional heartbeat of the team.

The first twenty minutes of the game were the worst twenty minutes of any international I had ever played. I dropped balls and made one basic error after another. I thought, oh God, please don't let this be a nightmare. I was doing things I just don't do. I don't drop balls. I don't make those sort of simple mistakes. It was over-eagerness. I was snatching at things. I never felt the occasion was getting the better of me. I thought it was just a matter of time before I settled into my rhythm. But I was trying so hard, too hard. And when that happens things that ordinarily you do instinctively, you start to think about. That's when the problems start.

England trailed 9-3 after twenty-five minutes because we could not keep hold of the ball for more than three phases. Mike Tindall and I had coughed up four turnovers in the first fifteen minutes, which had piled pressure on the team. But we never stopped trying to play, never retreated into our shells. By half-time the deficit was 12-9 and that was with Toby Flood missing two shots at goal. The mood in the changing room was that we could win the game if we maintained our high tempo.

For ten minutes straight after half-time we pounded at the French line but it held firm and we were forced back onto the edge of their 22. It was decision time. From the set-piece I got the ball and, looking up and seeing a forward in my path, I decided to have a dart. I slipped past Raphael Ibanez and up through the gears. The try line was in sight and I had Toby on my shoulder screaming for the ball. He did the rest and we led 16-12.

If we thought that was the turning point we were wrong. Two lapses of discipline enabled Dimitri Yachvili to kick France back in front and then Toby was forced off the field with a dead leg. On in his place came Shane Geraghty, my twenty-year-old team-mate from London Irish. Before the game I had told him, 'As soon as you get on and get the ball, you have to make an impact and give the team go-forward. Straight away. If you can do that, it makes such a difference to the players around you.' Within moments he had kicked a penalty to nudge us back in front 19-18. He then launched a dazzling, fearless break up through the guts of the French team. From our own half we were into the France 22. Shane looked left for support and found Mike Tindall, who crashed over under the posts. Shane converted and we held on to win 26-18.

Ali couldn't stop crying after the game. She burst into tears when she first saw me and I almost did the same. I felt such massive relief that I had not let down Brian Ashton, who had shown so much faith in me, and the rest of the squad. I had always thought that a week in rugby union was a long time and boy was that true of this week. In the space of seven days my whole life had changed. It had been that big an experience for me. I was shattered, more mentally than physically. Ali said she was so proud. She understood better than anyone what the day had meant because she had borne the brunt of all the crap that had gone on with me in the past. As much as it was for me, it was her moment of release.

I had press commitments to meet but my emotions were still raw.

LANDING ON MY FEET

Beforehand the media had questioned whether it was the right thing to make me captain of a team with eleven changes. And when the first question afterwards took me back to my difficult days with England I must admit I wanted to thump the guy who asked it. Had Richard Prescott, England's media manager, not called an early end to the interview I might well have blasted someone. Of course, in the cold light of day, I understand that the more provocative questions are only designed to get decent answers. But I was so hyped up at the time that I didn't see them as that, rather as people questioning my whole career as a rugby player.

Professional sport is a fickle business; fickle with a capital 'F'. Martin Corry told me that some bloke came up to him and said, 'I booed you in the autumn but you were absolutely brilliant today. Well done.' I've had exactly that experience numerous times, especially after the 2003 World Cup. 'Yeah I booed you at Twickenham that time but you saved us at the World Cup. Fantastic, mate. Can I have an autograph?' The temptation is to say, 'Fuck off.' That's how you feel inside. It's wrong of course, unprofessional, because fans who pay to watch you are entitled to air their view. But at a human level it can be difficult to take.

To my mind the only opinions outside of the squad that really count are those of former team-mates. Will Greenwood had handed out the England shirts before the game and when he gave me mine had said, 'You're an outstanding guy and a good mate.' After the game he then texted me to say that giving me my jersey had for him been on a par with winning a World Cup. That comment meant the world to me. It still does. There were also messages from Jerry Guscott, Jason Leonard and Will Carling, guys whom I have always looked up to, guys who don't dish out praise lightly, guys who fully appreciated the context of our achievement.

I went back to the changing room to gather up my stuff and to have a couple of moments to myself. It was then it started to sink in: the feeling that with the captaincy I had achieved absolutely everything I could on a rugby field. I had fulfilled every rugby dream I'd ever had. Winning the World Cup was one dream and until that moment I thought it was the ultimate one. But leading out England, and for us to have played the way we had in that match of all matches, I think topped even that.

At the official dinner afterwards I turned to Ali and said, 'You know what, I can retire now.'

'You're not going to, are you?' she replied, quick as a flash.

'No. But I am that satisfied. The way I'm feeling right now I could call a halt. I've had the most fantastic career and what I've been involved in today is the most awesome thing I've done.'

Not since working in Malcolm Pearce's newsagents to make ends meet during my first year at Bath had I been first at a paper shop on the Monday after a game, but on this occasion Ali insisted we check out the headlines. They were brilliant, great to see. But I could not dwell on them because Wales were waiting for us at the Millennium Stadium in five days' time and my hamstring and glutes were sore as hell. The coaches gave us time off until the Wednesday to allow us to each regroup mentally, and by the time we reassembled they had gone through the tapes and concluded that, well as we did, France had not really turned up.

We had not let them play but nor had they shown much appetite to do so. Wales, we knew, would be a completely different test, not least because they were yet to win a game and defeat would condemn them to a Six Nations whitewash. As a group, though, we felt we could go up another five levels. Had we gone through two or three more phases at certain times, we believed we could have crucified France. Our kicking game had not been great either. Brian said afterwards that it was a one-off win, just as Croke Park had been a one-off defeat. It would mean nothing if we didn't back it up.

He knew, as we all did, that winning at Twickenham was one thing, winning on the road quite another. It was of course satisfying to have won all three home games in the championship, a feat England had not managed since the 2003 Grand Slam, but since the World Cup that same year, England had won the grand total of three games away from headquarters. Since England's last away-day triumph in Italy thirteen months earlier, the team had lost in Edinburgh, Paris, Sydney, Melbourne and Dublin. If we were going to hope to make any sort of defence of our world title later in the year, we had to start fronting up on our travels.

Cutting straight to the bottom line, I challenged the boys to step outside the comfort zone when we played at the Millennium Stadium. 'Let's see if we, as a group of players and management, can handle it,' I said. We knew it would be tough, especially as Wales had lost in Italy the previous week and would be fired up but, as I put it, 'We need massive challenges at the stage we are at, building up to where we want to go.' I tried to pretend that the difference between playing at home and away was a state of mind and that as the young guys in the team didn't think that deeply, it would not be an issue for us.

But there was more to it than that. Against France there had been a desperation born out of fear of what happened in Ireland. We were now going to Wales on a high and to face a team in the same driven state as we had been in the week before. We needed to show that the performance against Ireland, rather than the one against France, was the one-off.

We didn't pull it off. Despite recovering from a disastrous start, we lost 27-18. Our set-piece play was poor and tactically we were naive. We played in the wrong parts of the pitch, especially in the second half. The real culprits were not the forwards but us backs. We knew Wales would come at us hard in the first twenty minutes and we needed to take the steam out of their performance. Instead, we just fuelled the fire by handing them turnover ball. We were 15-0 down after fourteen minutes with Chris Horsman, whom I had mentored when he first joined Bath, scoring a try for Wales.

We did pull it back to 18-18 before half-time. I made a decent break up the middle to set up a try for Harry Ellis and then Harry went himself to put Jason Robinson over in the left corner. But Wales came again and took the game away from us. 'It was an opportunity for us to become a pretty special side in the space of two weeks,' I told the papers. 'Unfortunately we didn't take it.'

I was mentally and physically knackered when I arrived home. I had a dead arse and my hamstring had gone. Yet still I felt strangely exhilarated. Twickenham had embraced me warmly and the media had been incredibly positive about me. It had given me a sense of closure. As a player I probably peaked in 2000 and 2001 as part of an England team that was putting 50 points on almost everybody. But as far as the media were concerned, that was the era of Jonny Wilkinson. The rest of us didn't get a look in. It's the way the media works. But now, with Jonny out injured, they had looked for a new leading man and they had given me the job. A fortnight earlier there had been a danger my career would finish without any sort of acknowledgement. Now when I went out and filled up my car with petrol there was somebody asking me for an autograph. When I walked into a shop someone was saying, 'Good on you, Catty.' It felt really good. In two weeks I had gone from feeling like a South African captaining England to feeling more English than I thought was possible. It was because I had been welcomed into the nation's heart, at least that's how it felt. It made me feel very proud. It also made me massively determined to make England successful again.

15

SHOCK THE WORLD

Royal Garden Hotel, Kensington, London,
22 January 2007

It had begun with a meeting, a simple ten-minute chat in which Brian Ashton, the England head coach, spoke and everybody else listened.

'I want people to be punctual, I want smiles on faces around the hotel, I don't want anyone to be grumpy,' he said. He then held up a little black book full of blank pages. 'It's up to you as individuals whether you write anything in here,' he added. Gone was the big black folder, containing 150 pages of various codes of conduct and do's and dont's, used first by Sir Clive Woodward, then Andy Robinson. 'I don't need that,' said Brian. 'We don't need all those meetings. Oh, and one other thing. This is our slogan. This is what we intend to do: Shock the World.'

I had always liked the no-frills, plain-speaking way in which Brian approached life and rugby. I had known him since I first came to England in the early 1990s when I joined Bath and found that the club shared the same playing philosophy as I did. But it was not until 2000, when Clive brought him into the England set-up, that we really struck up a close working relationship. Better than anyone, he understood my frustrations and empathised with my playing philo-sophies and maverick tendencies. The prospect of going to the 2007 World Cup as a senior member of his team massively excited me.

From the start it was a struggle, though not in the way it had been in 2003. Back then I had to win over Clive and convince him I had the form to make a difference to a team I had not played for in two years. This time that case was already made. I had captained England in the final two rounds of the Six Nations Championship and, but for a back injury, would have led them on tour to South Africa for two summer Test matches.

Unlike four years before, when my battle had been to get on board for a journey that I had a pretty good idea was bound for sporting immortality, this time the hard work began once the squad had formed. There was no momentum carrying the team to France. Quite the reverse in fact. If we were to win the race it would be from a standing start.

Brian had known this well enough when he agreed to succeed Andy Robinson as head coach at the turn of the year. At the age of sixty not much gets under his radar. But, like all of us, he has a strong sense of self-belief and he believed he could buck the odds. Hence his challenge to us, borrowing a quote from Muhammad Ali, to 'defy the impossible and shock the world'.

By the end of the Six Nations it was his conviction that was shaken. England had won all three games at Twickenham for the first time since the Grand Slam year of 2003 but on the road there were those heavy defeats in Dublin and Cardiff. However hard we tried to convince ourselves otherwise, there was a problem when it came to playing away from home. Statistics don't lie, not when you're talking twelve defeats in thirteen games. And next up were two Tests at altitude with only half a squad against a South African side that had won at Twickenham on its last outing and was determined to give us a bloody nose ahead of the World Cup.

At the best of times it would have been hard enough. Without thirty-odd players from Wasps, Leicester and Bath – all of whom were involved in European club finals the weekend before the First Test in Bloemfontein – the likelihood of England winning only their fourth away match since the World Cup was small. All the same, I was desperate to make the trip. To lead England back to the country of my birth would be an unbelievably proud moment for me and my family.

It didn't happen. Although Brian left the door open for me right up until the last minute, he eventually decided that it was just too big a risk to put me in the line of Springbok fire when I had not played a game of any sort in close on three months. He assured me I was inked into his World Cup plans and told me to concentrate on getting myself right. In my absence he asked Jason Robinson to lead the squad instead. Jason certainly had his hands full.

As the squad flew south to Johannesburg I headed west to Florida with Ali and Evie for a week at Disneyland. I was waving at Mickey and Donald when South Africa beat England 58–10 in the First Test in Bloemfontein, the second biggest margin of defeat ever inflicted on England, and I arrived home just in time to catch the highlights of the return in Pretoria seven days later. Fair play to the England boys, they actually led 19–17 at half-time and were still tied 22–22 with more than an hour gone. But then the floodgates opened and the Boks scored 33 unanswered points.

At the back of my mind I thought thank God I wasn't out there, particularly when I learned about the sickness bug which had decimated the squad. It was no joking matter. David Strettle, worst affected of all, had to be moved into the high dependancy unit of a local hospital after vomiting for eighteen hours solid and becoming gravely ill. England were so short of players that Anthony Allen was stuck on the bench for the First Test purely to make up the numbers. He was in no fit state to take to the field.

For all that, the competitor inside me felt that, had I been there, it could have been different. I had sent a text to Jonny Wilkinson before the squad was named saying, 'You go and I'll go.' He texted back telling me I had a deal. I then wasn't selected. Jonny later told me that after the First Test he was close to sending me a 'Thanks, mate' text but resisted the temptation.

My holiday ended the moment I got back from Disneyland. Every day I was at the gym at Twickenham doing pilates for an hour. I've always been a bit of a secret trainer. I love working hard by myself. Some people don't. Some people need to push themselves against other people. At my age, with so many young guys around, I need to make sure I'm right at the top fitness level. For a fortnight I combined training with coaching at London Irish. I had been offered a new contract which involved playing and coaching and I dived straight in.

By the time the England squad reassembled I was mentally exhausted, but I consoled myself with the thought that we were heading to the Algarve and would at least soak up some southern sun. We were told to meet at Bournemouth Airport to fly to Portugal. I thought it strange but it was an easy run from Sunbury so I got on with it. I threw on a tee-shirt, beach shorts and flip-flops and jumped in the car. The first two days were scheduled to be relatively easy and I thought that would give me time to get my head clear of the coaching stuff at Irish and get back into selfish mode again, just thinking about myself.

When I arrived we were ushered into a private room inside the airport where Viv Brown, our team manager, was waiting. With a big smile on her face she stood up in front of us all and said, 'Sorry, lads, the plane's cancelled.' She was accompanied by a physical training instructor from the Royal Marines. My heart sank. Instead of a sunshine flight to Faro we were diverted to Poole for four days of Commando training. I actually love doing all that and it was quite good fun but it was the last thing I needed at that time. I emerged from it mentally drained and physically shattered.

Brian's thinking was that the training would accelerate the squad bonding process and bring leaders to the fore. It was pretty shrewd on his part. Going from the Marines, where we slept under canvas, to two days of full-on training, four sessions a day in the intense heat of Portugal, was too much for me. We've got a saying that when you've had enough you ring the bell. Garath Archer did that before the 1999 World Cup and I must admit I came very close to doing the same.

I phoned Ali at home and said, 'I don't want to be here.' She listened to me and then replied, 'Well, we're here at home. It's up to you.' That wasn't what I wanted to hear. I wanted to be told I was being a dickhead and I shouldn't be thinking like that. I said I would call her later and rang off.

I then picked up the phone and dialled Dr Steve Peters. Steve is a forensic psychiatrist who had worked with the massively successful

British cycling team and is a renowned mental skills coach. He had already spoken to us as a group and told us to call him individually if he could help at all. He suggested I popped by and I did just that. I sat with him for half an hour and told him I was thinking of ringing the bell.

He looked at me and said that he thought I was being foolish. He then wrote the following down on a piece of paper: 'You're stupid. You're trying to do everybody else's job rather than just concentrating on your own.' He was right. I was worried about whether the other kickers in the England squad were getting the right information. I was also worried about my new coaching role at London Irish. When I signed the two-year contract – one year playing, one year full-time assistant backs coach – it had not occured to me that, perhaps, it was tantamount to being given a deadline to finish playing.

'Stop,' Steve said. 'Go talk to Brian, to Jon Callard and John Wells. See what they want from you as a player and a tactician but also from a physical point of view as well, because if you continue with what you're doing you're not going to last the next two weeks, let alone make it through to France. When you've done that, go talk to fitness coach Calvin Morriss and find out if he can alter your sessions for you. You know something, Mike, you're the king. You're the person who's going to be out on the pitch doing it. The coaches will listen to you.'

I didn't feel like the king at that moment but I did as I was advised. I sought out Jon Callard, our kicking coach and my old Bath team-mate. I told him I felt I had been undermining him. He would be taking a kicking session with some of the guys and I would pull him across and say, 'Look, try this or try that.' Because he's a good friend of mine he had taken it. He told me, 'The more information I can get the better. If we can work together that's brilliant.' But I was uncomfortable with what I had been doing. I knew in my heart of hearts that due to my new coaching responsibility at London Irish I was analysing everything with a coach's eye rather than a player's. I was watching what JC, forwards coach, John Wells, and Brian himself were or were not doing and getting caught up in it rather than just focusing on my own job. Jon and I had a good chat about it and I put my mind at ease.

But my body was in an altogether different place. We were into what Brian had said was as much a selection process as a training camp. He had made it clear after the South Africa tour that he knew only five players who would definitely start the World Cup. I liked to think that I was one of them but I had no way of knowing if that was true. So I went out all guns blazing in training, leaving nothing at all in the locker. On the first day we had pre-hab 7.30–8 a.m., which was core stability work in the gym, followed by two field sessions of kicking and defence, 10–1 p.m., then an hour back in the weights room. Two hours were designated for sleep and lunch, then we were back at it again. Between 4.30 and 6.30 p.m. we worked on exit plays – moves specifically designed to get us out of our own half – and conditioning.

After talking to Calvin I cut one of the four weekly weights sessions I had been alotted and replaced it with pilates. I also cut down on the amount of kicking I did. By doing that I felt I struck a better balance and physically I became far happier. My concern was then not for me personally, rather for the squad as a whole. Nine weeks out from the start of the World Cup, and it seemed to me that Brian did not have any idea who he was going to pick.

There were still forty-six players in the squad. I felt we needed to cut the number down to nearer thirty. In fact, I wanted Brian to pick his XV to play against Wales in the first of our three warm-up games and let them train together. The truth of the matter is that at that stage we didn't know how to play with each other on the pitch. There was not enough focus, not enough communication.

A senior players' meeting was called at which we voiced concern that time was running out and we were working with too big a squad. We were fine-tuning exit plays when we felt we needed to be working on overall attacking philosophy. Rather than spend too much time on specific things, we thought we needed to address the bigger picture: getting to know each other in an attacking frame-work, how best to combat a drift defence, what to do against a four-up defence. Brian listened to our concerns, then tried to assure us that everything we had asked for had been planned for the Bath leg of the training camp.

So we flew home from Portugal and, after a brief break, headed to Bath where we at last got a ball in our hands. But the squad was still too big for my liking. Had it been two people in each position we would have got so much more out of the sessions. Instead, working with forty-six players, in the fly-half and inside-centre positions Andy Farrell and Olly Barkley were swapping in and out with Charlie Hodgson, while Toby Flood and I were swapping in and out with Jonny Wilkinson. But I didn't get to work with Charlie, nor Olly with Jonny. It seemed far from ideal.

Julian White, perhaps the best tight-head scrummager in England, then decided to pull out of the squad to stay at home with his young family and his sheep-farming business. It was his choice and one I respected but it worried me that it sent out a negative message from our camp. And yet I still clung to the belief that if the rest of us were fit and in form we could make it to the semi-finals as, on paper at least, we had a hell of a squad.

Professional sportsmen tend, by nature, to be optimistic people. We had still not developed a well-drilled organised attack and, to be honest, the feeling was far more akin to going into the 1999 World Cup than 2003, in that we were hoping rather than expecting. 'If you guys don't believe, it won't happen,' Brian kept telling us. 'You guys have to start believing.'

Twickenham, 4 August 2007

England 62–5 Wales
Brian had only two games to finalise his World Cup squad, starting against Wales at Twickenham. Five months before, when the two teams met at the Millennium Stadium, I had been England captain. This time, I did not even make the squad. Brian said he wanted to see how Andy Farrell went with Dan Hipkiss, the uncapped Leicester centre. I was not happy about it. So close to the World Cup I felt he should have been playing the squad he wanted as his final XV, but he told me I would be starting against France the following week so I bit my lip.

I tried to lift my spirits by reminiscing over a previous England game against Wales at Wembley in 1999, the one that ended in heartbreak when Scott Gibbs cut through our defence to win the game in the final minute and deny us a Grand Slam. That wasn't remotely funny but what happened a couple of weeks later was. I received a small package with a Swansea postmark on it. I had sent my driving licence off to be renewed at the Driver and Vehicle Licensing Agency (DVLA) and it had been returned, but with an unexpected addition. Stuck on the document over the section containing my personal details was a yellow Post-It note onto which had been scrawled: 'Scott Gibbs for Prime Minister.' I almost wet myself laughing.

Eight years on and the joke was on Wales. Gareth Jenkins had chosen to bring a severely depleted team to Twickenham and it backfired pretty spectacularly. England ran out 62–5 winners, a record score for the fixture. Of the ten tries scored, nine went to England and four to Harlequins' Nick Easter, a first for an England number 8. His rival for the shirt, Lawrence Dallaglio, looked a little anxious watching from the bench, though he came on for the final quarter and grabbed one for himself. Lawrence is not used to being a peripheral figure. Sure enough, a week later he was back calling the shots.

Twickenham, 11 August 2007

England 15–21 France
Five months to the day since I had captained England against France at Twickenham I was re-appointed against the same opposition at the same venue. It was again a huge thrill for me but, unlike back in

March when I felt very much able to set the tone, this time it seemed different.

It began in the changing room beforehand when I was trying to talk. I could see Lawrence itching to say something, and get all motivational. That's the way he does things when he is in charge and I respect that. But I was skipper and I do it completely differently. I know he hadn't started a game for England for seventeen months and was excited, but I felt I didn't have his full support.

On the pitch our lines of communication were little better. We would make a call and Lawrence would go against it. The following morning Will Carling was on the radio saying that he felt Lawrence could become a 'divisive influence' within the camp. 'With a character like Lawrence it's not just about playing form, it's about him in a squad,' Will remarked. 'He's a natural leader, yet England are not picking him as captain.' Will's view, that it could be a problem if there are not 'very strong guys to keep him in check', led him to pose the question: 'If you take him does he end up being divisive if he's not in the team?'

Lawrence is a very good friend of mine, let me make that clear, and I've got the utmost respect for everything he's done. But at that point in time I did wonder whether Will perhaps had a point. I felt as though Lawrence was trying to control everything. My concern was not for me, it was for some of the less experienced players. Because Lawrence is such a strong personality I was afraid that some might go into their shells at a time when we badly needed everyone's games to develop.

A day which I should have spent anticipating a call from Brian to confirm my selection for a fourth World Cup, I instead spent wound up; sad and frustrated that my England team had lost its composure and, because of that, a hugely important game of rugby. When we were leading 15–11 inside the final quarter, Sébastien Chabal had come off the bench and bulldozed his way through Josh Lewsey and Nick Abendanon, making his debut at full-back, to score the only try of the game.

Had we all stuck to our tasks and not got upset, I believe we would have won. Instead we posted a loss which halted our momentum in its tracks at exactly a time we needed to be kicking on. As captain, I realised I needed to say something and at our next team meeting I posed the question: 'Was everyone happy with the communication on the pitch?' The next voice belonged to Lawrence, who stood up and started on about missed tackles and not kicking in the right parts of the field. Olly Barkley countered: 'We called certain calls and they were changed at the last second. We didn't go through with them.' Back came Lawrence. 'Yeah, but we didn't play in the right parts of the pitch.'

The meeting broke up with the situation unresolved and with me feeling, more strongly than ever, that I needed to sit down with Lawrence and urge him to pull his neck in a little while I was captain. I knew that he would not appreciate the conversation, but I felt it had to be done. As a squad we were not all pulling in the same direction and, given how much ground we had to make up before the tournament in our team development and game understanding, it was a nettle I knew I had to grasp.

The confrontation never took place. Steve Peters called a group session at which all the things I was upset about were brought up, mainly by Steve. I reckon he must have sat down with Lawrence beforehand and heard his side of the story, though I have no way of knowing that for sure. We all agreed that to progress and to improve as a team we had to all keep our composure.

That should have been that but I was still not happy. Building up to the French game I had felt really good. But with losing and the things that happened on the pitch, I had plunged into depression. I should be enjoying this, I really should, I thought. I've just won my seventieth cap and I led the team. But I'm not.

My consolation was that I would definitely be going to France to help defend the trophy. I was at home doing some stretching, watching Tiger Woods win another major title on telly, when Brian texted me to say: 'Congratulations, you're in the World Cup squad. Be at Bath, 11 o'clock Monday morning.'

It was a weird feeling. Finally I had done the job and achieved my goal. But because it had been such hard work the sense of achievement didn't really hit me. I had been in zombie land for the past eight weeks and when I got the text I was still unhappy about the France game. Still, there were positives; I had a game under my belt and had come through unscathed. I had not been able to say that for five months. I felt really comfortable knowing that I was bringing something different to the party because in the past I hadn't done that. I had just distributed and kicked well, but nobody really saw that. They were on the look-out for more individual stuff. All of a sudden I was actually being noticed on the pitch rather than just being the General behind the scenes. I had made four clean breaks since returning to the England team, creating tries against both France and Wales in the Six Nations.

My own pleasure at being selected was soon overtaken by my concern that the squad Brian had named seemed to me to be unbalanced in a key area. His decision to pick Andy Farrell ahead of Toby Flood puzzled me. Not because I have anything personal against Andy, but because it meant I was the only right-footed kicker in the number 10 – number 12 area. Farrell, Jonny Wilkinson and Olly Barkley are all left-footed. With Charlie Hodgson overlooked as well, it also meant that we had only three goal kickers, which left little room for manoeuvre in the event of injury.

Selection day for Marseilles was not one I remember with any pleasure. 'Catt axed by England' is a headline I have come to know pretty well, but to go from captaining the side to dropping out of the twenty-two took me completely by surprise. Brian said he wanted to see again how certain people, who had played in the win over Wales, responded under pressure because they had not been put under any that day at Twickenham. Among those chosen to face re-trial was Andy Farrell. Olly Barkley was given the bench spot.

I was spitting feathers. Brian knew what I could do because I had been involved in his teams so often in the past. But I didn't feel that was the point. I felt I had played reasonably well against the French and this was an important opportunity for me to play with Jonny Wilkinson and get that 10–12 relationship back on track. It had worked so well between us in the past, yet the last time we had played together was the 2003 World Cup final. I expressed my view to Brian, I told him I thought it would be better to play the ultimate World Cup team, build combinations and move the whole thing forward. I also felt that psychologically there was a big blow to be struck in Marseilles. Beating the World Cup holders in their own backyard three weeks before the tournament starts would be quite a statement of intent. Brian listened and then went with Andy Farrell.

Marseilles, 18 August 2007

France 22–9 England

The week before we should have beaten the French. We had the game in the bag and moments before Sébastien Chabal's score we blew a golden try opportunity at the other end. The fact France ended up with their biggest winning margin at Twickenham for thirty-two years did not overly concern us at the time. We believed we would put it right at Stade Vélodrome, even if only one visiting team, Argentina, had ever won an international there. We didn't appreciate that Chabal's try had shifted the momentum decisively in the direction of France.

Our performance in Marseilles, after a promising opening, degenerated horribly. In the first five minutes we went wide and caused them problems. Shaun Perry, breaking from scrum-half, almost put Jason Robinson over in the left corner. But then we seemed to retreat into our shell. Simon Shaw was very harshly sin-binned and during the ten minutes we were down to fourteen men, France scored 10 points. I had a long chat with Andy Farrell afterwards and asked why we had abandoned the plan so early to open France up in the wide channels. He said that Jonny had not wanted to go there. Apparently calls were being made and not executed, like the week before when we had three or four guys saying different things, rather than just going with one call and getting it right.

Matt Dawson, who called the game for BBC radio, made the point that Jonny was trying too hard. 'His work rate is phenomenal, better than probably anyone that plays the game, but on Saturday he was trying to do everything,' he said. 'He helped Tom Rees save a try in the corner, which was great. But he was also hitting rucks, standing round the fringes of rucks, taking the ball on and trying to make darting breaks when it was not on. It's just enthusiasm but in my mind, in my humble view, it needs to be tempered a little bit for the good of the team.'

I agreed with Matt, Jonny did appear to be trying too hard, trying to be everywhere, appearing not to trust the guys around him. The first half performance reminded me of the quarter-final against Wales in the 2003 World Cup where Jonny tried to do everything himself rather than delegating and trusting the guys around him. Four years on I could not come off the bench to help him because I was sitting in the stand. The whole evening was a huge disappointment. Individuals let themselves and the team down. We were nothing like clinical enough. It was unacceptable so close to the tournament. We had said we wanted to build more variety into our game and that we wanted to go in the wide channels. We did none of that.

Before the game I had said we were more than capable of reaching at least the semi-finals. But what happened in Marseilles made me wonder. As we headed home I really didn't know what to think. The only thing for certain was that we needed to face up to a few home truths, the biggest of which was that any form of success at the World Cup, given, I felt, the paucity of our preparation, would be a massive ask.

16

LOSING OUR WAY

Trianon Palace, Versailles, 4 September 2007

The backdrop was spectacular, our prospects were not. Less than a mile from Louis XIV's famed Château de Versailles the first day of England's World Cup campaign began with hope and ended with deep concern. In our opening training session Jonny Wilkinson damaged ligaments when he rolled his ankle with nobody near him. We did not know whether his tournament was over before it had begun.

By lunchtime the shockwaves were being felt all over the rugby world. News spread like wildfire that England's talismanic fly-half, the player whose extra-time drop-goal had won the World Cup for his country on his last appearance in the tournament, was injured. The consensus seemed to be that if England had little chance before of defending their title, our prospects were now considerably worse.

I did not quite go along with that however as I felt from the warm-up games that Olly Barkley was actually our in-form fly-half. Of greater concern to me was what I thought was dreadful preparation. I found it baffling that we did not seem to have done any analysis on our opening Pool A opponents, the United States, nor plan what to do against them. The reason, according to coach Brian Ashton, was that they did not have a defensive structure, that they jumped out of the line. I disagreed. I looked at the tapes of them in action and saw what I thought was a good defensive structure, with nobody jumping out of the line.

One way and another I thought it was a poor training week. We literally spent very little time with Brian in which he said he wanted us to play a simple game in order not to give anything at all away ahead of what everyone expected to be the pool decider against South Africa six days later. Brian told us to think up some really simple moves ourselves. I felt he should have imposed himself far more, walked into the team room and said, 'Right, this is how we play, this is how we do this, that and the other.' He did none of that.

Stade Félix-Bollaert, Lens, 8 September 2007

England 28–10 USA

In a word, unacceptable. Our campaign got off to a winning start but we muddled our way to victory. America finished the stronger and the second half was a 7–7 draw. We did not even get a bonus point. It was embarrassing. From my point of view I made two or three mistakes that I never normally make. My kicking wasn't great and I was pretty angry with myself.

I also felt a growing resentment towards the management. It saddened me the way that we had gone into our shells and also the way that I felt Brian had not coached us as he knew how. When you have coached a certain way with enormous success for twenty-five years surely you don't go and change it in the most important hour of your career. We were not understanding what we were trying to do. The backs were not getting quick ball, the forwards were standing in the way of us all the time. There was no structure, no accuracy, no clarity to our game.

Not until the Americans, a team of predominantly amateur players, lost a guy to the sin bin after half an hour did we break down their defence. Despite a 75 per cent territorial advantage we couldn't get a thing going until Josh Lewsey and Tom Rees combined to take the ball deep into the US 22, it was recycled and I kicked to the left corner for Jason Robinson to catch and dot down. Five minutes later, with the opposition still short of a man, Ben Kay put Olly Barkley over for try number 2 and a 21–3 half-time lead.

When Tom Rees added the third try from a quick free kick ten minutes after the restart to extend the margin to 27 points, that should have been that. With half an hour to get the fourth and final try that we needed for a bonus point, it should have been a matter of course. Ordinarily we would have relaxed and let our game flow. With no structure however, all we succeeded in doing was losing our way. Our line-out went to pot and everything else followed. Even before Lawrence Dallaglio was shown the yellow card for killing the ball three minutes from the end of normal time, America had taken control.

The final indignity, we thought, came when American replacement prop Matekitonga Moeakiola barged his way over our try line. Only it got even worse after the game had finished. Phil Vickery, our captain and a guy who does not have a malicious bone in his body, was charged with a deliberate trip on Paul Emerick. Phil had been wrong-footed, tried to reposition himself and only succeeded in catching the American centre on his knee. No way was there any intent involved but he was suspended for two matches.

When we got back to our hotel the players were very down. I sat up with Olly Barkley, who had been our best player, until half past two in the morning, talking about what had happened and how we could put it right against the Springboks. By the time we finished we had come up with a gameplan we believed would work. The question was whether we could convince the coaches to implement it.

Given that 90 per cent of our mistakes against America had come in attack we basically decided to take our attack out of the game. We knew there was no point trying to run against South Africa, who had stuck eight tries on Samoa in winning their opener 59–7, as we did not have the structure in place to do that. Attack you have to work on, you have to have practised, which we had not done to anything like the standard required to unlock a side like the Springboks, with an established and well organised rush defence.

So we devised a different plan centred around kicking and being far more streetwise. The idea was to follow the example set by Argentina in beating France in the opening game of the tournament: have our forwards meet South Africa head on and win us good ball with which we could pepper their back three with hanging kicks. The theory was that neither Percy Montgomery, Bryan Habana nor J. P. Pietersen were great under the high ball. Bombard them but accompany the aerial attack with a ground offensive. Get in their faces, give them no time or space to move.

In our first training session of the new week disaster struck again. Olly tore an abductor muscle and was ruled out of the game. With

Jonny Wilkinson still unavailable England had no fit specialist fly-half and no recognised goal kicker. The decision not to pick Toby Flood in the squad had come back to haunt Brian, and would require a late summons. Another rethink followed and at five o'clock I saw Andy Farrell in the team room and he told me that he had just had an hour's meeting with Brian and that he was now playing fly-half. I was gobsmacked. I had played international rugby at 10, Farrell had not even played one game of club rugby in the position. I phoned Brian and told him that I wanted to be at 10 controlling the game, that I wanted the ball in my hand early doors.

Brian seemed to me to be in a state of confusion. When I joined the rest of the squad for dinner that evening one of the lads told me that at ten o'clock on Monday night I had not been in the team at all. Apparently Brian had met with Olly and told him that he was going with him and Farrell at 10 and 12. In which case, by the morning Brian had changed his mind because he had Olly at 10 and me at 12, prior to Olly pulling up in training. When I heard that I thought of packing my bags and going home. The squad seemed to me to be rudderless. And people wondered why our communication was so poor on the field.

At Brian's press conference on the day before the South Africa game the newspaper boys pressed him about who exactly would be wearing the number 10 shirt. Brian tried to avoid giving a definitive answer, saying he saw both me and Andy Farrell as 'inside backs, mixing and matching during the game'. Pushed further, he eventually said: 'As an educated guess, Catt will play 10 and Farrell 12.'

It was hard to believe that this was the day before England played South Africa in the biggest match played by either country in four years. It was a match of enormous significance, given that whoever lost seemed likely, at least at that point, to have to take the southern hemisphere route through to the knock-out stages – Australia in the quarters, New Zealand in the semis – while the victor got Wales and either France or Argentina.

I had assumed that on the morning after the USA game we would have woken to find a sheet posted under the door containing all the moves for the South Africa game. There was nothing. We didn't even have any video clips. A week earlier I couldn't understand why we had not trained as we were going to play against South Africa. A week on, I felt the training sessions were no more instructive. I came up with the formation myself. Nobody even spoke to me about how I felt about calling the shots.

I found it very sad, not so much for myself, as it was my fourth World Cup, but for some of the others who were experiencing the tournament for the first time and were finding nothing to enjoy. They should have been buzzing, on top of the world, yet 99 per cent of the squad seemed to be unhappy. I didn't want to feel like that at this stage of my career.

It was my turn to face the media and I put on a brave face. I agreed that I was definitely facing one of the biggest challenges of my career. 'But how can I react other than positively?' I said. 'Whether it's playing with Faz at 12 or Olly at 10, it's more or less the same job that I've got. Faz and I have just got to control the game. We haven't been able to do much together in training. We've had one team run, that's about it. But we are the main decision-makers. It's down to us to put the team in the right parts of the pitch.

'We need to all pull together and make sure we understand where we're going and what we're doing. We are all realistic. It's going to be a massive ask, especially with the performances of the last three weeks. In that time we haven't performed as we know we're capable. But it is international rugby. It is a World Cup pool game and it is against South Africa. Believe me, we'll give it a good thrash. We are massive underdogs but we'll give it a very good go. We've still got a fantastic group of players. It's whether we perform on the day. A lot of individual errors against America have got to be wiped out because if we do that against South Africa the Habanas and Pietersens of this world are going to destroy us.'

Stade de France, Paris, 14 September 2007

England 0–36 South Africa

My worst fears could not prepare me for what unfolded on what turned into a night of almost unimaginable horror. It was as if it had been a car crash waiting to happen. All the concern expressed over the lack of a recognised goal kicker and we did not even win a kickable penalty. For the first time since the Tour from Hell in 1998 England did not register a point. The score in tries was three-nil. In every other sense it was a thrashing.

After the game I was fuming. John Wells, our forwards coach, had partially explained our poor performance against America the week before by saying we had spent too much time preparing for South Africa. Yet we had no gameplan, no strike moves, nothing. You've got to practise to prepare and we hardly practised anything. I felt that none of the sessions were thought out. We had done no meaningful analysis on South Africa, we went into the game with no direction, no shape and, consequently, with no belief. It was the worst week I had known in international rugby.

As a group of players we had tried to get ourselves going before the game, telling each other we could pull a performance out of the bag. But you can't do that with just good words. You need a structure, an idea. We had no pace to break them down whatsoever and there was nothing I felt I could have done on the pitch to change anything. Every time we looked up there were four South African guys back and I was thinking, where the flipping hell am I going to kick this ball without putting it down somebody's throat who's going to return it eighty metres back down the pitch? We couldn't exert any pressure on them. They just dropped back deep to field our kicks. And we didn't have any numbers to run against them because we were chucking five, six, seven, eight guys into rucks to try to win the bloody ball.

The Boks went ahead in the sixth minute when their right winger Pietersen broke up the short side from a line-out midway in his own half. He linked with his scrum-half Fourie du Preez who made ground before passing inside for flanker Juan Smith to go over. The only scoring opportunity we had all game came nine minutes later when I sliced a drop goal attempt. It might have appeared a waste of a good attacking platform to go for the posts but I had only hooker Mark Regan and a winger on the far touchline outside me. Before the ball came back from the ruck I yelled to Shaun Perry that I didn't want it but it seemed he didn't hear me as he threw it to me anyway.

By half-time the score was 20–0, Pietersen having again linked up with Du Preez, who was having a dominant game, to score in the final act of the half. Although we fared better in the second forty minutes the contest was already over. Du Preez made absolutely sure, scampering free to send Pietersen over for his second, ten minutes from time. A late penalty by Percy Montgomery gave him eight goals out of eight on the night.

We left Stade de France in sombre mood. Although our scrum actually fared okay, only Jason Robinson individually had really done himself justice and his game ended prematurely when he pulled a hamstring on the hour. Jason was carried off to a standing ovation from an 80,000 crowd assuming that they were witnessing the final episode in a wonderful rugby career. The rest of us were given no such reception at the end. At least half the stadium was filled with England supporters. On the final whistle many of them vented their displeasure.

A crisis meeting of the whole squad was called for the following morning, and I went in tired, having hardly slept. This meeting would later be credited for turning round our campaign. It began with a question from Brian. Why had we called 'off-the-top ball' at our second line-out? It was, he said, the wrong decision. I disagreed and I said so, arguing that it wasn't that our options were wrong, it was that we didn't execute anything. Others agreed. There was a lot of frustration in the room. As players, it was we who had gone out onto the field without any weapons, we who had got it in the neck for not performing. But I felt we had not been given sufficient structure to work with.

I've always said that I can take losing a game as long as we are creating, then it is down to individuals to finish things off. But against South Africa we didn't create anything. When the meeting broke up six of us got in a huddle to discuss strategy going forward.

From behind me Brian said, 'I can't believe that I've got a team of players here which don't play with width.'

I spun round on my heels. 'Brian, you've got a team here which wants to play with width but you're not coaching us to play with any,' I said. 'You need to coach the way you know how to.'

Having blown off some steam I headed into Paris for a Saturday night out with Ali and the Dallaglios and Farrells. It was a night we all needed and we had a brilliant time. The squad then came together for a team social the following evening in a local pub in Versailles, following a positive meeting involving Brian and the decision-makers – players who wear shirts numbered 8, 9, 10 and 12. Between us we devised a playing system, though it was Olly Barkley who came up with pretty well all the moves.

On the Monday we began practising what we had preached, then again the following day, making sure that every crease had been ironed out and everyone knew exactly what was happening. By Wednesday the session was very good. For what felt like the first time in the campaign there was a playing structure in place that we could hang our hats on. The structure from the coaches was also very good. John Wells took a little bit, so too Mike Ford. Brian was a lot more involved too.

The week leading into our third game against Samoa was not all sweetness and light however. On the Sunday morning after the South Africa game Jon Callard and Mike Ford had appeared at a press conference. JC had said a 'radical rethink' was required in England's kicking game. Ford went further, saying that England lacked world-class players. He also made some less than flattering observations about Andy Farrell and myself.

'A year out of the game has done him [Farrell] no favours,' said Ford. 'He is getting to grips with it but it is probably a bit too late, with his age, to be where he wants to be.' About me he said: 'Mike Catt has not played 10 in an international for a long while and you can't just expect him to step in and put in a first-class performance.'

I was pretty annoyed when I read it and Andy was particularly angry as he considers Mike a close friend. He had every right to feel the way he did. It is unacceptable to say that sort of stuff. We don't sound off in the press during a tournament that the coaches aren't up to it. You just can't turn round and say we've got no world-class players. That's rubbish, especially as we all knew what the problems were.

Mike apologised to me personally and to Andy Farrell as well. He then stood up in front of the whole squad and said sorry. For the next few days he walked around like a dog with its tail between its legs, which did none of us any good as Ford provides so much of the energy in the coaching team.

My mood was not improved twenty-four hours later when, after having had 'Happy birthday' sung to me by 3,000 locals watching us train, Brian marked my thirty-sixth birthday by informing me that I was one of seven players being dropped for a game which England had to win to stay alive in the tournament. There was no place for me on the bench either.

I enquired why and was told I was not in the team because I was not sharp enough and that Brian had preferred Farrell on the bench as he considered him a superior defender. 'Brian,' I said, 'I do not have a problem with that assessment but you need somebody on the bench who can come on and make the play to help win the game for you if need be.' He thought about it, then stood by his original decision.

Stade de la Beaujoire, Nantes, 22 September 2007

England 44–22 Samoa

The team bus pulled into the stadium parking lot and I looked up at the stands. Would this be where our World Cup dream died? It was a fleeting thought which I quickly dismissed. Yes, a defeat would almost certainly seal our fate and yes, we had changed half the team which seemed to me to be a knee-jerk reaction. But the structure put in place in training had given us a collective belief that we would beat Samoa. Jonny Wilkinson was fit at last, so too Olly Barkley, and there was a steely determination in the eyes of everyone as we headed into the ground. As in Paris six days earlier, there were thousands of England fans in attendance in Brittany. It was humbling to see such extraordinary support, especially as we had let everyone down against South Africa. This time would be different. It had to be.

Martin Corry led the boys out and the look on his face left little doubt that England meant business. He was totally focused, a fearsome sight to put even the Samoan Manu war chant in the shade. It was a statement of intent which he backed up with a try within eighty seconds of kick-off. Simon Shaw charged down an attempted clearance by Samoan fly-half Eliota Fuimaono-Sapolu, the bounce of the ball kicked away from the onrushing Joe Worsley.

Typical of our luck. But no, Nick Easter was there, then Matt Stevens who took it on before Martin Corry finished it off.

It was the ideal start and Jonny's boot put us 10 points clear before the sixth minute was out. A week before against the Boks we had trailed 10–0. We had also done so, for that matter, four years earlier against Samoa in the World Cup. Our lead didn't last. Two lapses of discipline allowed Loki Crichton to peg back the margin to 4 points. Again England regrouped. Jonny struck twice to punish Samoa for not rolling away at rucks and, in the thirty-third minute, threaded a grubber kick through the Islanders' midfield for Paul Sackey to score.

At 23–6 the match really should have been in the bag. But in the next sixteen minutes we hit the self-destruct button. Our tactical kicking game crashed. We started missing touches and giving the Samoans opportunities to run back at us. When the video ref awarded Junior Polu a highly dubious try seven minutes into the second half our lead was cut to 26–22. I was sitting in the stand and heard one frustrated fan yell at our bench: 'Brian, sort it out!'

On such moments are teams defined. Survive and it gives you the confidence to escape when you locate trouble again. Get affected by the situation and the panic is greater the next time. Our defence held firm and Andy Gomarsall, who was outstanding all game at scrum-half, marshalled us away from danger. Jonny, refusing to let some errant kicking out of hand subdue him, popped over a drop-goal to reach 1,000 points in international rugby, and then nailed a penalty from halfway.

We had weathered the storm and in stoppage time Martin Corry and Paul Sackey put icing on the cake with two superb tries. Dan Hipkiss, a late replacement, made ground up the left, Andy

Gomarsall threw out a long ball to Josh Lewsey and Corry was put in on an inside pass from Sackey. It had me on my feet and I was back up a few minutes later when Jonny checked inside in an attack from the right and, quick as a flash, Sackey was there on his shoulder to take the pass and scorch away for his second. Shape, structure, execution, it was all there. At last. At bloody last.

None of which did my chances of getting back into the team much good for our final pool game against Tonga, who had pushed South Africa hard in Lens and only lost 30–25 because the very last bounce of the ball went right into touch rather than left into the hands of a Tongan attacker. I had said all along that my overriding priority was for England to be successful and that remained true but I wanted so much to play a part in what would be a do-or-die clash back in Paris. The winner would go to Marseilles for a quarter-final against Australia, the loser would go home.

Sadly, I had also pulled something in the back of my right knee playing against South Africa and had not trained in the build-up to Samoa. So when Brian took me to one side shortly before he was due to announce the team for Tonga I knew what was coming. 'Catty,' he said, 'I haven't forgotten about you but because you didn't train all last week I'm going to go with the same team.'

I tried to change his mind, arguing that when England were in that hole at 26–22, really struggling to get out of our own half, he didn't have anyone on the bench who could come on and change things. 'This is where you need the balance of a left- and right-footer at 10 and 12,' I said. He didn't reply.

It would have been easy to spit out my dummy at that moment. But I knew there was still a big role for me to play. If not in front of the cameras, then behind the scenes. We had again done no worth-while analysis of our next opponents. We had got together on the Monday before leaving our camp in La Baule to return to Versailles and Brian merely said that the kickers needed to work on getting out of our own half. That was basically it.

I felt our back line play was terrible, yet there was no backs meeting. Almost every time Jonny caught the ball he seemed to stand still, yet no mention was made of it. I had to tell him and that is not my role. Understandably, he didn't particularly appreciate hearing it from me. It's not really for me to tell anyone else how to play the game, especially a world-class player like Jonny. On the train north, I sought out Brian for a chat and gave him what amounted to a twenty-minute presentation based on the information I believed the boys needed. I said to him that he had to start addressing things like that. He thanked me. I said, 'No problem. If you're not going to pick me, let me help. I will help you, I will do this stuff for you. Never mind my individual gripes, I want us to win.'

I then went to see John Wells after we arrived back at the Trianon Palace and said, 'Wellsy I don't want to step on anyone's toes here but we need this sort of analysis. Can I just talk to you about it and show you a couple of video clips?' My concern was with the forwards, a couple of whom were going from one ruck wide right to another wide left when there was no need for them to do so. They just needed to fill in and conserve their energy, sit back and wait for the ball to come to them, rather than chase it around the pitch. It was such a simple point but it needed to be brought to the players' attention. And I felt that if we could get such organisation sorted out it would give 10 and 12 far more options. John Wells listened and the following day used two of my clips. It then went straight into our training. Of course people were still going to get it wrong sometimes, but at least it had been drawn to everyone's attention and we were at last accountable if we were in the wrong place.

Parc des Princes, Paris, 28 September 2007

England 36–20 Tonga

It was about winning the game and staying alive. That was what mattered. For the second game running the options were stark. Lose and we were on a flight home. And this time it would not be on the plane which British Airways had rebranded 'Hope and Glory' for our flight out to France. Neither hope nor glory would be making the return trip.

Twenty minutes into the game that seemed a likely scenario. Tonga, whom England had beaten 101–10 the last time we met in the 1999 World Cup, had come out of the traps fast and proved that their wins over Samoa and the USA, not to mention their narrow 30–25 defeat to South Africa, were absolutely no fluke. These boys like to hit but they also like to throw the ball about.

Before the game Epi Taione, who has played for Newcastle and Sale, claimed poetically that 'all the angels in heaven' were willing his Tonga team to win. I guess it was just another take on the tedious 'everybody hates England' line. Nevertheless I can well imagine that a good proportion of the rugby world was on its feet when Taione burst past Jonny Wilkinson before offloading out of the tackle to his midfield partner Sukanaivalu Hufanga, who had enough pace and power to beat three white shirts to the line.

Trailing 10–3 was not the ideal start but England did not panic. Unlike against South Africa when we fell behind and the wheels rather came off, we had come into this game with a degree of belief and, as important, a playing structure which the boys understood. The team's growing confidence showed itself when Tonga conceded a penalty fifteen metres out from their own line. Jonny picked up the ball and, detecting that the Tongans were resigned to him going for goal, instead delivered a kick with pin-point accuracy into the right corner for Paul Sackey to catch on his knees and dot down.

It was outstanding skill by both men and Paul made it four tries in two games on the stroke of half-time when a Tongan move broke down in our 22, the ball ricocheted loose and he ran it back all of eighty metres for the score. All tournament people had raved about the finishing of the New Zealand, South African and Australian wings. Here was an Englishman to add to the list. Paul Sackey is a true athlete. He says he clocked 10.7 seconds for the 100 metres as a teenager. The Tongans certainly couldn't live with his pace.

England led 19–10 at half-time and put the game out of reach when Mathew Tait latched onto a pass from Nick Easter to score a third try on the hour. I was so pleased for him because he is a massive talent but had not seen much ball during the tournament. I was equally delighted for Andy Farrell when he went through two tackles to score his first England try in the seventieth minute.

Farrell had come off the bench to replace Olly Barkley and had a really good game. Given all the stick he had taken since coming over from rugby league, I was genuinely chuffed for him. He's a massively passionate guy and he tries his heart out every minute he is with England. I, for one, feel comfortable with him around but he knew his only way to answer critics who do not see all the hard graft he puts in, was to deliver on the pitch. He did that at Parc des Princes and good on him for that.

It was a shame we allowed Tonga a try with the last move of the game as it distorted the scoreline. I felt 36–13 was a more accurate reflection of the balance of play. Then again, we were disappointed with our defence at times, with simple tackles missed, and there was a realisation in the changing room afterwards that we would go no further in the tournament if we didn't tighten up. But we were through to the quarter-finals and not any old game; waiting for us were our old friends, Australia.

17

ALLEZ LES BLANCS!

World Cup quarter-final: Marseilles, 6 October 2007

England 12–10 Australia

There are certain days in life which catch you totally by surprise and are all the sweeter for that. This was one of those for me. Not only had I not seen the result coming, I had not even been selected to play in the game. But how many times in my career have I said a week is a long time in rugby? On the Wednesday before the game I was officially told I would not be playing and so was making plans to pick Evie up from school the following Monday, unable to see where a performance capable of toppling Australia would come from. Three days later, basking in the glory of an amazing victory, I was trying to find the words to tell my five-year-old daughter that I would not be home for another fortnight.

The drama for me began on Tuesday, a day after we had taken the TGV south out of Paris to Marseilles, the capital of the Provence-Alpes-Côtes d'Azur region. The city does not hold great memories for England, having lost both Test matches played there against France. The most recent, less than two months earlier, had been the final evidence many people needed that we were a team unable to

301

progress beyond the quarter-finals. We would find out soon enough, but first I had to make the team.

Having been out of the match squad since South Africa I was becoming increasingly restless and after training I confronted Brian. I'd had enough of carrying tackle pads and being an afterthought. I wanted to know what my fate was for the weekend and when he told me I was not going to be involved at all again for the third consecutive game I went potty. I unloaded two weeks of frustration first on him then on Mike Ford. I told Brian it seemed to me that he had one rule for me and one for everyone else. He had played me against South Africa in a completely different game plan to the one I enjoy playing, and in a position I had not played for ages. He had then dropped me like a hot coal and changed England's game plan to the way I really enjoy playing, and picked someone ahead of me because, he said, my defence was not up to scratch.

'Brian, you have never before spoken to me about defence in your life,' I said. 'It's always been about attack, attack. I can't work out what is going on any more. You also said to me before the Samoa game that I was not looking sharp enough. Barks and Wilko haven't looked their sharpest over the last two games either. I'm so frustrated, I can't tell you.'

I went back to my room satisfied at having said my piece, yet also convinced that I would never play for England again and that I would be left with the shocking memory of the South Africa game as my final cap. I dialled Ali, needing to hear a sympathetic voice. Evie picked up and said she wanted me to come home. She was fed up with her daddy being away. It had been too long. She got tearful and I promised I'd see her on Monday.

The following morning England's line-up was released to the media, with Andy Farrell at inside-centre and Olly Barkley named as his bench back-up. At Brian's press conference he was asked whether I had fallen off his radar. 'Mike Catt is still very much part of the overall picture,' came the reply. 'He does a hell of a lot of work at the moment with me behind the scenes in terms of developing game strategy. He's not out of the picture at all. We just felt this was the best option for the game.'

An hour later Brian was having to choose another option. Barkley had been clattered by Phil Vickery in a non-contact session and sustained a dead leg. Ten minutes later Farrell pulled a calf muscle while chasing a kick. At the end of the session Brian came to me and said I would start if Andy was unfit. They would know more the following morning when he underwent a clinical review and an MRI scan. Morning came, I was in. For the first time since the 2003 World Cup semi-final I would get to start a game for England alongside Jonny Wilkinson.

My emotions were all over the place. I had stockpiled a lot of bitterness over the way I felt I had been treated and yet suddenly I found myself in the line-up for a fourth World Cup quarter-final, twelve years on from my first, also against Australia, in Cape Town. I had to switch into positive mode and, frankly, I found it difficult.

On Friday morning I was presented to the media at a packed press conference in the breakfast room of our hotel in down-town Marseilles. It was the last place I wanted to be. Sitting right next to Brian, I could not bring myself to be all sweetness and light.

'Brian didn't have a choice, he had to pick me,' I said. 'It's been pretty disappointing personally for me over the last four weeks.' Was I surprised I had not played with Jonny in four years? 'It hasn't been my choice, believe me. I was out of the team and not selected. Other people had opportunities rather than myself. People have said we are the optimum 10–12 combination but it's not for me to say why it hasn't happened before now in this tournament.'

'I admit I did not perform well against South Africa but I have never seen a world-class player play two bad games in a row,' I continued. My inference was clear. I felt there had been too much chopping and changing in team selection during the tournament. I appreciate there had been injuries but when I came in for Farrell I was the twenty-fifth change in five matches.

I paused for breath then started again. 'Against South Africa we just had no structure in our game,' I said. 'We didn't know what we were doing. The understanding was not there. You put certain structures in a game so people understand where to go, where to stand, what to do, and they open up numerous opportunities for where to attack. Against South Africa we didn't have those options. We weren't getting guys playing to their strengths, whereas now the distribution is starting to get there. Guys are running good lines, guys are scoring tries. There has been a complete change in the gameplan and a huge shift in the understanding of it. A hell of a lot of water has passed under the bridge, a lot of talks and discussions have gone on, and we seem to be back on track. We're going in the right direction, but whether we are as far as we want to be I'm not really sure. Had it been in place earlier we would definitely be ahead of where we are at the moment. We are huge underdogs.'

In my column in the *Sunday Telegraph* the day after the game I admitted that 'I was not the only glass-half-empty man in the England team room before this game. If we are honest, most of us were fully expecting to be on the train home today.' It was the truth. The way things had progressed throughout the tournament a lot of the guys really thought we were going out. It wasn't meant to sound defeatist, I didn't mean it that way. We were all there to win a game of rugby but we knew we weren't firing on all cylinders. How remarkable then that the Australians should later say that we blew them away in the first thirty minutes.

There had been a couple of causes for optimism. First, there was all the hot air coming out of Australia, talking up the Wallabies and down the English. Of all people, the chief executive of the Australian Rugby Union led the way. John O'Neill said that when it came to sport 'all Australians hated England'. Lote Tuqiri, the Wallabies wing, added that Jason Robinson was England's only world-class back.

That was helpful but not as much as the discovery of a potential weakness in the Wallabies' game which the management believed was down to the easy run they had enjoyed in their pool, where only Wales had tested them at all. Having previously criticised the coaches over the quality of their analysis, this was a fantastic spot. It was John Wells who detected that Australia were becoming a bit lacklustre in the way they worked around rucks; that they had become so used to quick ball that their workrate had dropped off a little bit. The Aussies are such a well drilled side with not many weak links in their set up. So this was priceless information. The forwards poured all their focus into exploiting this apparent chink in their armour, while fine-tuning their set-scrummage. If we were going to beat the Wallabies we all knew it would need to be a bully-boy job. We would have to disrupt them at first phase and be a lot more streetwise.

The local weather forecast told of possible storms on match day. It was not the only prediction to be hopelessly wrong. Alex Evans, the Wallabies skill coach, said that Australia should win by 30 points. In the event there was hardly a cloud in the sky over Stade Vélodrome and the boys from Down Under did not win, let alone win well. History may well remember it as England's greatest World Cup comeback performance.

Looking back, I think the turning point for me was when I confronted Brian Ashton and Mike Ford in midweek. Nothing had materially changed but I had held nothing back. If I wasn't to play any further part in England's campaign, at least I knew I had told them exactly how I felt. Nobody could say, 'Why didn't you say something?' I had said everything and by doing so I had made peace with myself. My whole attitude changed. I still expected nothing but I was back to hoping for everything, and when I was then called into the side I stepped up with an incredibly positive frame of mind. I was absolutely buzzing.

On the morning of the game I was in the zone I wanted to be in. I had that adrenaline, that buzz about me that it means I'm spot on where I need to be mentally. Unlike before the South Africa match, when I was a complete mental mess, not knowing what to do, how to approach it, not feeling comfortable, I had a clear focus on how best to beat Australia.

In the changing room beforehand everyone was calm. This was our shot at redemption and nobody needed to be told. Phil Vickery and some of the others were stressing defence, defence, defence. 'Make the hits, stop him here, stop him there.' It was of course vital that we kept the Aussies on the back foot but I felt there needed to be more of an emphasis on us getting onto the front foot, so I started talking. As Stade Vélodrome filled up, I stood up and started preaching positivity.

'Boys, let's worry about what we're going to do to them. When Nick Easter picks up from the base and goes, be there in support, look to go wide, make sure we distribute right, then make sure we win that ruck out wide. Fuck what Australia do. Let's decide what we do.'

That was my mindset. If we just defended I knew that every time we looked up they would have three men back, just as South Africa had on that awful night at Stade de France three weeks earlier. We did not want to kick it to the Aussie back three any more than we did to the Springboks, not to Chris Latham, Lote Tuqiri and Adam Ashley-Cooper. The Wallabies management were so confident in the trio that they had dropped to the bench the tournament's leading try scorer, Drew Mitchell.

I spoke to Jonny Wilkinson. 'Mate, we have to play three or four phases before we kick. We've got to bring them up. If we don't, we're kicking straight down their throats and Latham is going to kick it seventy metres back.' He nodded. If this was going to be my last international I was going to go and do what I'm good at – and, more importantly, what I think this group of players is best at. We were going to go out and play, for ourselves

307

and for our amazing supporters, whom we knew we owed a big performance.

We caught Australia cold. From the start we were all over them. We hit them hard in the set-piece and at the breakdown, but it was the speed with which we moved the ball away and out wide that they had not anticipated. They did not expect an England team to go wide first. Lewis Moody broke blind and just failed to get the ball away to Nick Easter. I escaped but knocked-on attempting an offload. Lewis again, then Simon Shaw, sent runners through gaps. The final pass was missing but we were playing rugby. Little grubber kicks here, chips to the corners, phase play. The footwork of Jonny and Mat Tait, pulling two or three players one way, then putting team-mates into holes. All the time making the Wallabies think. Taking them out of their comfort zone, taking them into a mindset they had not prepared for.

Then there was the set-scrum. We had complete control, to an almost frightening degree. Matt Dunning, the Aussie loose-head prop, could not even stand up on his side. Andrew Sheridan absolutely munched him. Five of the first six scrums were collapsed. Yet in echoes of the 2003 final against Australia, when referee André Watson penalised England's dominant scrum, ref Alain Rolland awarded the first two scrum penalties to the Wallabies. Even more unbelievably, we were behind at half-time. Australia led 10–6 and had scored the only try, started and finished by Tuqiri in the thirty-sixth minute.

It was daylight robbery. But our concern was not so much with our gameplan as with our execution. Four times we had returned from the opposition 22 without a point to show for it. Seated calmly in the changing room the point was made, more than once, that we had to get the scoreboard moving. At no time did I think we would lose. I don't think any of us did. But because Australia's back three had not pushed up at all we had tried to play a little bit too much in our own half, and had got a taste for it. If we were going to continue playing like that we had to be more clinical.

Eight minutes into the second half we were laying siege to the Aussie line. I thought I was in, after our forwards had battered theirs in another scrum, but I could not hold a pass from Jonny thrown hard at my chest. Our pack wouldn't take no for an answer and set up camp until they drew a penalty which Jonny slotted. On the hour we were ahead. Again pressure at the set scrum told, again Jonny did the business.

With fifteen minutes to go I took a double hit to the side of my neck and to my mouth which would have cost me my front teeth had I not been wearing a gumshield. For the first time in my career I experienced a 'stinger', bruising to some of the nerves coming out of the neck and going into the shoulder. It can last for a few moments or for months. The physios brought me off and, true enough, I don't remember much of the final quarter. Stirling Mortlock had a kick to win the game for Australia, five minutes into stoppage time, from wide out just inside our half. I can't recall it. What I do vaguely remember is Phil Vickery hugging me on the bench soon after, saying, 'I can't believe it, Catty, I can't believe it.'

If anyone deserved the win it was Vickery. It had been tough on him being banned for two games for his trip against the United States, which might have been dangerous but was so obviously unintentional. To then be left out of the team to play Tonga, when he is captain of the squad, seemed like a further kick in the teeth. One night, over a game of pool, we agreed that we both had that I-wanna-go-home feeling.

But that's what makes World Cups unique. Things evolve. There are highs and there are lows during a tournament played out over seven pressure-filled weeks. You've got to strap yourself in for the ride. You can't just walk away, even though, heaven knows, there are times when the temptation is there. What kept this squad strong through good and bad was that we were, and remain, a close-knit group. Contrary to pre-tournament fears, there were no divisive influences, no animosity towards one another, just a bunch of brilliant guys.

At no time was that more true than when Andy Farrell was getting hammered in the press after being initially selected to start against Australia. The criticism was harsh and what hurt him most was that it was driven by former players, like Matt Dawson. The poor bugger didn't deserve it and the whole squad felt that way. Dawson is a great friend of mine but he used to get really upset when someone bagged him. Rightly so. It particularly grates when a former player slags off a current one, because they know what it feels like. After the game Nick Easter went on TV and, borrowing Nick Faldo's line from his 1992 Open Championship victory speech, thanked the press from 'the heart of his bottom'.

The truth is that as a team we had deserved pretty much all the criticism that had come our way. But as I sat on board a luxury cruiser in Marseilles' Vieux Port that night, sipping a beer and watching France beat tournament favourites New Zealand on a giant screen, along with 25,000 disbelieving others on the quayside, only one thing bothered me. How I was going to explain to Evie that I would not be home on Monday. I had a semi-final against the host nation to play.

It is amazing how one win had wiped the slate clean. Before Australia we had been a team living so far in the shadow of 2003 that we could barely see daylight. Every question fired at us referred to the past. Every performance was compared with the previous World Cup generation. Then we went and beat the Wallabies and the rugby world seemed to fall off its axis. Old rules and old judgments no longer applied. Yes, England had endured a torrid four years since that glorious night in Sydney, but New Zealand had beaten almost everything that moved in that same period and where had that got the two nations? England were through to the last four. The Kiwis were back home blaming the referee.

The only thing for certain was that having turned the corner in the tumultuous way England had, we were not about to settle for that. We knew we could beat France because we had done so in the Six Nations earlier in the year and should have done at Twickenham as recently as August. Okay, we had been well beaten by them in Marseilles the following week but we had none of the self-belief or structure to our game then that we had suddenly come upon, ironically in the very same stadium.

My mobile phone rang. 'Daddy, you're a winner!' shrieked an excited voice in my ear as we got off the train from Marseilles and headed for our new base in Neuilly-sur-Seine, a largely residential area ten minutes from the centre of Paris. It was Evie. It was also

Monday and I had told her I would be home. She had watched the game in a pub with Ali in Shepperton and the two of them were still flying as high as kites. 'Don't worry about today, daddy. I will see you very soon.'

Just when I thought life couldn't get better Evie had lifted me even higher. It was an absolutely brilliant call to get and I rang off with a smile on my face as wide as the Champs Elysées. As we drove around the imposing Arc de Triomphe it struck me that once again I had landed on my feet. One week a squad also-ran, the next preparing to become the first England player to start in a third World Cup semi-final.

My outlook became even more rosy when I sat down with Brian Ashton on the Tuesday to analyse the French. Where in the early pool matches there had been little or no analysis of the opposition, this time Brian had it all done. He had put a video together. He was on top of everything. He seemed like a different person. He was a lot more relaxed, his head was firmly on his shoulders.

Only time would tell if the preparation would translate itself into a performance to silence all of France and sweep us into another World Cup final; or whether the players would become over-confident and history would remember the Australia result as just a glorious one-off. But at that point in time it felt good. We had responded to an extreme test of our collective character. As a group of players and coaches we had been to the brink of humiliation together. We had come close to becoming the first world champions to fail to make the knock-out stages. But we had pulled back from the edge, dug deep into our characters and found a way not only out of trouble, but to within eighty minutes of reaching the final.

It could even be argued that we arrived at the semi-final in better shape than we had in Australia four years before when we made hard work of getting past Wales and had emerged from that night in Brisbane with little momentum to take us into the semis. To my mind our quarter-final victory over Australia was an even better performance than the one we gave against them to win the final in Sydney, because then we were expected to win and it was just a matter of executing on the day. Here we had completely turned the form book on its head. I can't overstate how much belief that one performance instilled in the squad.

But it would still not be good enough to beat the French, I was sure of that, and I was slightly concerned that the coaches gave a lot of praise to the forwards for their scrummaging display, richly deserved though it was. I wouldn't have given them any. This was not a time to hand out bouquets, we needed to keep our edge, to get angry again.

For four years people all over England had mourned Martin Johnson's decision to retire straight after the last World Cup. With each passing day his reputation had grown and every subsequent England captain was judged against his towering achievements. Lawrence Dallaglio had taken on the job in 2004 before himself retiring in September of that year. Then Jason Robinson, until he too stepped out of the international glare in 2005. Martin Corry, Pat Sanderson, Jonny Wilkinson and myself all had a go after that. None of us was called the new Johnno.

Phil Vickery would not have wanted that tag either as he is very much his own man, yet Phil was becoming a huge factor in the resurgence of the England team. He kept us tight and, like Martin

Johnson before him, he only spoke when something needed to be said.

One such occasion was the eve of the semi-final. We had pitched our preparations just right all week. Not too much physical work, not too many compliments, but no loss of focus either. There had been no repeat of 1995 when we beat the Aussies in the quarter-finals, then went on the booze for three days. Mentally we were right there this time.

Phil Vickery stood up in our Friday night team meeting and told us what our backs-to-the-wall comeback had meant to him. How proud he was and how proud we should all be. The Marines, Portugal, Bath, Versailles, we had been through so many tough times together, he said. People doubting us, people writing us off, people thinking we were good for nothing, we had shown them. He started welling up and there was certainly a lump in my throat.

Then he got to what he really wanted to say. He said that if we lost to France our win over Australia, our victories over Tonga and Samoa, four weeks of fighting for our self-respect, would mean nothing. As he put it: 'It would mean we might as well not have bothered really.'

He spoke of his confidence that we were where we needed to be in terms of a gameplan to beat the French. It was our mindset that was his concern. 'You can have gameplans galore,' he said. 'If you don't have the physicality, the guts, the bravery, it means nothing.

'You need to be able to use your brains on the field but if you haven't the will to sacrifice yourself body and soul on the field tomorrow night, then nothing will work. People are going to have to find performances within themselves they never knew were there or else we will not have a chance. This is the opportunity of a lifetime and I don't want us to miss it. I want to go home and be remembered for having achieved something. It's down to us now. We've put the hard work in. Let's go and play. We're not going home.'

World Cup semi-final: Stade de France, Paris, 13 October 2007

England 14–9 France

The first thought that struck me was how quiet it was inside Stade de France. The host nation were playing a semi-final. They had put out favourites New Zealand seven days earlier and were playing an England side they had beaten twice as recently as August. Yet there was a tension in the air. I liked the way it felt.

In the changing room beforehand I turned to Jonny Wilkinson. I knew it was a big night for him in particular, with so much expected of him. Jonny mania had taken off at home again in a major way. I also knew that the longer we stayed in the game the stronger Jonny would get. The guy is so bloody fit, and so focused. He doesn't fatigue mentally or physically. 'Mate,' I said, 'semi-finals and finals are what you are born for. This is your stage. You know this is your stage. This is your time to stand up.'

Out onto the pitch and the crowd found its voice. Phil Vickery pulled us into a huddle after the anthems and screamed and shouted something but I couldn't make it out. It didn't matter. We all had a pretty good idea what he was thinking. The game kicked off, the first scrum went down and we were awarded a free kick. Play moved to the next ruck where Andy Gomarsall swivelled and hoisted a box kick high into the French 22.

The ball bounced once, then twice. Damien Traille, a centre picked out of position at full-back, appeared to dither, then slip. Josh Lewsey, haring up the left touchline, took full advantage. The pair of them challenged for the ball but it was Josh who got hands on it and dived over the line. With seventy-eight seconds on the clock we led 5–0.

From there things quietened down. Brian Ashton had told us that when he looked up on the scoreboard after twenty minutes he wanted the points to belong to us. After two minutes they did but we then started conceding silly penalties. Our accuracy of a week ago was not quite there. By half-time we trailed by two penalties from Lionel Beauxis. Jonny had yet to land a kick.

For the second week running we were behind at the mid-point but, as in Marseilles, I saw no need to panic. In the first twenty minutes we had been hanging because of the way France ran at us. I had looked at Mat Tait and said, 'This is going to be a long night.' But then they stopped doing that and started attempting drop-goals from the halfway line. I asked myself what the hell they were doing, but I certainly didn't complain.

It was like the 2003 semi-final all over again. That night in Sydney they had put their faith in a young fly-half, Frédéric Michalak, and he had folded under the pressure of the occasion. This time they had gone for another number 10 in Beauxis, with no experience of an occasion of this size. It was not all his fault. That win over the All Blacks, achieved with more than 200 French tackles, had evidently sapped the energy from their legs. Their forwards looked tired.

Still we had to win the game and that meant kicking far better than we had done in the first half. We really hadn't put France under any pressure, the bombs to the full-back had not worked and Gomarsall was perhaps trying to do too much himself. There was a period when we panicked a little bit but Jonny and I said, 'Right, let's just slow it down, this is where we want to go, let's do this instead.' It alleviated a bit of pressure and France finally conceded a penalty in their own half which Jonny landed to get himself off the mark.

Then Michalak came on for Beauxis, who had missed with three drop goal attempts from miles out, and tried to do everything himself. What he didn't do was put pressure on us by pinning the corners. We would have retaken the lead on the hour but Jonny struck the post with an attempted drop-goal as the game degenerated into a pretty terrible spectacle.

France took charge again and when Yannick Jauzion saw a mismatch in numbers out wide and kicked left it seemed we could go under. But Joe Worsley, who had conceded a penalty in stoppage time against Australia which had given the Wallabies a kick to win the quarter-final, came to the rescue. As Julien Bonnaire tapped the ball back inside to Vincent Clerc, Joe dived at the winger and just managed to get finger tips to his trailing leg and tap tackle him.

My groin was giving me grief so I gave way to Toby Flood in the last ten minutes. We were still behind and facing a real challenge to get out of our own half and into position for Jonny to hopefully do his business. Then Danny Hipkiss, a half-time replacement for Josh Lewsey, made a line-break and Jason Robinson continued the move before being caught high by French hooker Dimitri Szarzewski. Jonny stepped up and kicked the penalty.

He would later say that he was so nervous that he could see his heartbeat pounding through his shirt. Also that as he lined up the kick he thought of what I had said to him beforehand about this being his stage, his time. 'When Mike said that to me, I knew exactly what he meant,' Jonny wrote in his column in *The Times*. 'That there are a few key things about semi-final and later-stage rugby, that it was going to be a tight game and it was going to have to be finished properly. He was saying: that's your accountability and responsibility, to ensure that we are the team with a couple more points than them.'

The game was still not over. We led 11–9 and France refused to go quietly. Sébastien Chabal launched a bullocking run but was forced into touch by Toby Flood and Paul Sackey. Better still, in the course of being evicted from the pitch, 'the Caveman' had aimed an elbow at one of his tacklers and was penalised. Jonny kicked to touch, Martin Corry took the line-out and the team worked its way into position infield to give Jonny a shot at the posts.

The similarities with the zig-zag move we had executed to set Jonny up for his winning kick in the 2003 final were uncanny. Sir Clive Woodward had always stressed the importance of thinking correctly under pressure. That, he said, was what separated great teams from good. Under the greatest pressure we were doing that again. An England team which a month ago had been condemned as unfit for purpose. Just watching it gave me goosebumps; and that was before Jonny drilled the ball between the sticks.

Up in the stands Ali, my brother Doug and his wife Catherine were on their feet. England were through to another final and I was on the verge of becoming the oldest ever World Cup finalist. Yet as a squad we were strangely unemotional. I can only think that none of us realised what we had achieved, not just by beating the hosts in their own backyard, but with our whole resurgence. Our win had not been pretty but tournaments are about winning not putting on a show. 'Sometimes in sport things happen that just don't make sense,' Phil Vickery told the watching world. 'Today was one of those special days where the underdog rises up.'

I didn't want to pinch myself in case I was dreaming. None of us did. Everyone was asking how we had turned it around, nobody really had an answer. We had stuck together, we had dug in, we had fought and we had given nothing away. We had said, 'We are still the world champions. If you want our crown you are going to have to take it off us.' Australia and France had not done enough to do so.

We just played the game and did not worry about the occasion. We didn't get caught up in it being a semi-final, in the same way as, against Australia, we had not worried about it being a quarter. It was all about going out there and beating the team in front of us. We always believed that the further we went in the tournament the more the experience in the England squad would come to the fore, and that had proved correct. It had proved invaluable. Guys who knew what it took, and what it was like, to win a World Cup were able to tell the rest of the group to live for the moment; to concentrate on today and let tomorrow look after itself.

After the gain came the pain. I had a tear in my groin and feared I might be unable to start in a World Cup final due to injury for the second time. Josh Lewsey had already been ruled out, having torn a hamstring, and his place on the left wing given to Mark Cueto. I was determined to avoid the same fate. But because a scan had revealed a small amount of bleeding I was concerned about my participation. I didn't sleep well on Saturday or Sunday night and on the Monday morning I had an injection. I then did not train on either Tuesday or Wednesday. Thankfully, the combination of rest and treatment did the trick. By Saturday I was fit to play my last game for England, in a World Cup final, against the country of my birth.

Five weeks earlier I also thought I had played my last Test against the Springboks. Whatever happened at the weekend, I knew I would be signing off on a far happier note. It was going to be a massive occasion for me and also my family. My three brothers all said they would be there and so too did dad, which was fantastic given that he had been absent in 2003. It was a close shave however. He missed his connecting flight from Port Elizabeth to Johannesburg. The four Catt boys were supposed to arrive together on a road trip from London. So dad flew direct to Paris, then got a flight to London, to make sure he would arrive in France with Doug, Pete and Rich.

A couple of days before the game I sat with Phil Vickery having a coffee in the hotel at Neuilly. For once we didn't know what to say to each other. Then, at exactly the same time, we came out with: 'One more game.' We had both been thinking the same thing: when is the bubble going to burst? I shook my head and laughed. 'You know what, mate, why does it have to burst at all? I honestly believe it's game-on this weekend. We know it. South Africa know it.'

Beating the Boks, however, was always going to be a greater challenge than either Australia or France, as they are a different kettle of fish; a very experienced and clinical side that knows exactly what it is doing. Then again we were going into the game with nothing to lose. People talked about us needing to repair the damage done by the 36–0 defeat. I completely disagreed. We had already repaired that by getting to the final. I didn't feel it was about repairing anything. It was just a one-off game that we needed to win and I was convinced we could. We had the right players in the right positions and, unlike when we met in the pool match, we were now playing the fifteen-man game we wanted to play. It would be interesting to see how South Africa played against us. In their earlier win they had not run at us. They had just driven and then banged the ball up in the air. It had worked very well. But this game was different in every way.

I had not had a good feeling about the semi-final, I don't know why. Perhaps I had played the game three nights before when we trained and I was flying. I had got myself up too early. By the Thursday and Friday I was coming down from that high a bit and I had to go and find it again. No such problems this time.

Just thinking about playing in the final gave me a warm feeling. Yet, if anything, I was equally pleased for Brian Ashton. We had had our differences earlier in the campaign, but like the rest of us he had come through strongly and was now a lot more controlled and firmly in charge.

World Cup final:
Stade de France, Paris, 13 October 2007

England 6–15 South Africa

Focus on the process, not the outcome. That's what the management told us as we prepared for the biggest occasion in all of rugby; one made even bigger for me by the country standing between England and the Webb Ellis Cup.

The theory was sound. It had served us well against both Australia and France. But this time was different. However much we told ourselves that we had come through four 'cup finals' to reach this point and we would treat this as we had the rest, it *was* different this time. It was *the* final.

We all knew what was at stake. We had an opportunity to make history; to become the first country to win back-to-back titles. We spoke with pride of how far we had come in the thirty-six days since we had conceded 36 unanswered points to the same opposition in the stadium. And we made a commitment to each other not to leave anything in the changing room.

Shortly before leaving the room we shook hands and embraced one another, knowing that it was the last time as England players that we would stand together in a huddle. I had made up my mind that it would be my last international. Others had come to the same decision. Nothing was said but everyone knew.

Messages of support had flooded in all week. The media liked the one from 007 actor Daniel Craig which gave us, as one of them quipped, license to kill. From James Bond to the Prime Minister, Gordon Brown, who had borrowed a line from Sir Winston Church-ill: 'Courage is the first of human qualities because it is the quality which guarantees all others.'

If there was one quality our squad did not lack it was courage. We had been to the brink and back on this trip, stared humiliation in the face and not blinked. Quite how we had done it nobody was altogether sure, but done it we had. Our renaissance was now complete. We all genuinely believed that we could beat South Africa. As we headed into the tunnel Phil Vickery issued one simple instruction: 'Go out and make this a special time.'

Out onto an international field for one last time, the roar straightened the hairs on the back of my neck. My nearest and dearest were in the crowd. I was about to play in my second World Cup final. Life had been worse. 'God Save the Queen' played first, then 'Nkosi Sikelel' iAfrika'. One last time I touched my ear as the camera passed me along the line, my way of acknowledging my family's support.

And then we were playing. Immediately our line-out was in trouble and Percy Montgomery kicked the Springboks ahead. Jonny Wilkinson levelled but Lewis Moody obstructed Butch James as he kicked ahead and Montgomery struck again.

We were kicking a lot out of hand but unable to gain a firm foothold in the game. Then a chance. A throw to the tail of the line-out was taken by Lewis who popped a pass inside to Simon Shaw who made ground. Jonny was waiting in the pocket. The ball came back, the drop goal attempt went wide.

We needed points but we couldn't get close enough to strike. Increasingly it was South Africa in possession, England fighting fires in defence. Mathew Tait made a huge tackle on François Steyn. Paul Sackey and Martin Corry followed suit. But the half ended with Montgomery extending the lead to 9–3 with his third penalty.

Still we believed. We knew we had come from behind to win the previous two matches, we just needed to score first when play resumed. The chance came. Andy Gomarsall's pass missed Jonny Wilkinson and went to ground, Mathew Tait picked up the loose ball and set off upfield. Stepping off his left foot, then his right, he powered past four defenders. It was a fabulous run and he looked to be in when Victor Matfield snared him and then Schalk Burger dived all over him.

I flashed a glance at referee Alain Rolland, convinced he would penalise Burger for killing play and either send him to the sin-bin or award us a penalty try. Jonny Wilkinson was otherwise engaged. He got to the breakdown and flipped a pass out to Mark Cueto on the left wing. Cueto dived for the line and, from where I stood, appeared to beat Danie Rossouw's cover tackle.

Rolland didn't award the try, but signalled for the television match official to rule on whether Cueto's left leg had brushed the sideline before his hands touched the ball down. For more than three minutes we stood waiting, our fate in the hands of Australian ref Stuart Dickinson, locked away in a room studying the various angles available to him on a TV monitor.

I thought the try was good and Cueto was convinced it was. It would pull us back to within a point with Jonny's touchline conversion to come. We would be back in the game and the momentum would be with us. But the call went against us. Rolland instead chose to punish Burger, but not with a yellow card or a penalty try either, only a penalty.

Even though Jonny kicked it over via a post to make it a 9–6 ball game, we had not gained the injection of belief that a try would have brought. Had it been awarded, South Africa would have been chasing the game and we would have been able to sit back a little bit.

My game ended soon after when my calf packed in. Moments later Jason Robinson was hit hard on his right shoulder and a second England career was brought to a premature halt. By the time the team regrouped, Montgomery and Steyn had each kicked penalties and the game was out of reach.

The final whistle sparked celebrations among players wearing the Springbok jersey I had once held so dear. I felt strangely numb. Not distraught, not anything really. It didn't feel like we had lost a World Cup final, more just a game of rugby. I guess that's what comes of focusing on the process.

On the smallest margin a World Cup had been won and lost. It had come down to inches. For so long England had been miles away from where we needed to be. But we never lost sight of the target. And when it mattered most we had made up almost all the lost ground. We were neck and neck with South Africa and we just lost out on the dip.

Brian Ashton called us into a circle on the pitch. 'You've got nothing at all to regret,' he said. 'You've given everything over the last four months. You ought to be incredibly proud of the way you have conducted yourselves both on the field as players and off it as people. You are a special group of people, not just rugby players.'

We collected our silver medals and then I looked across to where my family was sitting and saw Evie on Ali's lap. I wanted her to share the moment with me and went across and lifted her up and put my medal around her neck. With my daughter in my arms I walked around the pitch with the rest of the boys, whilst Evie waved to the England supporters in her pink woolly gloves.

The night had ended in defeat. Our quest for World Cup glory had come up just short. But in all other respects I was as happy as I had ever been. I had achieved everything I could hope for and more. This one defeat could not take that away from me.

Mike Catt Career Record

MIKE CATT'S TEST CAREER FOR THE BRITISH/IRISH LIONS

- **Catt, M J** *(Bath and England)* 1997 SA 3
- One Test, one defeat.

TEST 3: LOST 16-35 v SOUTH AFRICA, 5th July 1997, Ellis Park, Johannesburg
British/Irish Lions: N R Jenkins; J Bentley, I S Gibbs, J C Guscott (rep A G Bateman), T Underwood (rep T R G Stimpson); M J Catt, M J S Dawson (rep A S Healey); T J Smith, M P Regan, P S Wallace, M O Johnson *(captain)*, J W Davidson, R I Wainwright, L B N Dallaglio, N A Back
Lions Scorers *Try:* Dawson *Conversion:* Jenkins *Penalty Goals:* Jenkins 3

MIKE CATT'S CAP CAREER FOR ENGLAND

- **Catt, M J** *(Bath, London Irish)* 1994 W (R), C (R), 1995 I, F, W, S, [Arg, It, WS, A, NZ, F in the RWC], SA, WS, 1996 F, W, S, I, It, Arg, 1997 W, Arg 1, A 1,2, NZ 1, SA, 1998 F, W (R), I, A 2(R), SA 2, 1999 S, F, W, A, C (R), [Tg (R), Fj, SA (R) in the RWC], 2000 I, F, W, It, S, SA 1,2, A, Arg, 2001 W, It, S, F, I, A, R (R), SA, 2003 [Sm(R), U, W(R), F, A(R) in the RWC], 2004 W(R), F(R), NZ1, A1, 2006 A1, 2, 2007 F1, W1, F2, [US, SA1, A, F, SA2 in the RWC]
- 75 Tests, 50 wins, one draw and 24 defeats. He was on the winning side in all of his first ten Tests for England.
- He captained England three times in 2007: to victory over France in the Six Nations match at Twickenham and to defeats against Wales (Cardiff in the Six Nations) and against France (Twickenham in the RWC warm-up match in August).
- He scored 142 Test points for England: seven tries, 16 conversions, 22 penalty goals and three dropped goals.

- He played in 19 games at Rugby World Cup finals. Only Jason Leonard (for England) and George Gregan (for Australia) have played more matches in the tournament.
- He played in one World Cup third/fourth place play-off (1995), was a World Cup winner in 2003 and a runner-up in the 2007, when he became the first 36-year-old to appear in a final.
- Only two England backs have won more caps: Rory Underwood (85) and Matt Dawson (77).
- His Test career span (1994 to 2007) is the longest of any England back player.
- He was the first England player to start Test matches in the No 15, No 14, No 13, No 12 and No 10 jerseys.

CAP 1: WON 15-8 v WALES, 19th March 1994, Twickenham
England: I Hunter; T Underwood, W D C Carling (*captain*), P R de Glanville, R Underwood; C R Andrew (rep M J Catt), C D Morris; J Leonard, B C Moore, V E Ubogu, M O Johnson, N C Redman, T A K Rodber, D Richards, B B Clarke
England scorers *Tries :* R Underwood, Rodber *Conversion :* Andrew *Penalty Goal:* Andrew

CAP 2: WON 60-19 v CANADA, 10th December 1994, Twickenham
England: P A Hull (rep M J Catt); T Underwood (rep P R de Glanville), W D C Carling (*captain*), J C Guscott, R Underwood; C R Andrew, K P P Bracken; J Leonard, B C Moore, V E Ubogu, M O Johnson, M C Bayfield, T A K Rodber, D Richards, B B Clarke
England scorers *Tries :* R Underwood 2, Catt 2, T Underwood, Bracken *Conversions :* Andrew 6 *Penalty Goals:* Andrew 6

CAP 3: WON 20-8 v IRELAND, 21st January 1995, Lansdowne Road, Dublin
England: M J Catt; T Underwood, W D C Carling (*captain*), J C Guscott, R Underwood; C R Andrew, K P P Bracken; J Leonard, B C Moore, V E Ubogu, M O Johnson, M C Bayfield, T A K Rodber, D Richards, B B Clarke
England scorers *Tries :* Carling, T Underwood, Clarke *Conversion :* Andrew *Penalty Goal:* Andrew

CAP 4: WON 31-10 v FRANCE, 4th February 1995, Twickenham
England: M J Catt; T Underwood, W D C Carling (*captain*), J C Guscott, R Underwood; C R Andrew, K P P Bracken; J Leonard, B C Moore, V E Ubogu, M O Johnson, M C Bayfield, T A K Rodber, D Richards, B B Clarke
England scorers *Tries :* T Underwood 2, Guscott *Conversions :* Andrew 2 *Penalty Goals:* Andrew 4

CAP 5: WON 23-9 v WALES, 18th February 1995, Cardiff Arms Park
England: M J Catt; T Underwood, W D C Carling (*captain*), J C Guscott, R Under-
wood; C R Andrew, K P P Bracken; J Leonard, B C Moore, V E Ubogu, M O Johnson,
M C Bayfield, T A K Rodber, D Richards, B B Clarke
England scorers *Tries :* R Underwood 2, Ubogu *Conversion :* Andrew *Penalty Goals:*
Andrew 2

CAP 6: WON 24-12 v SCOTLAND, 18th March 1995, Twickenham
England: M J Catt; T Underwood, W D C Carling (*captain*), J C Guscott, R Under-
wood; C R Andrew, K P P Bracken (temp rep C D Morris); J Leonard (temp rep G C
Rowntree), B C Moore, V E Ubogu, M O Johnson, M C Bayfield, T A K Rodber, D
Richards (rep S O Ojomoh), B B Clarke
England scorers *Penalty Goals:* Andrew 7 *Dropped Goal :* Andrew

CAP 7: WON 24-18 v ARGENTINA, 27th May 1995, King's Park, Durban
England: M J Catt; T Underwood, W D C Carling (*captain*) (rep P R de Glanville), J C
Guscott, R Underwood; C R Andrew, C D Morris; J Leonard, B C Moore, V E Ubogu,
M O Johnson, M C Bayfield, T A K Rodber, S O Ojomoh (temp rep N A Back), B B
Clarke
England scorer *Penalty Goals:* Andrew 6 *Dropped Goals :* Andrew 2

CAP 8: WON 27-20 v ITALY, 31st May 1995, King's Park, Durban
England: M J Catt; T Underwood, P R de Glanville, J C Guscott, R Underwood; C R
Andrew (*captain*), K P P Bracken; G C Rowntree, B C Moore, J Leonard, M O
Johnson, M C Bayfield, T A K Rodber, B B Clarke, N A Back
England scorers *Tries :* R Underwood, T Underwood *Conversion :* Andrew *Penalty
Goals:* Andrew 5

CAP 9: WON 44-22 v WESTERN SAMOA, 4th June 1995, King's Park, Durban
England: J E B Callard; I Hunter, W D C Carling (*captain*) (rep D P Hopley), P R de
Glanville, R Underwood; M J Catt, C D Morris; G C Rowntree (rep J Mallett), R G R
Dawe, V E Ubogu, M O Johnson, R J West, S O Ojomoh, D Richards (rep B C
Moore), N A Back (rep T A K Rodber who was temp rep by K P P Bracken)
England scorers *Tries :* R Underwood 2, penalty try, Back *Conversions :* Callard 3
Penalty Goals: Callard 5 *Dropped Goal :* Catt

CAP 10: WON 25-22 v AUSTRALIA, 11th June 1995, Newlands, Cape Town
England: M J Catt; T Underwood, W D C Carling (*captain*), J C Guscott, R Under-
wood; C R Andrew, C D Morris; J Leonard, B C Moore, V E Ubogu, M O Johnson, M
C Bayfield, T A K Rodber, D Richards (temp rep S O Ojomoh), B B Clarke
England scorers *Try :* T Underwood *Conversion :* Andrew *Penalty Goals:* Andrew 5
Dropped Goal : Andrew

CAP 11: LOST 29-45 v NEW ZEALAND, 18th June 1995, Newlands, Cape Town
England: M J Catt; T Underwood, W D C Carling (*captain*), J C Guscott, R Under-wood; C R Andrew, C D Morris; J Leonard, B C Moore, V E Ubogu, M O Johnson, M C Bayfield, T A K Rodber, D Richards, B B Clarke
England scorers *Tries :* R Underwood 2, Carling 2 *Conversions :* Andrew 3 *Penalty Goal:* Andrew

CAP 12: LOST 9-19 v FRANCE, 22nd June 1995, Loftus Versfeld, Pretoria
England: M J Catt; I Hunter, W D C Carling (*captain*), J C Guscott, R Underwood; C R Andrew, C D Morris; J Leonard, B C Moore, V E Ubogu, M O Johnson, M C Bayfield, T A K Rodber, S O Ojomoh, B B Clarke
England scorer *Penalty Goals:* Andrew 3

CAP 13: LOST 14-24 v SOUTH AFRICA, 18th November 1995, Twickenham
England: J E B Callard; D P Hopley, W D C Carling (*captain*) (rep P R de Glanville), J C Guscott, R Underwood; M J Catt, K P P Bracken; J Leonard, M P Regan, V E Ubogu, M O Johnson, M C Bayfield, T A K Rodber (rep L B N Dallaglio), B B Clarke, R A Robinson
England scorers *Try :* de Glanville *Penalty Goals :* Callard 3

CAP 14: WON 27-9 v WESTERN SAMOA, 16th December 1995, Twickenham
England: M J Catt; D P Hopley, W D C Carling (*captain*), J C Guscott, R Underwood; P J Grayson, M J S Dawson; G C Rowntree, M P Regan, J Leonard, M O Johnson, M C Bayfield, T A K Rodber, B B Clarke, L B N Dallaglio
England scorers *Tries :* Dallaglio, Underwood *Conversion :* Grayson *Penalty Goals :* Grayson 5

CAP 15: LOST 12-15 v FRANCE, 20th January 1996, Parc des Princes
England: M J Catt; J M Sleightholme, W D C Carling (*captain*), J C Guscott, R Underwood; P J Grayson, M J S Dawson; G C Rowntree, M P Regan, J Leonard, M O Johnson, M C Bayfield, S O Ojomoh, B B Clarke (temp rep D Richards), L B N Dallaglio
England scorer *Penalty Goals :* Grayson 2 *Dropped Goals :* Grayson 2

CAP 16: WON 21-15 v WALES, 3rd February 1996, Twickenham
England: M J Catt; J M Sleightholme, W D C Carling (*captain*) (rep P R de Glanville), J C Guscott, R Underwood; P J Grayson, M J S Dawson; G C Rowntree, M P Regan, J Leonard, M O Johnson, M C Bayfield, T A K Rodber, B B Clarke, L B N Dallaglio
England scorers *Tries :* Underwood, Guscott *Conversion :* Grayson *Penalty Goals :* Grayson 3

CAP 17: WON 18-9 v SCOTLAND, 2nd March 1996, Murrayfield, Edinburgh
England: M J Catt; J M Sleightholme, W D C Carling (*captain*), J C Guscott, R Underwood; P J Grayson, M J S Dawson; G C Rowntree, M P Regan, J Leonard, M O Johnson, G S Archer, B B Clarke, D Richards (rep T A K Rodber), L B N Dallaglio
England scorer *Penalty Goals :* Grayson 6

CAP 18: WON 28-15 v IRELAND, 16th March 1996, Twickenham
England: M J Catt; J M Sleightholme, W D C Carling (*captain*) (rep P R de Glanville), J C Guscott, R Underwood; P J Grayson, M J S Dawson; G C Rowntree, M P Regan, J Leonard, M O Johnson, G S Archer, B B Clarke, D Richards, L B N Dallaglio (temp rep T A K Rodber)
England scorers *Try :* Sleightholme *Conversion :* Grayson *Penalty Goals :* Grayson 6 *Dropped Goal :* Grayson

CAP 19: WON 54-21 v ITALY, 23rd November 1996, Twickenham
England: T R G Stimpson; J M Sleightholme, W D C Carling, P R de Glanville (*captain*), A A Adebayo; M J Catt, A C T Gomarsall (rep K P P Bracken); G C Rowntree, M P Regan (rep P B T Greening), J Leonard (rep R J K Hardwick), M O Johnson, S D Shaw, T A K Rodber, C M A Sheasby, L B N Dallaglio
England scorers *Tries :* Gomarsall 2, Sleightholme, Johnson, Dallaglio, Rodber, Sheasby *Conversions :* Catt 5 *Penalty Goals :* Catt 3

CAP 20: WON 20-18 v ARGENTINA, 14th December 1996, Twickenham
England: N D Beal; J M Sleightholme, W D C Carling, J C Guscott, T Underwood; M J Catt, A C T Gomarsall; G C Rowntree, M P Regan, J Leonard (*captain*), M O Johnson, S D Shaw, T A K Rodber, C M A Sheasby (rep B B Clarke), L B N Dallaglio
England scorers *Try :* Leonard *Penalty Goals :* Catt 5

CAP 21: WON 34-13 v WALES, 15th March 1997, Cardiff Arms Park
England: T R G Stimpson; J M Sleightholme (rep J C Guscott), W D C Carling, P R de Glanville (*captain*), T Underwood; M J Catt (rep C R Andrew), A S Healey; G C Rowntree (rep D J Garforth), M P Regan (rep P B T Greening), J Leonard, M O Johnson, S D Shaw, B B Clarke (rep C M A Sheasby), T A K Rodber, R A Hill
England scorers *Tries :* Stimpson, Underwood, Hill, de Glanville *Conversions :* Catt 4 *Penalty Goals :* Catt 2

CAP 22: WON 46-20 v ARGENTINA, 31st May 1997, Buenos Aires

England: J Mallinder; J M Sleightholme, P R de Glanville (*captain*), N J J Greenstock, A A Adebayo; M J Catt, K P P Bracken; K P Yates, P B T Greening (rep R Cockerill), D J Garforth, M Haag, N C Redman, M E Corry (rep C M A Sheasby), A J Diprose, B B Clarke

England scorers *Tries:* Adebayo 2, Greenstock, Catt, Diprose, Clarke *Conversions:* Catt 5 *Penalty Goals:* Catt 2

CAP 23: LOST 6-25 v AUSTRALIA, 12th July 1997, Sydney Football Stadium

England: T R G Stimpson; J Bentley, N J J Greenstock, P R de Glanville (*captain*), N D Beal; M J Catt, M J S Dawson (rep A S Healey); G C Rowntree, M P Regan, D J Garforth, N C Redman, S D Shaw, L B N Dallaglio, T A K Rodber, R A Hill (rep B B Clarke)

England scorers *Penalty Goal:* Stimpson *Dropped Goal:* Catt

CAP 24: DREW 15-15 v AUSTRALIA, 15th November 1997, Twickenham

England: M B Perry; D L Rees, W J H Greenwood, P R de Glanville (temp rep P J Grayson), A A Adebayo (rep A S Healey); M J Catt, K P P Bracken; J Leonard, A E Long (rep R Cockerill), W R Green, M O Johnson, G S Archer, L B N Dallaglio (*captain*), A J Diprose, R A Hill

England scorer *Penalty Goals:* Catt (5)

CAP 25: LOST 8-25 v NEW ZEALAND, 22nd November 1997, Old Trafford, Manchester

England: M B Perry; D L Rees, W J H Greenwood, P R de Glanville, A A Adebayo (rep A S Healey); M J Catt, K P P Bracken; J Leonard, R Cockerill, D J Garforth, M O Johnson, G S Archer, L B N Dallaglio (*captain*), A J Diprose (rep N A Back), R A Hill

England scorers *Try:* de Glanville *Penalty Goal:* Catt

CAP 26: LOST 11-29 v SOUTH AFRICA, 29th November 1997, Twickenham

England: M B Perry; J Bentley (rep A S Healey), W J H Greenwood, N J J Greenstock, D L Rees; M J Catt (rep P J Grayson), M J S Dawson; J Leonard, R Cockerill, D J Garforth, D J Grewcock (rep S D Shaw), G S Archer, L B N Dallaglio (*captain*), R A Hill (rep C M A Sheasby), N A Back

England scorers *Try:* Greenstock *Penalty Goals:* Catt (2)

CAP 27: LOST 17-24 v FRANCE, 7th February 1998, Stade de France, Paris

England: M J Catt; D L Rees, W J H Greenwood, J C Guscott, A S Healey; P J Grayson, K P P Bracken; J Leonard, M P Regan (rep D E West), D J Garforth, M O Johnson, G S Archer, L B N Dallaglio (*captain*), R A Hill, N A Back

England scorers *Try :* Back *Penalty Goals :* Grayson (4)

CAP 28: WON 60-26 v WALES, 21st February 1998, Twickenham

England: M B Perry; D L Rees, W J H Greenwood (rep P R de Glanville), J C Guscott, A
S Healey; P J Grayson (rep M J Catt), K P P Bracken (rep M J S Dawson); J Leonard, R
Cockerill, P J Vickery (D J Garforth), M O Johnson (D J Grewcock), G S Archer, L B
N Dallaglio *(captain)*, R A Hill (rep A J Diprose), N A Back

England scorers *Tries :* Rees (2), Back, Bracken, Dallaglio, Healey, Greenwood, Dawson
Conversions : Grayson (7) *Penalty Goals :* Grayson (2)

CAP 29: WON 35-17 v IRELAND, 4th April 1998, Twickenham

England: M B Perry; M J Catt (rep J P Wilkinson), W J H Greenwood (rep P R de
Glanville), J C Guscott, A S Healey; P J Grayson, M J S Dawson; J Leonard, R
Cockerill, D J Garforth, M O Johnson, G S Archer (rep D J Grewcock), L B N
Dallaglio *(captain)*, A J Diprose, N A Back

England scorers *Tries:* Perry, Catt, Cockerill, de Glanville *Conversions:* Grayson (3)
Penalty Goals : Grayson (3)

CAP 30: LOST 11-12 v AUSTRALIA, 28th November 1998, Twickenham

England: M B Perry; T Underwood, P R de Glanville, J C Guscott, A S Healey; P J
Grayson (rep M J Catt), M J S Dawson; J Leonard, R Cockerill, D J Garforth, M O
Johnson, T A K Rodber, L B N Dallaglio *(captain)*, R A Hill, N A Back

England scorers *Try:* Guscott *Penalty Goals:* Catt (2)

CAP 31: WON 13-7 v SOUTH AFRICA, 5th December 1998, Twickenham

England: N D Beal; T Underwood (rep D L Rees rep A S Healey), P R de Glanville (rep A
D King), J C Guscott, D D Luger; M J Catt (temp rep M E Corry), M J S Dawson; J
Leonard, R Cockerill, D J Garforth, M O Johnson, T A K Rodber (rep D J
Grewcock), L B N Dallaglio *(captain)*, R A Hill, N A Back

England scorers *Try:* Guscott *Conversion:* Dawson *Penalty Goals:* Dawson (2)

CAP 32: WON 24-21 v SCOTLAND, 20th February 1999, Twickenham

England: N D Beal; D L Rees, J P Wilkinson, J C Guscott, D D Luger; M J Catt, M J S
Dawson (K P P Bracken); J Leonard, R Cockerill, D J Garforth, M O Johnson (rep D J
Grewcock), T A K Rodber, L B N Dallaglio *(captain)*, R A Hill, N A Back

England scorers *Tries:* Rodber, Luger, Beal *Conversions :* Wilkinson (3) *Penalty Goal:*
Wilkinson

CAP 33: WON 21-10 v FRANCE, 20th March 1999, Twickenham

England: M B Perry; D L Rees (rep N D Beal), J P Wilkinson, J C Guscott, D D Luger; M
J Catt, K P P Bracken (rep M J S Dawson); J Leonard, R Cockerill, D J Garforth (rep V
E Ubogu), M O Johnson, T A K Rodber, R A Hill (rep M E Corry), L B N Dallaglio
(captain), N A Back

England scorer *Penalty Goals:* Wilkinson (7)

CAP 34: LOST 31-32 v WALES, 11th April 1999, Wembley

Wales: S P Howarth; G Thomas (rep N J Walne), M Taylor, I S Gibbs, D R James; N R Jenkins, R Howley (*captain*); P J D Rogers (rep A L P Lewis), G R Jenkins, B R Evans (rep D Young), J C Quinnell, C P Wyatt, C L Charvis, L S Quinnell, B D Sinkinson

England scorers *Tries:* Howarth, Gibbs *Conversions :* N Jenkins (2) *Penalty Goals :* N Jenkins (6)

CAP 35: LOST 15-22 v AUSTRALIA, 26th June 1999, Stadium Australia, Sydney

England: M B Perry (rep N D Beal); D L Rees, M J Catt (rep P R de Glanville), J C Guscott, D D Luger; J P Wilkinson, K P P Bracken (rep M J S Dawson); J Leonard, R Cockerill (rep P B T Greening), D J Garforth (rep V E Ubogu), M O Johnson (*captain*), T A K Rodber (rep D J Grewcock), R A Hill, M E Corry (rep B B Clarke), N A Back

England scorers *Tries:* Perry (2) *Conversion:* Wilkinson *Penalty Goal:* Wilkinson

CAP 36: WON 36-11 v CANADA, 28th August 1999, Twickenham

England: M B Perry (rep T R G Stimpson); A S Healey (rep N D Beal), W J H Greenwood, J C Guscott (rep M J Catt), D D Luger; J P Wilkinson, M J S Dawson; G C Rowntree (rep J Leonard), P B T Greening (rep R Cockerill), P J Vickery (rep D J Garforth), M O Johnson (*captain*) (rep M E Corry), D J Grewcock, R A Hill, L B N Dallaglio, N A Back

England scorers *Tries:* Greenwood (2), Perry, Luger, Dawson *Conversions:* Wilkinson (4) *Penalty Goal:* Wilkinson

Cap 37: WON 101-10 v TONGA, 15th October 1999, Twickenham

England: M B Perry; A S Healey, W J H Greenwood (rep M J Catt), J C Guscott, D D Luger; P J Grayson, M J S Dawson (rep N D Beal); G C Rowntree, P B T Greening, P J Vickery, M O Johnson (*captain*) (rep D J Grewcock), G S Archer, J P R Worsley, L B N Dallaglio (rep R Cockerill), R A Hill

England scorers *Tries :* Greening (2), Luger (2), Greenwood (2), Healey (2), Guscott (2), Hill, Dawson, Perry *Conversions :* Grayson (12) *Penalty Goals :* Grayson (4)

Cap 38: WON 45-24 v FIJI, 20th October 1999, Twickenham

England: M B Perry; N D Beal, W J H Greenwood, M J Catt, D D Luger (rep P R de Glanville); J P Wilkinson (rep P J Grayson), A S Healey (rep M J S Dawson); J Leonard (rep G C Rowntree), P B T Greening (R Cockerill), D J Garforth, M O Johnson (*captain*), G S Archer (rep T A K Rodber), J P R Worsley (temp rep R A Hill), L B N Dallaglio, N A Back

England scorers *Tries:* Greening, Luger, Back, Beal *Conversions :* Wilkinson, Dawson *Penalty Goals :* Wilkinson (7)

334

CAP 39: LOST 21-44 v SOUTH AFRICA, 24th October 1999, Stade de France, Paris
England: M B Perry; N D Beal (rep A S Healey), W J H Greenwood, P R de Glanville (rep M J Catt), D D Luger; P J Grayson (rep J P Wilkinson), M J S Dawson (rep M E Corry); J Leonard, P B T Greening, P J Vickery, M O Johnson (*captain*), D J Grewcock, R A Hill, L B N Dallaglio, N A Back
England scorers *Penalty Goals:* Grayson (6), Wilkinson

CAP 40: WON 50-18 v IRELAND, 5th February 2000, Twickenham
England: M B Perry (rep I R Balshaw); A S Healey, M J Tindall, M J Catt, B C Cohen; J P Wilkinson, M J S Dawson (*captain*); J Leonard (rep T J Woodman), P B T Greening, P J Vickery, G S Archer, S D Shaw (rep M E Corry), R A Hill, L B N Dallaglio, N A Back
England scorers *Tries:* Healey (2), Cohen (2), Back, Tindall *Conversions:* Wilkinson (4) *Penalty Goals :* Wilkinson (4)

CAP 41: WON 15-9 v FRANCE, 19th February 2000, Stade de France, Paris
England: M B Perry (rep I R Balshaw); A S Healey, M J Tindall, M J Catt, B C Cohen; J P Wilkinson, M J S Dawson (*captain*); J Leonard, P B T Greening, P J Vickery, G S Archer, S D Shaw, R A Hill (rep M E Corry), L B N Dallaglio, N A Back
England scorer *Penalty Goals :* Wilkinson (5)

CAP 42: WON 46-12 v WALES, 4th March 2000, Twickenham
England: M B Perry; A S Healey, M J Tindall, M J Catt, B C Cohen; J P Wilkinson, M J S Dawson (*captain*); J Leonard, P B T Greening, P J Vickery, G S Archer, S D Shaw (rep M E Corry), R A Hill, L B N Dallaglio, N A Back
England scorers *Tries:* Greening, Back, Cohen, Hill, Dallaglio *Conversions:* Wilkinson (3) *Penalty Goals :* Wilkinson (5)

CAP 43: WON 59-12 v ITALY, 18th March 2000, Stadio Flaminio, Rome
England: M B Perry; A S Healey, M J Tindall (rep I R Balshaw), M J Catt, B C Cohen; J P Wilkinson (rep A D King), M J S Dawson (*captain*) (rep A C T Gomarsall); J Leonard (rep T J Woodman), P B T Greening (rep N McCarthy), D J Garforth, G S Archer (rep M E Corry), S D Shaw, R A Hill (rep J P R Worsley), L B N Dallaglio, N A Back
England scorers *Tries:* Healey (3), penalty try, Cohen (2), Dawson (2) *Conversions :* Wilkinson (4), King *Penalty Goals :* Wilkinson (2) *Dropped Goal:* Back

CAP 44: LOST 13-19 v SCOTLAND, 2nd April 2000, Murrayfield
England: M B Perry; A S Healey, M J Tindall, M J Catt, B C Cohen (rep I R Balshaw); J P Wilkinson, M J S Dawson (*captain*); J Leonard, P B T Greening, P J Vickery, G S Archer (rep M E Corry), S D Shaw, R A Hill (rep J P R Worsley), L B N Dallaglio, N A Back
England scorers *Try:* Dallaglio *Conversion:* Wilkinson *Penalty Goals:* Wilkinson (2)

CAP 45: LOST 13-18 v SOUTH AFRICA, 17th June 2000, Loftus Versfeld, Pretoria
England: M B Perry; T R G Stimpson, M J Tindall, M J Catt (rep L D Lloyd), D D Luger; A S Healey, K P P Bracken; J Leonard, P B T Greening, J M White (rep D L Flatman), M O Johnson (*captain*) (rep S D Shaw), D J Grewcock (rep J P R Worsley), R A Hill (temp rep M P Regan), L B N Dallaglio, N A Back
England scorers *Try:* Luger *Conversion:* Stimpson *Penalty Goals:* Stimpson (2)

CAP 46: WON 27-22 v SOUTH AFRICA, 24th June 2000, Free State Stadium, Bloemfontein
England: M B Perry; A S Healey, M J Tindall (rep L D Lloyd), M J Catt, B C Cohen; J P Wilkinson, K P P Bracken; J Leonard, P B T Greening, J M White (rep D L Flatman), M O Johnson (*captain*), D J Grewcock (rep S D Shaw), R A Hill (rep J P R Worsley), L B N Dallaglio, N A Back
England scorer *Penalty Goals:* Wilkinson (8) *Dropped Goal:* Wilkinson

CAP 47: WON 22-19 v AUSTRALIA, 18th November 2000, Twickenham
England: M B Perry; A S Healey (rep I R Balshaw), M J Tindall, M J Catt, D D Luger; J P Wilkinson, K P P Bracken (rep M J S Dawson); J Leonard, P B T Greening (rep M P Regan), P J Vickery (temp rep D L Flatman), M O Johnson (*captain*), D J Grewcock, R A Hill, L B N Dallaglio, N A Back
England scorers *Try:* Luger *Conversion:* Wilkinson *Penalty Goals:* Wilkinson (4) *Dropped Goal:* Wilkinson

CAP 48: WON 19-0 v ARGENTINA, 25th November 2000, Twickenham
England: I R Balshaw; B C Cohen, M J Tindall (rep W J H Greenwood), M J Catt, D D Luger; J P Wilkinson, M J S Dawson; J Leonard (rep D L Flatman), M P Regan (rep D E West), J M White (rep P J Vickery), M O Johnson (*captain*), D J Grewcock, R A Hill (rep M E Corry), L B N Dallaglio, N A Back
England scorers *Try:* Cohen *Conversion:* Wilkinson *Penalty Goals:* Wilkinson (3) *Dropped Goal:* Wilkinson

CAP 49: WON 44-15 v WALES, 3rd February 2001, Millennium Stadium, Cardiff
England: I R Balshaw (rep M B Perry); B C Cohen, W J H Greenwood, M J Catt (rep M J Tindall); D D Luger (rep A S Healey); J P Wilkinson, M J S Dawson; J Leonard (rep T J Woodman), D E West, P J Vickery, M O Johnson (*captain*), D J Grewcock, R A Hill, L B N Dallaglio (rep M E Corry), N A Back
England scorers *Tries:* Greenwood (3), Dawson (2), Cohen *Conversions:* Wilkinson (4) *Penalty Goals:* Wilkinson (2)

CAP 50: WON 80-23 v ITALY, 17th February 2001, Twickenham
England: I R Balshaw; A S Healey, W J H Greenwood, M J Catt, B C Cohen (rep J Robinson); J P Wilkinson, M J S Dawson (rep K P P Bracken); J Leonard (rep T J Woodman), D E West (rep M P Regan), P J Vickery, M O Johnson (*captain*), D J Grewcock (rep M E Corry), R A Hill, L B N Dallaglio, N A Back (rep J P R Worsley)
England scorers *Tries:* Healey (2), Balshaw (2), Cohen, Regan, Worsley, Greenwood, Wilkinson, Dallaglio *Conversions:* Wilkinson (9) *Penalty Goals:* Wilkinson (4)

CAP 51: WON 43-3 v SCOTLAND, 3rd March 2001, Twickenham
England: I R Balshaw; A S Healey, W J H Greenwood, M J Catt (rep J Robinson), B C Cohen; J P Wilkinson, M J S Dawson (rep K P P Bracken); J Leonard, D E West (rep M P Regan), P J Vickery, M O Johnson (*captain*), D J Grewcock, R A Hill, L B N Dallaglio, N A Back (rep J P R Worsley)
England scorers *Tries:* Dallaglio (2), Balshaw (2), Hill, Greenwood *Conversions:* Wilkinson (5) *Penalty Goal:* Wilkinson

CAP 52: WON 48-19 v FRANCE, 7th April 2001, Twickenham
England: I R Balshaw (rep M B Perry); A S Healey, W J H Greenwood, M J Catt, B C Cohen (rep J Robinson); J P Wilkinson, M J S Dawson (rep K P P Bracken); J Leonard (temp rep D L Flatman), P B T Greening (temp rep D E West), J M White, M O Johnson (*captain*), S W Borthwick (rep M E Corry), R A Hill (rep J P R Worsley), L B N Dallaglio, N A Back
England scorers *Tries:* Balshaw, Hill, Greenwood, Greening, Catt, Perry *Conversions:* Wilkinson (6) *Penalty Goals:* Wilkinson (2)

CAP 53: LOST 14-20 v IRELAND, 20th October 2001, Lansdowne Road, Dublin
England: I R Balshaw; D D Luger (rep A S Healey), W J H Greenwood, M J Catt, J Robinson; J P Wilkinson, M J S Dawson (*captain*) (rep K P P Bracken); J Leonard, P B T Greening (rep D E West), J M White (rep G C Rowntree), S D Shaw, D J Grewcock, M E Corry (rep L W Moody), R A Hill, N A Back
England scorers *Try:* Healey *Penalty Goals:* Wilkinson (3)

CAP 54: WON 21-15 v AUSTRALIA, 10th November 2001, Twickenham
England: J Robinson; A S Healey, W J H Greenwood, M J Catt, D D Luger; J P
   Wilkinson, K P P Bracken; G C Rowntree, D E West, P J Vickery, B J Kay, D J
   Grewcock, R A Hill, J P R Worsley, N A Back (*captain*)
Scorers *Penalty Goals:* Wilkinson (5) *Dropped Goals:* Wilkinson (2)

CAP 55: WON 134-0 v ROMANIA, 17th November 2001, Twickenham
England: J Robinson; B C Cohen, W J H Greenwood (rep M J Catt), M J Tindall, D D
   Luger; C Hodgson, A S Healey (rep K P P Bracken); G C Rowntree (rep J White), M P
   Regan, J Leonard, B J Kay (rep D J Grewcock), S W Borthwick, L W Moody, J P R
   Worsley, N A Back (*captain*) (rep A Sanderson)
England scorers *Tries:* Robinson (4), Cohen (3), Luger (3), Hodgson (2), Moody (2),
   Tindall (2), Healey, Sanderson, Regan, Worsley *Conversions:* Hodgson (14) *Penalty
   Goals:* Hodgson (2)

CAP 56: WON 29-9 v SOUTH AFRICA, 24th November 2001, Twickenham
England: J Robinson; A S Healey, W J H Greenwood, M J Catt (rep M J Tindall), D D
   Luger; J P Wilkinson, K P P Bracken; G C Rowntree, D E West, P J Vickery, M O
   Johnson (*captain*) (rep B J Kay), D J Grewcock, R A Hill (rep L W Moody), J P R
   Worsley, N A Back
England scorers *Try:* Luger *Penalty Goals:* Wilkinson (7) *Dropped Goal:* Catt

CAP 57: WON 35-22 v SAMOA, 26th October 2003, Telstra Dome, Melbourne
England: J Robinson; I R Balshaw, S Abbott (rep M J Catt), M J Tindall, B C Cohen; J P
   Wilkinson, M J S Dawson; J Leonard, M P Regan (rep S Thompson), J M White (rep P
   J Vickery), M O Johnson (*captain*), B J Kay, J P R Worsley (rep L W Moody), L B N
   Dallaglio, N A Back
England scorers *Tries*: Back, penalty try, Balshaw, Vickery *Conversions*: Wilkinson (3)
   Penalty Goals: Wilkinson (2) *Dropped Goal:* Wilkinson

CAP 58: WON 111-13 v URUGUAY, 2nd November 2003, Suncorp Stadium, Brisbane
England: O J Lewsey; I R Balshaw (rep J Robinson), S Abbott, M J Catt, D D Luger; P J
   Grayson (rep W J H Greenwood), A C T Gomarsall (rep K P P Bracken); J Leonard, D
   E West, P J Vickery (*captain*) (rep J M White), M E Corry (rep M O Johnson), D J
   Grewcock, J P R Worsley, L B N Dallaglio, L W Moody
England scorers *Tries*: Lewsey (5), Balshaw (2), Robinson (2), Catt (2), Gomarsall (2),
   Moody, Luger, Abbott, Greenwood *Conversions*: Grayson (11), Catt (2)

CAP 59: WON 28-17 v WALES, 9th November 2003, Suncorp Stadium, Brisbane

England: J Robinson; D D Luger (rep M J Catt), W J H Greenwood (rep S Abbott), M J Tindall, B C Cohen; J P Wilkinson, M J S Dawson (rep K P P Bracken); J Leonard (rep T J Woodman), S Thompson, P J Vickery, M O Johnson (*captain*), B J Kay, L W Moody, L B N Dallaglio, N A Back

England scorers *Try*: Greenwood *Conversion*: Wilkinson *Penalty Goals:* Wilkinson (6) *Dropped Goal:* Wilkinson

CAP 60: WON 24-7 v FRANCE, 16th November 2003, Telstra Stadium, Sydney

England: O J Lewsey; J Robinson, W J H Greenwood, M J Catt (rep M J Tindall), B C Cohen; J P Wilkinson, M J S Dawson (rep K P P Bracken); T J Woodman (rep J Leonard), S Thompson (rep D E West), P J Vickery (temp rep J Leonard), M O Johnson (*captain*), B J Kay, R A Hill (rep L W Moody), L B N Dallaglio, N A Back

England scorer *Penalty Goals:* Wilkinson (5) *Dropped Goals:* Wilkinson (3)

CAP 61: WON 20-17 v AUSTRALIA, 22nd November 2003, Telstra Stadium, Sydney

England: J Robinson; O J Lewsey (rep I R Balshaw), W J H Greenwood, M J Tindall (rep M J Catt), B C Cohen; J P Wilkinson, M J S Dawson; T J Woodman, S Thompson, P J Vickery (rep J Leonard), M O Johnson (*captain*), B J Kay, R A Hill (rep L W Moody), L B N Dallaglio, N A Back

England scorers *Try:* Robinson *Penalty Goals:* Wilkinson (4) *Dropped Goal:* Wilkinson

CAP 62: WON 31-21 v WALES, 20th March 2004, Twickenham

England: J Robinson; O J Lewsey, W J H Greenwood (rep M J Catt), M J Tindall, B C Cohen; O Barkley, M J S Dawson; T J Woodman, S Thompson, P J Vickery (rep J M White), D J Grewcock, B J Kay, C M Jones (rep J P R Worsley), L B N Dallaglio (*captain*), R A Hill

England scorers *Tries:* Cohen (2), Worsley *Conversions:* Barkley (2) *Penalty Goals:* Barkley (4)

CAP 63: LOST 21-24 v FRANCE, 27th March 2004, Stade de France, Paris

England: J Robinson; O J Lewsey, W J H Greenwood (rep M J Catt), M J Tindall, B C Cohen; O Barkley, M J S Dawson; T J Woodman, S Thompson, P J Vickery (rep J M White), D J Grewcock (rep S W Borthwick), B J Kay, J P R Worsley, L B N Dallaglio (*captain*), R A Hill

England scorers *Tries:* Cohen, Lewsey *Conversion:* Barkley *Penalty Goals:* Barkley (3)

CAP 64: LOST 3-36 v NEW ZEALAND, 12th June 2004, Carisbrook, Dunedin

England: O J Lewsey (temp rep S Abbott); J D Simpson-Daniel, M J Tindall, M J Catt (rep S Abbott), B C Cohen; C C Hodgson, M J S Dawson (rep A C T Gomarsall); T J Woodman, S Thompson (rep M P Regan), J M White (rep M J H Stevens), S D Shaw, D J Grewcock (rep S W Borthwick), C M Jones (rep J P R Worsley), L B N Dallaglio (*captain*), R A Hill

England scorer *Penalty Goal:* Hodgson

CAP 65: LOST 15-51 v AUSTRALIA, 26th June 2004, Suncorp Stadium, Brisbane

England: O J Lewsey; T M D Voyce, M J Tindall (rep F H H Waters), M J Catt (rep O J Barkley), B C Cohen; C C Hodgson, A C T Gomarsall (rep M J S Dawson); T A N Payne (rep M A Worsley), M P Regan (rep S Thompson), J M White, S D Shaw, S W Borthwick, J P R Worsley (rep M E Corry), L B N Dallaglio (*captain*), R A Hill (rep M R Lipman)

England scorers *Tries:* Dallaglio, Hill *Conversion:* Hodgson *Penalty Goal:* Hodgson

CAP 66: LOST 3-34 v AUSTRALIA, 11th June 2006, Telstra Stadium, Sydney

England: I R Balshaw; T W Varndell, M Tait, M J Catt (rep J D Noon), T M D Voyce; O J Barkley (rep A J Goode), P C Richards (rep N P J Walshe); G C Rowntree (rep T A N Payne), L A Mears (rep G S Chuter), J M White, L P Deacon, A Brown (rep C M Jones), M B Lund (rep J P R Worsley), P H Sanderson (*captain*), L W Moody

England scorer *Penalty Goal:* Barkley

CAP 67: LOST 18-43 v AUSTRALIA, 17th June 2006, Telstra Dome, Melbourne

England: I R Balshaw; T W Varndell, J D Noon, M J Catt (rep O J Barkley), M Tait (rep S Abbott); A J Goode, P C Richards; G C Rowntree (rep M B Lund rep by L A Mears), G S Chuter, J M White (T A N Payne), C M Jones, B J Kay, J P R Worsley (rep L P Deacon), P H Sanderson (*captain*), M R Lipman (rep N P J Walshe)

England scorers *Tries:* Varndell, Chuter *Conversion:* Goode *Penalty Goal:* Goode *Dropped Goal:* Goode

CAP 68: WON 26-18 v FRANCE, 11th March 2007, Twickenham

England: O J Lewsey; D Strettle (rep M Tait), M J Tindall, M J Catt (*captain*) (rep S Perry), J T Robinson; T Flood (rep S Geraghty), H A Ellis; T A N Payne, G S Chuter, J M White, M E Corry, T Palmer (rep L P Deacon), J P R Worsley (rep M B Lund), N Easter, T Rees

England scorers *Tries:* Flood, Tindall *Conversions:* Flood, Geraghty *Penalty Goals:* Flood (3), Geraghty

CAP 69: LOST 18-27 v WALES, 17th March 2007, Millennium Stadium, Cardiff

England: M J Cueto; D Strettle, M Tait, M J Catt (*captain*) (rep S Geraghty), J T Robinson; T Flood, H A Ellis (rep S Perry); T A N Payne (rep S Turner), G S Chuter (rep L A Mears), J M White, M E Corry, T Palmer (rep L P Deacon), J Haskell, J P R Worsley (rep M B Lund), T Rees

England scorers *Tries:* Ellis, Robinson *Conversion:* Flood *Penalty Goal:* Flood *Dropped Goal:* Flood

CAP 70: LOST 15-21 v FRANCE, 11th August 2007, Twickenham

England: N Abendanon; P H Sackey, J D Noon, M J Catt (*captain*) (rep J P Wilkinson), O J Lewsey; O J Barkley, S Perry (rep A C T Gomarsall); A J Sheridan, M P Regan (rep L A Mears), M J H Stevens (rep P J Vickery), S D Shaw (rep M E Corry), B J Kay, J Haskell, L B N Dallaglio, J P R Worsley

England scorers *Penalty Goals:* Barkley (4) *Dropped Goal:* Gomarsall

CAP 71: WON 28-10 v UNITED STATES, 8th September 2007, Stade Félix Bollaert, Lens

England: M J Cueto; O J Lewsey, J D Noon, M J Catt (rep A Farrell), J T Robinson (rep M Tait); O J Barkley, S Perry (rep P C Richards); A J Sheridan, M P Regan (rep G S Chuter), P J Vickery (*captain*) (rep M J H Stevens), S D Shaw (rep M E Corry), B J Kay, J P R Worsley (rep L W Moody), L B N Dallaglio, T Rees

England Scorers *Tries*: Robinson, Barkley, Rees *Conversions:* Barkley (2) *Penalty Goals*: Barkley (3)

CAP 72: LOST 0-36 v SOUTH AFRICA, 14th September 2007, Stade de France, Paris

England: J T Robinson (rep M Tait); O J Lewsey, J D Noon (rep P C Richards), A Farrell, P H Sackey; M J Catt, S Perry (rep A C T Gomarsall); A J Sheridan (rep P T Freshwater), M P Regan (rep G S Chuter), M J H Stevens, S D Shaw (rep S W Borthwick), B J Kay, M E Corry (*captain*), N Easter, T Rees (rep L W Moody)

CAP 73: WON 12-10 v AUSTRALIA, 6th October 2007, Stade Vélodrome, Marseilles

England: J T Robinson; P H Sackey, M Tait, M J Catt (rep T Flood), O J Lewsey; J P Wilkinson, A C T Gomarsall (temp rep P C Richards); A J Sheridan, M P Regan (rep G S Chuter), P J Vickery (*captain*) (rep M J H Stevens), S D Shaw, B J Kay, M E Corry N Easter (rep L B N Dallaglio), L W Moody (rep J P R Worsley)

England Scorer *Penalty Goals*: Wilkinson (4)

CAP 74: WON 14-9 v FRANCE, 13th October 2007, Stade de France, Paris
England: J T Robinson; P H Sackey, M Tait, M J Catt (rep T Flood), O J Lewsey (rep D
Hipkiss); J P Wilkinson, A C T Gomarsall (rep P C Richards); A J Sheridan, M P
Regan (rep G S Chuter), P J Vickery (*captain*) (rep M J H Stevens), S D Shaw, B J Kay,
M E Corry N Easter (rep L B N Dallaglio), L W Moody (rep J P R Worsley)
England Scorers *Try:* Lewsey *Penalty Goals*: Wilkinson (2) *Dropped Goal:* Wilkinson

CAP 75: LOST 6-15 v SOUTH AFRICA, 20th October 2007, Stade de France, Paris
England: J T Robinson (rep D Hipkiss); P H Sackey, M Tait, M J Catt (rep T Flood), M
J Cueto; J P Wilkinson, A C T Gomarsall; A J Sheridan, M P Regan (rep G S Chuter),
P J Vickery (*captain*) (rep M J H Stevens), S D Shaw, B J Kay, M E Corry N Easter (rep
L B N Dallaglio), L W Moody (rep J P R Worsley; rep P C Richards)
England Scorer *Penalty Goals*: Wilkinson (2)

Index